Voices of the Civil War

Voices of the Civil War · Chickamauga

By the Editors of Time-Life Books, Alexandria, Virginia

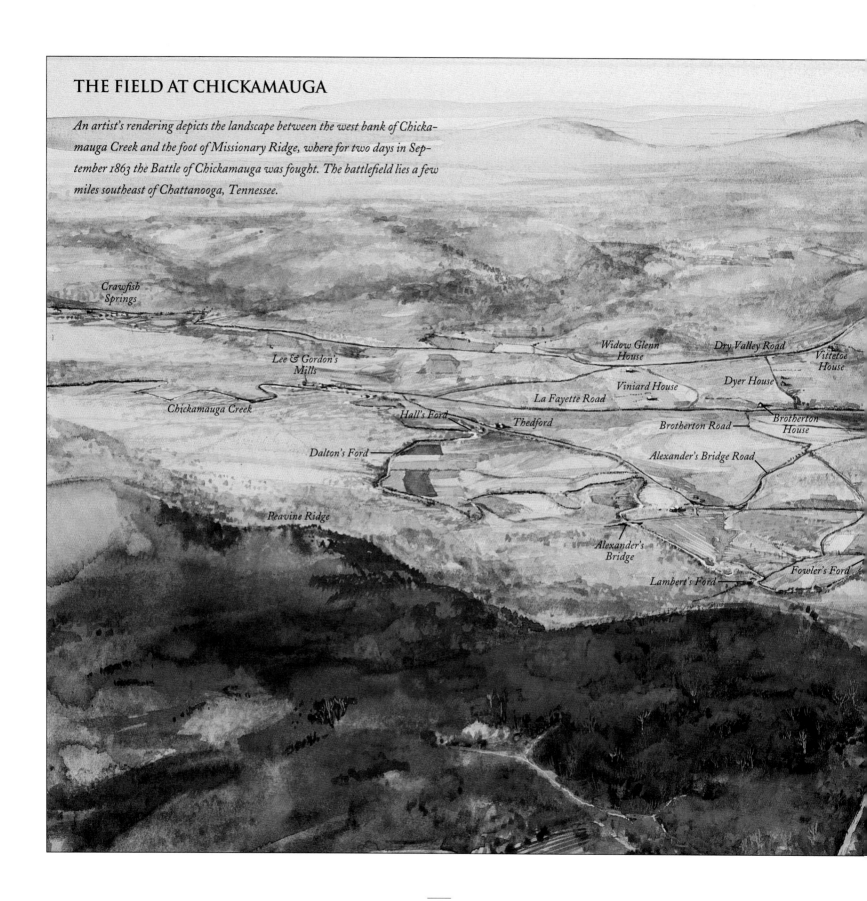

THE FIELD AT CHICKAMAUGA

An artist's rendering depicts the landscape between the west bank of Chicka-
mauga Creek and the foot of Missionary Ridge, where for two days in Sep-
tember 1863 the Battle of Chickamauga was fought. The battlefield lies a few
miles southeast of Chattanooga, Tennessee.

Crawfish
Springs

Widow Glenn
House

Dry Valley Road

Vittetoe
House

Lee & Gordon's
Mills

Viniard House

Dyer House

La Fayette Road

Chickamauga Creek

Hall's Ford

Thedford

Brotherton Road

Brotherton
House

Dalton's Ford

Alexander's Bridge Road

Peavine Ridge

Alexander's
Bridge

Fowler's Ford

Lambert's Ford

The Tullahoma Campaign

The objective of Major General William S. Rosecrans' Army of the Cumberland in the spring of 1863 was vitally important for the Union cause: to thrust southward through eastern Tennessee and capture the town of Chattanooga, junction point for four vital railroad lines that carried a large percentage of the Confederacy's arms, munitions, food, and other supplies. If Rosecrans and his troops could take the town, they would put a damaging crimp in the Southern war effort.

Chattanooga, a town of 3,500 people on a bend in the Tennessee River, was also a prime gateway into northern Georgia and the routes leading to Atlanta and the heart of the middle South. With Chattanooga in Union hands, President Abraham Lincoln wrote, "I think the rebellion must dwindle and die."

The campaign to fulfill the president's prophecy would unfold after long delays and

....

Private John Munson, shown astride his mount, Col. John Mosby, and sporting a seven-shot Spencer rifle, served with the 72d Indiana, a regiment of Wilder's Lightning Brigade, which played a key role in the Tullahoma and Chickamauga campaigns.

proceed with a series of Union successes. Then its meandering path would lead to the rough hill country south of Chattanooga. There the Union and Rebel armies would confront each other in one of the crucial battles of the Civil War, a confused, desperate, and violent fight near a creek known to the area's Cherokee people as Chickamauga, or River of Blood.

The campaign got under way sluggishly, however. By mid-January 1863 Rosecrans and his army were camped in and around Murfreesboro, Tennessee, 85 miles from Chattanooga. They had already defeated, if just barely, the Confederate force facing them, General Braxton Bragg's Army of Tennessee, in a three-day battle along the banks of the nearby Stones River at the turn of the year, December 31 to January 2. Now Bragg's badly wounded army was only about 30 miles to the southeast, camped behind the Duck River. Too weak to attack—he had lost one-third of his force at Stones River—Bragg was reorganizing and mustering reinforcements as best he could to meet Rosecrans' inevitable move south.

But Rosecrans, despite having the larger and better-equipped army, stubbornly refused to move. A large, jovial West Pointer,

Old Rosy—as he was affectionately known to his troops, partly for his heroically large red nose—had proved a brave and decisive leader in battle. At Stones River he had ridden furiously through the worst of the enemy cannon fire from one front-line unit to another, a battered black hat jammed on his head, a cigar stub clamped in his teeth, advising and encouraging his hard-pressed troops.

Between battles, however, Rosecrans had already proved maddeningly deliberate, driving his superiors in Washington to distraction with his refusal to take action until he was entirely ready. It had happened in the fall of 1862, before Stones River, and now it was happening again as the muddy, frigid Tennessee winter gave way to spring.

The delays prompted a barrage of telegrams urging him to move from the army's chief back in Washington, Major General Henry W. Halleck. Halleck wanted Chattanooga taken, and soon. He was also concerned about another campaign currently being waged 400 miles to the west. There, General Ulysses S. Grant was laying siege to Vicksburg, the Confederate bastion guarding the Mississippi River. Halleck feared that unless Rosecrans attacked toward Chattanooga, Bragg might detach part of his army and send it westward to hammer at Grant, thwarting the Union campaign for Vicksburg.

Rosecrans fired back his own barrage of telegrams, belittling the threat to Grant and blandly pointing out that in military matters, as in others, haste makes waste. He wanted to be perfectly ready before he moved so that, as he put it, he would not have to "stop and tinker" along the way. He would be campaigning through "country full of natural passes and fortifications" that demanded "superior forces to advance with any success," he informed Washington. He needed more of everything: troops, artillery, cavalry. Besides, he complained, his communications were threatened, rations were low, and his men were worn out.

In fact, Rosecrans' men were worn out from waiting. To occupy their time, the troops built snug log huts for themselves and even planted rows of trees along the company streets. But boredom was endemic. There was little to do, complained an Indiana artillery officer, except for "talking, eating, sleeping and fighting flies." Another Federal soldier noted that the men "were simply rusting away."

Bragg's Confederates were not much better off. Perpetually short of rations, they spent much of their time shooting rabbits and otherwise scrounging about the countryside for food. They were also in a state of chronic discontent; they despised their commanding general—a dour, crabbed, sickly looking martinet—for the harsh discipline he imposed.

The Southern officers held Bragg in open contempt for retreating when victory might have been won at Stones River—and boldly told him so in a series of extraordinary letters advising him to step down. They even petitioned Richmond to have him removed. But Confederate president Jefferson Davis could find no other general able to take Bragg's place, so he stayed on by default.

While the infantrymen moldered in their camps, the cavalry on both sides got strenuous workouts. Bragg had 15,000 horsemen in his 47,000-man army, and they were led by some of the South's most daring cavalry commanders, including Nathan Bedford Forrest, Joseph Wheeler, and John Hunt Morgan. The Rebel raiders shot up transports on the Cumberland River and demolished virtually every bridge and trestle on the railroads—the Louisville & Nashville and the Louisville & Chattanooga—that Rosecrans depended on for supplies. They also savaged depots, freight cars, and locomotives.

Rosecrans tried to fight back, mostly in vain, with his 9,000 overmatched horsemen. To increase his numbers, he converted some foot soldiers into mounted troops. This produced one of the hardest-fighting units of the western war, a brigade of 1,500 men made up of two infantry regiments from Illinois and two from Indiana. The leader of this brigade was a brave and exceedingly determined Hoosier, Colonel John T. Wilder, successful proprietor of an iron foundry before the war.

It was no easy task for Wilder to organize the new brigade. The troops had to scrounge their own horses—and then learn how to ride them. But, initially at his own expense, Wilder provided excellent weapons: Spencer seven-shot repeating rifles that gave the new riders firepower far beyond their numbers. Wilder and his made-over infantry would be in the thickest of the fighting in the months to come.

By June 1863 Rosecrans' cavalry was holding its own, protecting his supply lines, and reinforcements had enlarged his army to almost 80,000 men. Still the methodical general showed few signs of moving. The continued procrastination produced a bizarre exchange of messages. "I deem it my duty," telegraphed General Halleck from Washington on June 11, "to repeat to you the great dissatisfaction felt here at your inactivity."

When Rosecrans ignored him, Halleck wired again on June 16: "Is it your intention to make an immediate move forward? A definite answer, yes or no, is required." Rosecrans answered this message with perhaps unconscious humor. "If immediate means to-night or to-morrow, no," he wired. "If it means as soon as all things are ready, say five days, yes."

Rosecrans was not quite as good as his word, but eight days later, on June 24, he suddenly got his army in motion. And once started, he moved with speed, skill, and energy, dodging and feinting his way south in a masterly series of maneuvers—the so-called Tullahoma campaign, named after the town where General Bragg had his headquarters.

Bragg, studying maps of the area, had positioned his forces as best he could to meet the expected assault. A long ridge, an extension of the Cumberland Plateau, rose between Murfreesboro and the Confederate positions on the Duck River. Cutting through the barrier were four passes: Guy's Gap on the west, then Bellbuckle Gap, Liberty Gap, and Hoover's Gap. Hoover's Gap ran through especially rough country, but the other three appeared to be more easily negotiable by marching troops, and they were aimed right at Bragg's defensive line.

To cover the approaches, Bragg placed the larger of his two corps, commanded by Lieutenant General Leonidas Polk, on the left near Shelbyville, facing Guy's and Bellbuckle Gaps. On the right he stationed Lieutenant General William J. Hardee's corps to protect against an assault by way of Hoover's and Liberty Gaps. He also dispatched most of Nathan Bedford Forrest's cavalrymen to the west to cover a roundabout route that avoided the ridge, a path that Bragg thought Rosecrans might favor.

But Rosecrans had been studying hard, too, and he had come up with what he hoped was a way to deceive the enemy. He had no intention of taking the easy western route or of sending his main force down Bellbuckle and Liberty Gaps for a frontal assault. Instead he would confuse Bragg, feinting one way and then attacking another.

By way of a main feint, Rosecrans sent

Major General David Stanley's Cavalry Corps and Major General Gordon Granger's Reserve Corps through Bellbuckle Gap toward Shelbyville and Polk's corps on the Confederate left—exactly where Bragg expected an attack. At the same time Rosecrans sent a column, initially a single division, toward the town of McMinnville, well to the east beyond Hoover's Gap. Bragg soon learned of this movement but, assuming it was a diversion, ignored it.

This was precisely what Rosecrans wanted. Following right behind the lone division way to the east marched Major General Thomas L. Crittenden's XXI Corps, which was to punch through a Confederate cavalry screen on the Cumberland Plateau and then head south for Manchester, a dozen miles from Tullahoma, in Hardee's right rear. At the same time Major General George H. Thomas' XIV Corps plunged into Hoover's Gap. To complete the deception, parts of Major General Alexander McCook's XX Corps headed through Liberty Gap to threaten Hardee's troops around Wartrace and fix them in place. If the deception worked, Rosecrans' left wing would get behind Bragg's army and cut it off from Chattanooga.

Despite deluges of rain that turned the roads to ankle-deep mud, the Federal columns moved with amazing speed. By the afternoon of the 24th, McCook's advance brigade, led by Brigadier General August Willich, had gotten much of the way through Liberty Gap—and ran head-on into a Confederate division commanded by Major General Patrick R. Cleburne.

Cleburne's troops stopped the Federals cold. But Willich's men, abandoning their frontal attack, scrambled up the hills on either side of the pass and outflanked the defenders. Riddled by enfilading fire, Cleburne's men were forced to fall back and abandon the gap.

At Hoover's Gap, General Thomas' corps

was spearheaded by the 1,500 infantry-turned-horsemen of John Wilder's brigade. Wilder had been ordered to trot into the gap and then wait for infantry units to come up in support. Instead, the rookie troopers galloped full tilt through the pass, chasing the astonished enemy pickets before them and leaving the Federal infantry 10 miles to the rear.

Units from General Hardee's corps responded quickly. Brigadier General William Bate's brigade, along with Brigadier General Bushrod Johnson's troops and three batteries of artillery, all moved fast to meet the 72d Indiana and Wilder's other regiments at the southern end of the gap. Suddenly hit by shellfire, Wilder's troopers dismounted and formed a line of battle supported by the guns of Captain Eli Lilly's 18th Indiana Battery.

Hammered by Bate's and Johnson's brigades, Wilder's hard-pressed troopers soon copied Willich's men, taking cover on the rocky slopes overlooking the gap. There, despite murderous blasts from the enemy guns, the Federals held on, beating back the Confederate assaults with sheets of fire from their fast-shooting Spencer rifles. One of the brigade's officers, Major James A. Connolly, recalled that "each enemy shell screamed so close to us as to make it seem that the next would tear us to pieces." But when the Confederates made a charge, the Union troops were "on their feet in an instant and a terrible fire from the Spencers" quickly caused "the advancing regiment to reel and its colors to fall to the ground."

In late afternoon Wilder's division commander, Major General Joseph J. Reynolds, fearful that the exposed troopers would be wiped out, sent forward a message ordering them to retire. But Wilder refused to budge, insisting he and his men could hold out. About seven o'clock in the evening a battery of artillery clattered up from the rear. This sign of help, Major Connolly recalled, "nerved the men to maintain the unequal conflict a little longer." Then 30 minutes later two brigades of Reynolds' infantry finally arrived, the men exhausted but hurrying as best they could. They were greeted, Connolly said, "by such lusty cheers as seemed to inspire them with new vigor."

As Wilder's men fell back to rest, Thomas himself appeared. A Virginia-born West Pointer who had remained faithful to the Union, "Pap" Thomas was normally quiet and undemonstrative, but now he grabbed Colonel Wilder's hand and announced, "You have saved the lives of a thousand men by your gallant conduct today," adding that "I didn't expect to get this gap for three days."

That night Bragg in his Tullahoma headquarters was still baffled by what Rosecrans was doing. Reports kept coming in of Federal cavalry and infantry heading for Shelbyville on the Confederate left. Strangely, no reports filtered through from the gaps on the Confederate right, despite all the fighting there.

On the next day, the 25th, the fighting continued on the Rebel right. Generals Bate and Johnson smashed away again at Reynolds' division of Thomas' corps coming through Hoover's Gap, and the exceedingly combative Cleburne launched a furious all-out assault on Willich's brigade, still in the vanguard of the division of McCook's corps trying to hold the hills around Liberty Gap.

At last, on the 26th, it dawned on Bragg that the real danger was on his right. In midafternoon he ordered General Polk to shift his corps eastward and go to the aid of Hardee's hard-pressed troops.

But it was too late. That night, almost three days after the fighting began, a dismayed Bragg finally realized that his army was in mortal danger. Colonel Wilder's hard-fighting unit—now dubbed the Lightning Brigade for its headlong ride through Hoover's Gap—had broken through the Confederate line and, with the rest of General Thomas' corps following, was heading for Manchester to join up with Crittenden's corps already there, well beyond Hardee's right flank. There was nothing for Bragg to do except order Polk and Hardee to abandon their positions and fall back on Tullahoma itself as fast as their men could march.

Tullahoma provided few comforts for the bedraggled Rebel soldiers. The unfortunate little railroad town, soaked by incessant downpours and overrun by troops and horses and mule-drawn wagons, had become an ever-worsening quagmire. When one wet-to-the-skin member of Hardee's staff was asked the source of the town's name, he acidly said it came from two Greek words, *tulla,* meaning "mud," and *homa,* meaning "more mud."

Despite the rain, Wilder's Lightning Brigade reached Manchester on the morning of June 27, followed soon by other elements of Thomas' corps. At dawn on the 28th, Wilder's midwesterners splashed their way south once again, heading for the town of Decherd. Although soon chased away by a good-sized detachment of Confederate infantry, the Federals managed to tear up track and destroy trestles on two branch lines of the Nashville & Chattanooga Railroad, at least partially crippling Bragg's supply-and-communications line with Chattanooga.

By the 29th Bragg was deep in the throes of indecision. He had his army concentrated around Tullahoma, ready to fight, but there were few signs that Rosecrans' main force was bearing down on the town with intentions to attack. Instead, reports kept filtering in from the east, indicating the Federals might be trying to get in behind the Confederate army once again.

Bragg called a council of war that night, but he, Polk, and Hardee could come to no decision about what to do. By the next day, however, there were fresh reports: elements of three Union corps—Thomas', Crittenden's, and part of McCook's—were on their way toward Hillsboro, farther in the Confederate rear. At the same time, Granger's Reserve Corps and Stanley's Union cavalry had reached the old Confederate line on the Duck River and were bearing down on Tullahoma from the northwest.

Clearly the Confederates were in trouble, and on the night of June 30 Bragg ordered his forces to abandon Tullahoma and fall back once more, this time behind the next natural defensive line of the Elk River. Polk and Hardee's men had hardly begun to dig in there on July 1, however, before Bragg realized that the several Federal corps to the east could still easily turn his flank by simply continuing their swift march south. He had evaded one trap, but another one threatened.

Finally there was nothing for Bragg to do but make another humiliating retreat. On July 3 he ordered his bedraggled army to start marching to the southeast along the roads that led to crossing points on the Tennessee River and thence to Chattanooga. Riding south from Tullahoma with his troops, his thin face looking even more cadaverous than usual, Bragg fell into talk with one of his army's chaplains. "This is," he said in a sepulchral whisper, "a great disaster."

A far more cheerful Rosecrans reached Tullahoma on the same day, July 3. In an almost flawless nine-day campaign, executed despite appalling weather, he had swept Bragg and his force from much of middle Tennessee—and at the astonishingly modest cost of 84 dead and 476 wounded.

Rosecrans' huge success came, however, at exactly the wrong moment for him to receive credit. July 4, 1863, was the day of all days for the Federal cause. Out west, Grant captured Vicksburg on the Fourth, ending a long, anguishing siege. In Pennsylvania, also on the Fourth, after three days of desperate fighting around Gettysburg, a Federal army stopped Robert E. Lee's second invasion of the North.

Amid the wild rejoicing over those huge victories, Rosecrans' capture of Tullahoma received little notice or praise from the press, the public, or the high command in Washington. So little impressed was Secretary of War Edwin M. Stanton, in fact, that on July 7, only three days after Rosecrans reached Tullahoma, he sent off a barbed telegram. "Lee's army overthrown; Grant victorious," the wire read. "You and your noble army now have the chance to give the finishing blow to the rebellion. Will you neglect the chance?"

Rosecrans immediately fired off a sarcastic reply. "You do not appear to observe the fact," it read, "that this noble army has driven the rebels from Middle Tennessee. I beg in behalf of this army that the War Department may not overlook so great an event because it is not written in letters of blood."

Rosecrans' troops, justifiably elated, settled down to rest, find some protection from the rain, and cook some hot rations. But knowing Chattanooga was next, they were ready to move when Old Rosy gave the word. Rosecrans himself, unabashed by Stanton's wire, was not a bit inclined to take up the march. Much reorganization and planning needed to be done before the next stage in his campaign, and he settled down comfortably, for six weeks this time, to attend to every detail.

CHRONOLOGY

December 31, 1862 and January 2, 1863	*Battle of Stones River (Murfreesboro)*
May 18	*Siege of Vicksburg begins*
June 23	*Tullahoma campaign begins*
June 24-26	*Skirmishes at Hoover's Gap*
June 24-27	*Skirmishes at Liberty Gap*
June 27	*Federals occupy Manchester*
June 30	*Bragg evacuates Tullahoma, beginning retreat to Chattanooga*
July 1	*Rosecrans occupies Tullahoma*
July 1-3	*Battle of Gettysburg*
July 4	*Vicksburg surrenders*
July 7	*Bragg encamps in Chattanooga*
August 21	*Federals begin shelling Chattanooga*
September 7-9	*Confederates evacuate Chattanooga*
September 9	*Federals occupy Chattanooga*
September 11-13	*Skirmishes at or near Davis' Crossroads, Ringgold, Rock Spring, and Lee and Gordon's Mills*
September 18	*Skirmishes at Pea Vine Ridge, Reed's and Alexander's Bridges*
September 19-20	*Battle of Chickamauga*
September 21-22	*Federals retreat to Chattanooga*
September 30	*Wheeler raid on Federal communications*
October 3	*Federals reinforce Chattanooga with troops from Army of the Potomac and from Vicksburg*
October 16	*Grant takes command of the Military Division of the Mississippi and replaces Rosecrans with Thomas*

ORDER OF BATTLE

ARMY OF TENNESSEE (Confederate)

Bragg 66,300 men

Left Wing Longstreet

Buckner's Corps

Stewart's Division	Preston's Division	Hindman's Division
Bate's Brigade	*Gracie's Brigade*	*Anderson's Brigade*
Clayton's Brigade	*Kelly's Brigade*	*Deas' Brigade*
Brown's Brigade	*Trigg's Brigade*	*Manigault's Brigade*

Hood's Corps

Kershaw's Division	B. Johnson's Division	Law's Division
Kershaw's Brigade	*Fulton's Brigade*	*Sheffield's Brigade*
Humphreys' Brigade	*Gregg's Brigade*	*Robertson's Brigade*
	McNair's Brigade	*Benning's Brigade*

Right Wing Polk

Hill's Corps

Cleburne's Division	Breckinridge's Division
Wood's Brigade	*Helm's Brigade*
L. E. Polk's Brigade	*Adams' Brigade*
Deshler's Brigade	*Stovall's Brigade*

Walker's Corps

Gist's Division	Liddell's Division
Colquitt's Brigade	*Govan's Brigade*
Ector's Brigade	*Walthall's Brigade*
Wilson's Brigade	

Polk's Corps

Cheatham's Division
Jackson's Brigade
Maney's Brigade
Smith's Brigade
Wright's Brigade
Strahl's Brigade

Cavalry

Wheeler's Corps

Wharton's Division	Martin's Division
Crews' Brigade	*Morgan's Brigade*
Harrison's Brigade	*Russell's Brigade*
	Roddey's Brigade

Forrest's Corps

Armstrong's Division	Pegram's Division
J. T. Wheeler's Brigade	*Davidson's Brigade*
Dibrell's Brigade	*Scott's Brigade*

ARMY OF THE CUMBERLAND (Federal)

Rosecrans 58,200 men

XIV Corps Thomas

1st Division Baird	2d Division Negley	3d Division Brannan	4th Division Reynolds
Scribner's Brigade	*J. Beatty's Brigade*	*Connell's Brigade*	*Wilder's Brigade*
Starkweather's Brigade	*Stanley's Brigade*	*Croxton's Brigade*	*E. King's Brigade*
J. King's Brigade	*Sirwell's Brigade*	*Van Derveer's Brigade*	*Turchin's Brigade*

XXI Corps Crittenden

1st Division Wood	2d Division Palmer	3d Division Van Cleve
Buell's Brigade	*Cruft's Brigade*	*S. Beatty's Brigade*
Wagner's Brigade	*Hazen's Brigade*	*Dick's Brigade*
Harker's Brigade	*Grose's Brigade*	*Barnes' Brigade*

Cavalry Corps R. Mitchell

1st Division E. McCook	2d Division Crook
Campbell's Brigade	*Minty's Brigade*
Ray's Brigade	*Long's Brigade*
Watkins' Brigade	

XX Corps A. McCook

1st Division Davis	2d Division R. Johnson	3d Division Sheridan
Post's Brigade	*Willich's Brigade*	*Lytle's Brigade*
Carlin's Brigade	*Dodge's Brigade*	*Laiboldt's Brigade*
Heg's Brigade	*Baldwin's Brigade*	*Bradley's Brigade*

Reserve Corps Granger

1st Division Steedman	2d Division D. McCook
Whitaker's Brigade	*D. McCook's Brigade*
J. Mitchell's Brigade	

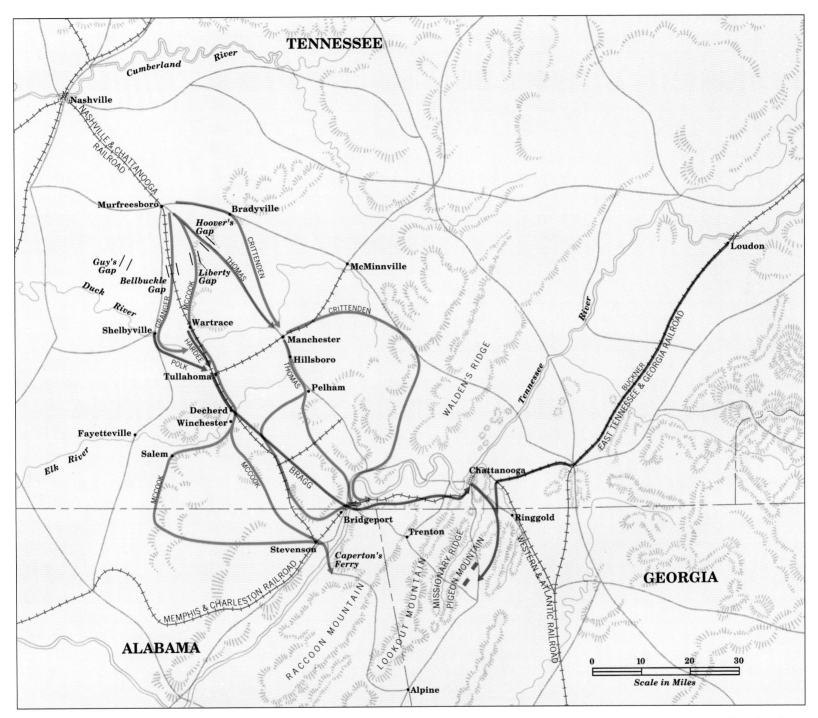

After the Union victory at Stones River in January 1863, Bragg's Confederates retired to positions around Tullahoma. In late July, Rosecrans launched a series of flanking moves that threatened Bragg's supply lines and forced him to retreat across the Tennessee River to Chattanooga. Rosecrans followed, and by early September most of his army was across the river below Chattanooga and moving east in three columns. Bragg evacuated the town, fell back to the south, and turned to fight.

CORPORAL GEORGE S. WILSON
17TH INDIANA INFANTRY, WILDER'S BRIGADE

Wilson and his comrades took advantage of the six-month hiatus that followed the Federal victory at Stones River in January 1863 to confiscate horses and mules from the countryside around Murfreesboro for use in Wilder's mounted infantry brigade—an action that infuriated local Tennesseans. His droll descriptions of the neophyte horsemen belie the fact that Wilder's Yankees soon evolved into one of the most daring units of the western war.

In our eagerness for riding animals we paid no attention to age, color, size, sex, or previous condition of servitude. Blooded racers, awkward plow-horses, sway-backed plugs, brood mares, stallions, ponies, and mules of assorted dimensions and uncertain tricks, all went to make up the mount of a company; while our drummer-boy was happy in the possession of a little brown jackass, which he contentedly rode until the melancholy-looking creature came to an untimely end at the hands of an exasperated veteran, whose only pair of trousers had served for its midnight tiffin. Whenever we found an animal, hornless and with deck-room for a saddle, we took it; and if some fellow was not riding it before night, it was for the very good reason that the beast would be riding him. We were an infantry command, many of the members of which had never straddled a horse, and this last contingency was not of infrequent occurrence. But in time our mount improved. We got things straightened out and finally presented a tolerable appearance. In tactics and drill we were indifferent, but soon learned enough to use great caution in approaching a mule to go abroad, and never to entirely trust in his well-simulated intention of good behavior. Early in the season I got a lesson from a little specimen of the seemingly meek and lowly variety. He had a tired, resigned manner about him, a sort of "If you want to lick me, you can, but I wish you wouldn't" expression, that altogether inspired me with confidence and recklessness. But you should have seen that mule and me the first time our opinions happened to differ on some point or other, which he deemed of importance.

In April, about the time we were all mounted, another fortunate circumstance resulted in our being armed with the Spencer magazine rifle, using metallic ammunition. At that time no other large body of troops was so well armed; in fact, I doubt if there was then . . . another entire brigade in all the West using metallic cartridges. Our services up

Colonel John T. Wilder showed the same resourcefulness in arming his 1,500-man brigade that he did in running his iron foundry in civilian life before the war. When Washington was slow to buy new repeating rifles, he arranged for a personal loan from his hometown bankers.

to this period had been arduous, while we had had considerable experience under fire, so now, with our Spencer rifles, we felt ourselves to be wellnigh invincible, and anxiously awaited an opportunity to broaden our field of operations.

MAJOR GENERAL HENRY W. HALLECK
GENERAL IN CHIEF, U.S. ARMY

An armchair general dubbed Old Brains in the prewar army, Halleck was widely disliked by the generals in the field, who doubted his military acumen. He dispatched these telegrams in an effort to spur the methodical Rosecrans to move faster against Bragg.

> "I deem it my duty to repeat to you the great dissatisfaction that is felt here at your inactivity."

War Department,
Washington, June 11, 1863—3 p.m.
Major-General Rosecrans,
Murfreesborough, Tenn.:
I deem it my duty to repeat to you the great dissatisfaction that is felt here at your inactivity. There seems to be no doubt that a part of Bragg's force has gone to Johnston.
H. W. Halleck,
General-in-Chief.

War Department,
Washington, June 16, 1863—2 p.m.
Major-General Rosecrans,
Murfreesborough, Tenn.:
Is it your intention to make an immediate movement forward? A definite answer, yes or no, is required.
H. W. Halleck,
General-in-Chief.

MAJOR GENERAL WILLIAM S. ROSECRANS
COMMANDER, ARMY OF THE CUMBERLAND

Having outgeneraled Braxton Bragg at Stones River, Rosecrans had won the respect of his men for his personal courage and strategic cunning, and he was not about to be bullied into hasty action by Washington. He did not share the administration's fear that the Confederates might gamble on his inactivity and transfer troops from eastern Tennessee to Vicksburg, the critical Mississippi River port where General Ulysses S. Grant was preparing to attack.

Murfreesborough, Tenn.,
June 16, 1863—6.30 p.m.
Maj. Gen. H. W. Halleck, *General-in-Chief:*
In reply to your inquiry, if immediate means to-night or to-morrow, no. If it means as soon as all things are ready, say five days, yes.
W. S. Rosecrans,
Major-General.

Headquarters Army of the Cumberland,
June 24, 1863—2.10 a.m.
Major-General Halleck, *General-in-Chief:*
The army begins to move at 3 o'clock this morning.
W. S. Rosecrans,
Major-General.

Major General William S. Rosecrans (hatless, left) disciplines a subordinate (hatless, right). Painted by Adolph Metzner, topographical engineer for Willich's brigade, the scene depicts one of the administrative chores the energetic general performed daily during the army's long encampment at Murfreesboro. A journalist described Rosecrans as of "middle stature, with a broad upper body and rather short, bow legs (owing to which peculiarities he presented a far better appearance when mounted than on foot)."

MAJOR GENERAL DAVID S. STANLEY
COMMANDER, U.S. CAVALRY CORPS

An 1852 graduate of West Point, David S. Stanley, Rosecrans' blunt-speaking cavalry chief, turned down a commission in the Confederate army in the spring of 1861 to remain a U.S. Army officer. The anecdote he relates here occurred during the opening phase of the Tullahoma campaign. Racked with dysentery for months, Stanley gave up his command two days before the Battle of Chickamauga and headed home to Ohio to recover.

In a severe skirmish on that day, one of those ridiculous things that sometimes happen to lighten up the deathroll, occurred. The Confederates made a charge on our line of skirmishers, but recoiled when they met a brisk fire. One trooper continued to charge straight down on our lines. As he passed across the line of the skirmishers of the First Tennessee cavalry (Union), every man took a shot at the bold horse soldier. He dashed into our ranks with his gray clothes full of bullet holes but skin whole, when it was discovered that a bullet had cut both reins, and it was the horse that did the charging, the trooper being an unwilling participant.

PRIVATE FRANCIS A. KIENE
49TH OHIO, WILLICH'S BRIGADE

Kiene and the men of Willich's brigade, carrying 12 days' rations, began their advance toward Liberty Gap at 7:00 a.m. on June 24. Kiene would serve throughout the Tullahoma campaign, the Battle of Chickamauga, and subsequent fighting around Chattanooga, but he was wounded in the left elbow in the Atlanta campaign in May 1864. He received a medical discharge in November 1864.

June the 24th—Wednesday. . . . we went out on the Shelbyville Pike about 5 miles when we turned to the left takeing the Liberty gap road . . . on this road we had marched onley a short distance when we found rich Fields of corn and Wheat . . . it commenced to rain prety briskley and the road got slipry and martching became hard and tedisome . . . one Battalion of the 39th Ind mounted Infantry came with us and as they reached the foot of the Hills they met the first rebels 3 or 4 of whome they captured while they ware at work in a harvest Field working at 3 Dollars a day. When we got up the 15th Ohio Reg. deployed to the right of the road while we deployed to the left and so advanced on the rebel piguid line who were . . . at fences a long the foot of two steap hills on each side of the road and covert with woods . . . after Capt. Good Speed had thrown a fiew shells along the fences makeing it a little unpleasant for the rebels. Than we commenced moveing acrost the open fields and driveing the rebels up the side of the hills but it was found that the rebels were prety strong and our lines were lengthened out by deploying parts of the 32nd Ind. and 89th Ill. Regts. We prest

The men of Battery A, 1st Ohio Light Artillery, commanded by Captain Wilbur Goodspeed, stand beside their three 6-pounder James guns for a photograph taken by the Nashville firm of A. S. Morse. Goodspeed's battery, part of Brigadier General Absalom Baird's division in Major General George H. Thomas' XIV Corps, was in the thick of the fighting during the Tullahoma campaign.

forwards while the rebels stubernley resisted but we drove them up the hill. The rebels tried to flank us with 4 companies but they were met by the 39th boys who were protecting our left flank . . . when we had nearley gained the hill the rebels made one more effort to drive us back and for a moment our line in the center wavert but just than our gallant Adjutant dashed forward and urged the men onward . . . the move was successful . . . one more dash and the Hill was ours and a hearty cheer told us that we were gaining. Company I had been a reserve till now but now we relieved Company C. and deployed out when we again moved forward on this side of the hill we found the Camp of the 15th Arkansas regiment whome we had been fighting on the hill . . . they had left most of their Tents sitting and meny knapsacks were left . . . a table was left setting that was set for supper . . . after we had pushed on a little when we were called in and the 2nd Brigade went to the front . . . we campt close to a meeting house. The rebels now got some reinforcements and a short Artillery fight took place but night stopt fighting . . . we lost 14 killed and wounded in the 49th . . . among the killed was Capt Chance . . . no one hurt in Company I.

Brigadier General August Willich (mounted) directs his troops at Liberty Gap. A graduate of the military academy at Potsdam, the Prussian aristocrat immigrated to the United States after the failed revolution of 1848. At the onset of the Civil War, he joined the 9th Ohio as a private but was made an officer when his background became known. "In time of action," a soldier wrote, "all looked to General Willich as the directing mind, trusted him with the utmost confidence and followed him implicitly."

"The country varied as we drew near, the hills bunching up close together and separating into single knobs, the valleys between becoming little more than narrow winding ravines."

COLONEL THOMAS E. ROSE
77TH PENNSYLVANIA INFANTRY, DODGE'S BRIGADE

On the afternoon of June 24, the 77th Pennsylvania reinforced Willich's brigade at Liberty Gap. By scaling the slopes on either side of the pass, the Federals outflanked their foe and forced them to withdraw. Plagued by gout, Rose sometimes went into battle with one foot shoeless. Captured at Chickamauga, he went on to lead one of the most celebrated escapes of the war from Richmond's notorious Libby Prison.

We left the turnpike and continued on a dirt road through Millersburg toward Wartrace until we arrived at Liberty Gap, at which place we arrived, after a toilsome march through the mud, at about 3 p.m. At this time the enemy's pickets were encountered by General Willich's brigade, which was in advance of our own. The firing soon became quite spirited, and finally assumed the form of a skirmish, when the Twenty-ninth Regiment Indiana Volunteers, of our own brigade, was ordered forward to try and flank the enemy, which order was promptly and spiritedly executed. In a few minutes after, I received orders to move up for the same purpose. I immediately moved up in column by company to the main entrance of the gap, where the enemy were posted, and then, piloted by Lieutenant Sheets, of General Johnson's staff, moved up on the opposite slope of a ravine which extended around the elliptical base of the hill on which the left wing of the enemy was posted. I proceeded along this ravine for several hundred yards under a sharp fire from the enemy's sharpshooters, which did us but little damage, until I had gained what was deemed a proper position, when I was ordered by Colonel Miller, now commanding the brigade, to move directly on the enemy, who was posted on a hill of from 80 to 100 feet elevation, on the opposite side of the ravine, which ravine was about 300 yards wide, quite level and muddy. I at once formed line of battle, and moved half way across the ravine, throwing two companies of skirmishers nearly to the foot of the hill . . . and found the hill very steep, so

much so that we were obliged to scramble up by laying hold of the bushes and saplings in order to effect progress; in fact, it was equal to scaling the Heights of Abraham, but the enemy did not offer as much resistance as I had expected from the fire that he had kept up on my regiment from the time we had first approached the gap; for while we scrambled up one side of the hill he scrambled down on the other in great confusion, leaving his camps without attempting to move anything.

We pursued the enemy over the hills and up through the gap for about a mile, as nearly as I can judge, when we were halted by order of General Johnson, and relieved by the Third Brigade.

PRIVATE PHILIP D. STEPHENSON
13TH ARKANSAS INFANTRY, GOVAN'S BRIGADE

On June 24, unaware that they had been outflanked, Stephenson and his comrades left the hill they were occupying at Liberty Gap in high spirits, thinking they had witnessed a victory by the 2d Arkansas. Stephenson wrote this account decades later, when he was a Presbyterian minister.

The country varied as we drew near, the hills bunching up close together and separating into single knobs, the valleys between becoming little more than narrow winding ravines. These knobs were steep and quite high. We had barely gotten there before the fight was on us. Stray shots came among us and wounded some of us, I think, and, of course there was response, but the fight proper was between the 2nd Arkansas of our brigade and several regiments of Yankees. We saw the whole thing as mere spectators!

Our position was good for it. The knob we were on (where we lay supporting a section of artillery, two pieces of Swett's battery, I think) was one of three which were to each other as the corners of a triangle. Ours was the west knob, the 2nd's was the south knob, and the Yankees', the north knob. So as they charged down their hill through the little valley and up the 2nd's hill we were on their flank, but a few hundred yards off. The whole scene was before us—a thrilling and beautiful picture it was! Not often is it given for a soldier to be a mere looker on in battle. We had opportunity to see the whole fight from beginning to end and to note every move and every incident. Although we could have enfiladed them with artillery and musketry, we took no part— only looked on! Why, I know not. Perhaps our commander thought the 2nd could manage them. But we ought to have enfiladed them when they fell back, it seems to me.

Down came their line of blue from the knob, a single line of two ranks, into the little valley where it was open. A long line of several regiments with their right flank to us. Up and down it we could look, and the order was pretty good, the line only a little "wobbly" and their flags like square flames of crimson (I never saw the Stars and Stripes look so

beautiful before or since). They got a little way into the valley and then started on the charge with a cheer.

Not a sound from our side! Only when they got across the valley and a little way up the base of the 2nd's knob, *then* came the crash of musketry from the hill. Like the loud increasing crackling of a conflagration in the woods, it continued and continued. Before it in a very little while, that line recoiled, gave way, broke into bits and poured back a disordered mob, every fellow for himself, back to the shelter of their own hill. *Then* came our men's time to yell. No cheer, but a yell—the prolonged, unbroken "rebel yell!" We *all* yelled, *our* hill as well as the 2nd's hill. To see that blue line go out, go across, go up, so long so straight, so orderly, so beautiful, with its flags glancing in the sunlight— and then, see it in a minute or two come streaming in frantic haste back across the valley, filling it at once from hill to hill like separate particles of individual men, the fastest the first, the wounded or the bravest the last—was a sight to see!

But one repulse did not whip them. Again they formed, perhaps with reinforcements. Again they crossed the little valley. But each time with the same result, each time feebler, less spirited, each time getting less close. This they did, two or three times. A useless sort of thing it was. Finally day began to close and they ceased.

Many a man lay in the little valley, dead or wounded. We lost scarcely any. I never knew, or at least do not remember, what brigade or division that was. They went in gallantly enough, but did not have enough persistency. That night we fell back to Bellbuckle.

Such moves of course confused us of the ranks. We had just gained an undoubted victory—why retreat? However, we were in good humor over the fact that "we had whipped em," and so, stumbling along in the dark, we talked and laughed over the fight and left the rest to the future. We cut across fields and through woods, leaving the roads. Perhaps our tarrying to make that fight may have exposed us to a flank movement. We were tired enough when we got to Bellbuckle.

The brigade of Brigadier General St. John R. Liddell (left) suffered 120 casualties defending Liberty Gap, half of them in the 2d Arkansas, which ran out of ammunition and lost its flag on June 25. "Two color-bearers of the 2d were killed," Liddell reported, "and the third, standing on a declivity of the hill, was fatally struck, and falling forward headlong, cast his colors toward the base, in close proximity to the line of the enemy."

MAJOR JAMES A. CONNOLLY

123D ILLINOIS INFANTRY, WILDER'S BRIGADE

The audacious charge through Hoover's Gap by Wilder's brigade, vividly described by Connolly, took the Confederates completely by surprise. Connolly's last military duty was to help escort Lincoln's body back to Springfield in April 1865. After the war he set up a successful law practice in Illinois and was elected to two terms in Congress.

Developed by the ingenious New England gunsmith Christopher M. Spencer, the 47-inch Spencer repeating rifle (below) proved its worth at Hoover's Gap, where the innovative weapon helped Wilder's brigade hold off a force several times its size. The rifle was loaded by inserting the tubelike magazine containing seven copper cartridges through the butt plate. The rifle was immensely popular. "Our men adore them as the heathen do their idols," exclaimed one trooper.

oon after daylight a heavy rain commenced falling which continued without interruption all day and night, and has continued ever since, with only a few hours cessation at a time. About noon the first gun was fired, and then we pushed ahead rapidly, for we were nearing the formidable "Hoover's Gap," which it was supposed would cost a great many lives to pass through, and our brigade commander determined to surprise the enemy if possible, by a rapid march, and make a bold dash to pass through the "Gap" and hold it with our brigade alone until the rest of the army could get up. We soon came into the camp of a regiment of cavalry which was so much surprised by our sudden appearance that they scattered through the woods and over the hills in every direction, every fellow for himself, and all making the best time they could bareback, on foot and every other way, leaving all their tents, wagons, baggage, commissary stores and indeed everything in our hands, but we didn't stop for anything, on we pushed, our boys, with their Spencer rifles, keeping up a continual popping in front. Soon we reached the celebrated "Gap" on the run.

This "Gap" is formed by a range of hills that run westwardly from the Cumberland mountains, and the pike runs for about two miles through between these hills; the valley is barely wide enough to admit the passage of two wagons side by side, and the hills upon either side command the valley completely; as we swept through the valley with our 1,500 horsemen on a gallop we noticed the lines of entrenchments crowning the hills, but they were deserted; the enemy was surprised and flying before us, so we pushed onward until we passed entirely through the "Gap," when a puff of white smoke from a hill about half a mile in front of us, then a dull heavy roar, then the shrieking of a shell told us we could advance no further as we had reached their infantry

"You took the responsibility to disobey orders, did you? Thank God for your decision."

The main body of Major General George H. Thomas' XIV Corps hurries along the road through Hoover's Gap and up the nearby hills to reinforce the foothold secured several miles ahead by Wilder's mounted brigade on June 24, 1863. When the first regiment of footsore infantry reached Wilder about 7:00 that evening, they were greeted by lusty cheers, which according to one of Wilder's men, "seemed to inspire them with new vigor." The soldier-artist who depicted this scene, Horace Rawden of the 105th Ohio, was among those first reinforcements to arrive. The self-taught watercolorist apparently chose not to attempt to illustrate the rainy weather.

and artillery force. But we had done enough, had advanced 6 miles further than ordered or expected possible, and had taken a point which it was expected would require a large part of the army to take; but the serious question with us now was: "Could we alone hold it in the presence of superior force?" . . . we [here] learned that we were confronted with 4 brigades of infantry and 4 batteries. . . .

. . . As soon as the enemy opened on us with their artillery we dismounted and formed line of battle on a hill just at the south entrance to the "Gap," and our battery of light artillery was opened on them, a courier was dispatched to the rear to hurry up reinforcements, our horses were sent back some distance out of the way of bursting shells, our regiment was assigned to support the battery, the other three regiments were properly disposed, and not a moment too soon, for these preparations were scarcely completed when the enemy opened on us a terrific fire of shot and shell from five different points, and their masses of infantry, with flags flying, moved out of the woods on our right in splendid style; there were three or four times our number already in sight and still others came pouring out of the woods beyond. Our regiment lay on the hill side in mud and water, the rain pouring down in torrents, while each shell screamed so close to us as to make it seem that the next would tear us to pieces.

Presently the enemy got near enough to us to make a charge on our battery, and on they came; our men are on their feet in an instant and a terrible fire from the "Spencers" causes the advancing regiment to reel and its colors fall to the ground, but in an instant their colors are up again and on they come, thinking to reach the battery before our guns can be reloaded, but they "reckoned without their host," they didn't know we had the "Spencers," and their charging yell was answered by another terrible volley, and another and another without cessation, until the poor regiment was literally cut to pieces, and but few men of that 20th Tennessee that attempted the charge will ever charge again. . . .

On that part of the field an incident occurred worthy of mention, for it shows the spirit of the men of this brigade. A corporal of the [17th] Ind. was shot through the breast at the first fire; he had always said, as indeed all our men do, that the enemy should never get hold of his "Spencer" to use it; he hadn't strength to break it so he took out his knife, unscrewed a part of the lock plate and threw it away, rendering the gun entirely useless, he then fell back amid the storm of bullets, lay down and died.

COLONEL JOHN T. WILDER
BRIGADE COMMANDER, ARMY OF THE CUMBERLAND

Wilder explains how his command won the nickname Lightning Brigade at Hoover's Gap. His superiors had expected it would take several days and heavy losses to capture the vital pass. Yet Wilder's bold action allowed the Federals to seize it in just one day. Armed with Spencer repeating rifles, his vastly outnumbered brigade inflicted 146 Confederate casualties while losing only 14 killed and 47 wounded of its own.

Captain Rice, Adjutant-General of the division, came riding speedily to the front with orders from General Reynolds to me to fall back immediately, as the division was six or eight miles in our rear, having stopped to repair a bridge without letting me know of it. I told him I would hold this position against any force, and to tell General Reynolds to come on without hurrying, as there was no danger of our being driven out of the position. Captain Rice repeated his order for me to fall back, and I told him I would take the responsibility of remaining where I was, and that if General Reynolds were on the ground he would not give such an order. Captain Rice said that he had no discretion in the matter, and that if I did not obey the order he would put me in arrest and give the command to Colonel Miller, who would fall back as ordered.

I declined to obey the order of arrest, and requested Captain Rice to return to General Reynolds and tell him we had driven their force back, and could not be driven by any forces that could come at us. He then left just as the second attack was being made. This move was repulsed without difficulty, and when the enemy had fallen back out of range, General Rosecrans, with General Thomas and General Garfield, came riding up with their staff and escort. General Rosecrans came up to me and asked what we had done, and I told him in a few words, and also told him I had taken the responsibility of disobeying the order of General Reynolds to fall back, knowing that we could hold the position, and also felt sure that General Reynolds would not order us to retire if he were present.

General Rosecrans took off his hat and handed it to an orderly, and grasped my hand in both of his, saying: "You took the responsibility to disobey orders, did you? Thank God for your decision. It would have cost us two thousand lives to have taken this position if you had given it up."

General Reynolds just then came riding up in advance of his forces, and General Rosecrans said to him: "Wilder has done right. Promote him, promote him," and General Reynolds, after looking over the position, said to me: "You did right, and should be promoted and not censured."

The next morning an order was read at the head of every regiment of the Fourteenth Corps describing the attack of my command, saying that the conduct of the brigade should be emulated by all, and recommended my promotion as a Brigadier-General, and directing that the command should thereafter be known as Wilder's Lightning Brigade.

CORPORAL GEORGE S. WILSON
17TH INDIANA INFANTRY, WILDER'S BRIGADE

Corporal Wilson and other members of his company were advancing as dismounted skirmishers near the southern entrance to Hoover's Gap when they were pinned down by Confederate sharpshooters and caught in the middle of an artillery duel. It was at that moment that the Confederates launched a powerful counterattack. Wilson remained in the U.S. Army until his death on January 12, 1897. His final rank was major.

We were hurriedly dismounted and assigned positions. My regiment was posted on a wooded hill to the right of the road; the other regiments were assigned positions and the battery took station on high ground retired from the center. My company was thrown forward to a rail fence as skirmishers, and was at once hotly engaged by a battalion of Georgia Sharpshooters, who had cover behind a sharp ridge about 200 yards to the front. At the same time a Rebel battery opened on ours, and at once elicited a reply. Both friendly and unfriendly projectiles passed over our heads. This state of affairs had gone on about ten minutes, when there suddenly burst from a thicket a short distance to our left front two Rebel regiments, who bore down on us at a run, with their accustomed yell. About this time I developed a sudden desire to retire to the seclusion of the wood-covered hill where the regiment lay, and looked around to see if the other fellows were not of the same mind. They were. If we didn't make tracks to the rear at the same speed, it was because some of the boys couldn't run as fast as the rest of us.

SERGEANT BENJAMIN F. MAGEE
72D INDIANA INFANTRY, WILDER'S BRIGADE

As regimental historian, Magee recorded this account of how Lewis E. Wilhite of Company E saved the lives of three children at Hoover's Gap. The 72d Indiana—described by Magee as "in the front rank of all the regiments that went from the noble old State of Indiana"—was among the first Federal units to enter the infamous Confederate prison at Andersonville, Georgia, in May 1865.

Just then the rebel artillery began to rake their position and the skirmishers also began to fire on them. The company started to move across the woods and immediately came upon three little children who were bewildered in their efforts to escape from the dangers and awful noise of the battle; two little girls aged about seven and nine, and a little boy aged five. These were veritable babes of the woods. The girls could out-run the boy, but every minute would stop, turn, and cry, "come on, bubby, come on!" Sergt. Wilhite, amid a shower of bullets, dismounted, helped them over the fence, placed the boy between the girls and started them towards a house, out of the range of the fire, remounted his horse while the bullets rattled against the fence and rode away unhurt. At such an act of tenderness would not the angels smile through the smoke of battle and protect the brave man who did it?

Wearing a cavalry jacket with the yellow taping removed to mark him as mounted infantry, Private William N. Rogers, 98th Illinois, Wilder's brigade, holds his precious Spencer rifle. The weapon, which could deliver a .52-caliber bullet accurately the distance of a mile, held up well in its first combat test at Hoover's Gap. The rifle, one of Rogers' comrades claimed, "never got out of repair. It could be taken all to pieces to clean, and hence was little trouble to keep in order."

LIEUTENANT A. PIATT ANDREW III

21ST INDIANA BATTERY, CROOK'S BRIGADE

Crook's brigade moved into the front lines at Hoover's Gap on the evening of June 24. Among Crook's soldiers was Andrew, who had enlisted in August 1862 after completing his sophomore year at Wabash College. In 1860 he had been among the throng of spectators watching Abraham Lincoln accept the nomination for the presidency at the Republican Convention in Chicago.

LIEUTENANT ROBERT M. COLLINS

15TH TEXAS CAVALRY (DISMOUNTED), DESHLER'S BRIGADE

Perhaps because of his difficult youth—he was orphaned as a child and his guardian also died—Collins developed survival skills early on, not the least of which was a keen sense of humor, as revealed by this anecdote from his popular "Unwritten History" of the Civil War, published in 1892. Despite suffering a serious thigh wound at Peachtree Creek that pained him for the rest of his life, the self-educated Collins never lost his wit. After the war he became a respected businessman and newspaper editor in Texas.

It had rained all day and unfortunately the rain did not depart with the day but continued to fall during the night. It is not difficult to imagine the condition of our clothing and our feelings.

At the break of day all were up and at their posts, prepared for whatever might be in store. But though the enemy were plainly in sight not a shot was fired from either side until about eight o'clock, when artillery firing commenced, continuing for half an hour or more with considerable activity. One shot struck both wheels of one of Loomis' pieces (which had been placed upon our left a short time before), cutting a spoke from each wheel and stunning two of the cannoniers. Only one of our company was injured, and his wound was slight—a finger being broken by a piece of shell. A number of the infantry were killed and wounded during the firing. For a short time all was quiet. Then rebel infantry were seen advancing and immediately the Ninety-second Ohio moved forward as skirmishers, one or two companies at a time, till nearly the whole regiment was engaged. For the remainder of the day firing was quite active a few hundred yards to our left and front. Quite a number were killed and wounded on both sides. In the afternoon about four o'clock, the rebs again opened with artillery from four different points, all centering upon the batteries. Their guns were stationed on our front, left flank, and at two points between these positions. It was their hope to drive us from our position and their pieces were well sta-

tioned for their purpose, but the want of skill on the part of their gunners prevented the completion of their plan. Fourteen of our pieces opened upon them, and for a short time shot and shell flew thick and fast. Their guns ceased firing and the contest was closed for the day.

After ten minutes' notice on the morning of June 28th, we had packed our traps and were in line moving with the head of our column going toward Blue Bird Gap. The Federal army under command of Gen. Rosencrans was on the move pressing, we supposed, all along Bragg's front, whose right was somewhere near McMinville and his left at Shelbyville. When our brigade arrived at the Gap already named, quite a lively skirmish was going on. We were put in line in a wheat field on the safe side of a hill. Woods' Mississippi Brigade were in line a few spaces lower down the hill and in our rear. The Texas boys here got in some work on the "mud-heads" as we called them. The ground was covered with a sort of iron ore pebbles; the Texans would flip these pebbles right over the heads of the Mississippians in such manner as to make them sing like a minnie ball, and they stuck their heads so close to the ground that their mustaches took root and commenced to grow. We had fun enough for all until they caught us in the trick. That night we were marched back to the camp we had left in the morning; passing through a little town called Bellbuckle, on the 29th the whole army seemed to be on the move towards Tulahoma.

"If we haven't been in any of the fights, we have been in enough mud to make up for it."

PRIVATE JAMES G. WATSON
25TH ILLINOIS INFANTRY, HEG'S BRIGADE

For Watson and the rest of the 25th Illinois, Rosecrans' elaborate plan to drive Bragg from the ridge between Murfreesboro and Duck River consisted only of slogging through the rain and mud at the rear of McCook's XX Corps. Nearly deaf from "the firing of cannon and the bursting of shell" at Pea Ridge in early 1862 and wounded in the right shoulder by shrapnel at Chickamauga, Watson served through the Atlanta campaign, mustering out in September 1864.

June 30, 1863, Manchester, Tennessee ". . . We left camp on the 24th and marched in rear of our train as guard . . . rained hard . . . some hard fighting during the day . . . it rained all night; next day . . . only marched three miles. The next day we marched through Greys Gap and camped in Beech Grove . . . the next day we marched to this place . . . probably will go to Tullahoma tomorrow 12 miles off . . . our Brigade has been the rear guard for the whole corps and wagon train so if we haven't been in any of the fights, we have been in enough mud to make up for it.

LIEUTENANT WILBUR F. HINMAN
65TH OHIO, HARKER'S BRIGADE

Having reduced their route gear to a bare minimum, and with supply trains slowed by heavy rains and dismal roads, the men of the 65th Ohio, typical of any soldiers on the march, supplemented their meager supplies any way they could. Hinman was wounded on the first day of fighting at Chickamauga.

We were ordered to march at five o'clock Friday morning. We were ready, but after standing around in the mud till noon were directed to pitch tents and spend the night there. Two or three professedly loyal denizens of the neighborhood made so much disturbance on account of the work of our foragers, that Colonel Harker, in a state of unwonted excitement, directed Lieutenant-colonel Whitbeck to cause the arrest of all offenders in the Sixty-fifth. The storm-center seemed to be over Company D, which was enveloped in the incense arising from sizzling ham and tenderloin. Every member of that company seemed to be engaged in cooking a tidbit from a freshly slaughtered pig. I happened to be the first officer upon whom Whitbeck's eye rested, and he ordered me to proceed at once to company D, ferret out the offenders, and arrest them in the name of the United States of America. Buckling on my "toad-stabber," to give myself an impressive appearance, I put on a stern look and proceeded upon my mission. That one or more pigs had come to an untimely end through the agency of Company D, individually or collectively, was an obvious fact. The evidence was cumulative and undeniable. But where that fresh pork came from no man knew—at least that is what everybody said. I appealed to Lieutenant Gardner, whom I found squatting under a "pup" tent, gnawing a savory spare-rib.

"Well," he said, as he wiped the grease from his mustache and smacked his lips, "you've heard that it sometimes rains toads and angle-worms! The fact is it rained pieces of fresh pork this morning, and my boys just held out their gum blankets and caught 'em. Fact, sure's my name's Asa Gardner!"

Clearly, the only way by which the wrongs of outraged justice could be avenged was to arrest the whole company. I did not feel myself sufficiently numerous to do this. . . . I traveled back and made to Colonel Whitbeck an official report in writing, setting forth the singular freak of nature by which the pork had found its way to Company D, and venturing to suggest that it was a dispensation of Providence to save that excellent company from starvation. I was afraid the colonel would order me under arrest for not discharging my duty better, but he didn't. He just winked and said he guessed the matter might drop there. How he settled the account with Colonel Harker, I never learned. Lieutenant Gardner sent to my quarters a nicely-cooked and fragrant section of pig, and I devoured it with a thankful heart—and stomach.

SERGEANT BENJAMIN F. MAGEE
72D INDIANA INFANTRY, WILDER'S BRIGADE

On the morning of June 28, Magee and his comrades set off on one of their most exhausting missions of the war. From the town of Manchester, some 15 miles northeast of Tullahoma, they rode a 45-mile-long, circuitous route through Hillsboro, Pelham, and Hawkinsville, to Decherd, nearly 10 miles southeast of Tullahoma, where the Army of Tennessee was concentrated. After destroying much of the town, the Federals made their escape into the Cumberland Mountains, where the bone-tired men slept on the rocky slopes under a steady downpour.

Duck and Elk rivers were so swollen by the rains as to swim all the mules and small horses; at one place we carried the artillery ammunition across on our horses, and at the other made a raft to ferry the artillery over. We reached Decherd at nine o'clock at night. The bulk of Bragg's army was at Tullahoma, 15 miles north of this place, and hence we are right in the rear of Bragg's army. We found Decherd garrisoned by a small force of rebels in stockade, and scattered them with a few shots from our howitzers. . . .

A detachment of Wilder's mounted brigade trots past a Federal outpost in this sketch made for Frank Leslie's Illustrated Newspaper. The artist shows the horses kicking up dust when in fact they were slogging through mud as they drove southward behind Confederate lines to raid the village of Decherd, a rail junction on the Nashville & Chattanooga Railroad line. There, on June 28, Wilder's men destroyed a bridge and tore up track, temporarily cutting off Bragg's communications with Chattanooga.

116 FRANK LESLIE'S ILLUSTRATED NEWSPAPER. [Nov. 14, 1863.

THE ARMY OF THE CUMBERLAND—WILDER'S MOUNTED INFANTRY PASSING A BLOCKHOUSE ON THE NASHVILLE AND CHATTANOOGA RAILROAD.—FROM A SKETCH BY OUR SPECIAL ARTIST, J. F. E. HILLEN.

While this was going on Capt. Rice started through the village to give directions to scouts who were burning the water tank, tearing up the railroad and working all possible mischief in a great hurry. He had dismounted and was quietly leading his horse when suddenly some rebels began to fire on him from a stockade; the bullets rattled against a fence and scared his horse, which jerked loose from him, leaving him in quite an unpleasant predicament, and his chances for Libby prison good. His horse did not run from him, but just as he caught the bridle another volley, and another rattle of balls against the fence, and again the horse broke away. This was repeated, the Captain's hair standing on end, until the horse got out of range of the bullets, and then the Captain mounted and went out of there like a bird flying. He regards this as his most daring feat during the war, but confesses that he was a little scared. . . .

. . . The depot was burned, a short section of the railroad torn up and a bridge burned. The command then hurried away six mile, north-east, to a point on the Cumberland Mountains, and as Records has it, "ambushed for the night;" that is, simply stopped in the bushes and lay down to sleep, holding our horses' bridles in our hands. We had put in another hard day's work in the rain, and our beds were on the mountain side on the sharpest of rocks. The mountain was so steep that we had to get our feet against the trees or rocks to keep from slipping down. And had not the surroundings been so desperate it would have been funny to see us try to sleep. You see a big, stout, long-legged soldier lay down flat of his back, his legs stiff and his feet braced against a tree; in two minutes he is asleep, his muscles begin to relax, his knees fly up, and down he goes a-straddle of the tree. With many the remainder of the night is worn away in sliding down the hill and climbing up again; while others more fortunate, find a hole or depression, the rain still pouring down, and two hours later they are called up to find themselves in water six inches deep.

LIEUTENANT GRANVILLE C. WEST
4TH KENTUCKY (U.S.) INFANTRY, CROXTON'S BRIGADE

On July 1, Colonel John T. Croxton (below, right) ordered Lieutenant Granville West to storm the Confederate stronghold at Tullahoma, defended by the rear guard of Bragg's army. West had been with his regiment less than two months at the time; he went on to live a long life, serving as clerk in the War Department through World War I.

After a couple of days' maneuvering and some pretty hard fighting Hardee was driven out of and away from the Gap. He retreated on the road to Manchester and Tullahoma and for several days we followed him in almost a continuous skirmish. Whenever the ground offered a favorable place he would make a stand, and we would have to form line and drive him out. When night came we bivouacked then and there on the ground we had won that day. He was finally driven to his stronghold at Tullahoma which had been fortified by formidable earthworks, behind which Fort Bragg stood a tremendous bulwark, all of which was guarded by fallen trees, sharpened limbs and abatis of all descriptions. We had driven his skirmish line to within probably one-half mile of his outer works. Here the enemy made a tenacious and defiant stand against our line of skirmishers. Company A of my regiment being on the skirmish line, Company B was deployed and sent forward to reinforce the line, but the enemy still stubbornly held his ground. The rattle of the musketry fire and frequently the wounded coming back indicated quite a fierce struggle. The regiment stood in line of battle a few rods in the rear. The Brigade commander galloped up to my front, called me by name and gave me the order, "deploy your company, go forward and pass through our skirmish line and assail those fellows in the woods, drive them into their works and assault the works and take them."

This order was plain and imperative and admitted no doubtful construction.

I turned to my company, commanded, "Attention company, forward, deploy as skirmishers, quick step, march!" and we were off.

The Major of my regiment was in command of the skirmish line where the battle was in progress. When he saw my line advancing he galloped up to me and asked my orders; when I told him he was silent for a moment, settled back in his saddle and remarked that he thought I had a serious job before me. I replied that might be the case, but I

"The line of battle had come through the woods into the open and the long line of bayonets glistening in the bright sun presented a scene of warlike splendor."

was going into those works or be brought out on a stretcher. As I passed through the skirmish line they ceased firing and gave my line a rousing cheer and made all kinds of complimentary and encouraging remarks. This was one of those situations that I thought it doubtful that I would get out of alive, for, if the enemy held to his position, under my orders I could not stop and did not intend to. As we moved forward the enemy, hearing the cheers and seeing my line boldly coming through the woods, gave us a parting shot and began to give way, and we drove them into their works and out, and as we moved through the fallen trees and sharpened limbs, the sun was shining intensely hot, and we suffered severely. But the enemy was fleeing and the tension relaxed. As I mounted the works I turned to look back, the line of battle had come through the woods into the open and the long line of bayonets glistening in the bright sun presented a scene of warlike splendor. I assembled my company near Fort Bragg, and in a few minutes Gen. J. B. Steadman, the grand old hero, rode up from another part of the field, now a General commanding a division. He had been Colonel of the 14th Ohio in our Brigade and knew me, and he called me by name and said, "I see you here;" and asked "did you lead the advance into the works in your front." I told him "yes;" that I had taken the advance half a mile back and drove the skirmish line of the enemy into the works and out, when they moved off immediately in retreat, and he then ejaculated "Quite an honor, sir, quite an honor, and you should have official recognition of it." The whole rebel army had taken flight and was gone.

Although Colonel John T. Croxton (left) had no formal military training, his corps commander, Major General George H. Thomas, called the Yale graduate, lawyer, and Republican politician the "best soldier Kentucky has furnished to the war." Croxton recovered from a leg wound at Chickamauga to attain the rank of brigadier general in 1864. He died 10 years later, while serving the Grant administration as minister to Bolivia.

PRIVATE JAMES TURNER
6TH TEXAS INFANTRY, DESHLER'S BRIGADE

After putting up fierce resistance at Liberty Gap, Deshler's brigade pulled back to Tullahoma, where it formed a rear guard for Bragg's army. Turner and his comrades were among the last Confederates to cross the Tennessee River. Turner was captured at the Battle of Franklin in November 1864 and remained in Union hands until he was exchanged in May of the following year.

Slowly we retreated in the rain back to Tullahoma where we arrived at about noon on [June 30], completely worn out and covered with mud. Rations of corn meal and bacon were issued to us, and having no cooking utensils we baked our bread on flat fence rails turned up to the fire, making the well known johnny cakes, and we cooked our bacon on forked sticks. We enjoyed the feast for we had been without food since leaving Wartrace. We remained in line at Tullahoma until night, thinking we would make a stand at that point, for the place was fortified, but after dark the order to march was given and the retreat to Chattanooga began.

Our brigade acted as rear guard and on the next day we halted at Bethpage Bridge on Elk River, near the town of Allisonia, where we held the enemy in check until our retreating army could get well started over the bridge, which was immediately burned, and fell back to the foot of the mountains where we remained in line until the following evening when we, too, started over the mountains.

We retreated down the Sequatia Valley, crossed the Tennessee River on a pontoon bridge and went into camp near Tiners Station, about nine miles east of Chattanooga. As we had had nothing to eat since leaving Tullahoma except green apples and an occasional ear of corn picked up in the road, we were somewhat hungry and were glad to get the green corn issued to us on our arrival.

All of our tents having been burnt up at Tullahoma, we built brush arbors for shelter and made ourselves as comfortable as possible. The great quantity of commissary stores which Bragg had been collecting for so many months at Tullahoma had also been burned up to keep them from falling into the hands of the enemy, so we had to live for a week or more on green corn, which soon became tiresome, and we were delighted to receive the corn meal and bacon which finally came to us, and we came near eating up a week's rations at one meal.

PRIVATE LEVI WAGNER
1ST OHIO INFANTRY, BALDWIN'S BRIGADE

Having been under artillery fire at Liberty Gap, but suffering no losses, the 1st Ohio Infantry was ordered to march on Manchester and then on Tullahoma. Wagner recalled, "This march was very disagreeable to both men and horses, on account of the constant rain, which made the ground so soft that it was almost impossible for teams to pull through." The unit would remain in Tullahoma until August 16, when Rosecrans began his move on Chattanooga.

On the 1st of July we passed on to Tullahoma, Bragg having vacated the place, going toward Chattanooga. We got into town about 1 A.M. that night. Here the indications were that Bragg had left in a hurry. I cannot see why he delayed his going until the last moment, unless he expected the rain to check our advance. Vain expectations, for when the army of the Cumberland once started, nothing would stop it. . . .

Our regiment camped on the north side of the railroad, and just opposite the station. Nearly all the town was located on the north side.

Colonel Philemon P. Baldwin was killed attempting to rally his brigade at the Battle of Chickamauga on September 19, 1863. Having grabbed the colors of the 6th Indiana, he jerked his horse around to face the Confederates and yelled, "Follow me!" A hail of bullets then struck him, and he fell dead from the saddle.

There were but a few dwellings on the north side, and a large school building just at the right of our camp. I think likely the 2nd Division was all that was left here, while the rest of the army followed up the Rebels, as I can remember seeing sick and wounded being brought back and placed in houses, after being there a few days. On the 2nd of Aug. our Co. was detailed to clean out this schoolhouse and prepare it for a hospital, as there was no place for the many wounded being brought back there. Along in the afternoon when we had just finished our task and were lounging about in the yard talking and resting, with several perched upon the front fence, which same was a board fence, among which was a man named Bennett, from about New Holland, O. suddenly for some unknown cause, a large lot of shell that had been left lying scattered around in the store room of the depot, by the Rebels, exploded with a shock more startling to the nerves than the firing of a hundred cannon, because of its unexpectedness. A piece of shell came speeding across the way and struck Bennett on the breast. He was knocked off the fence and killed so quickly that his spirit passed from one realm to the other like a flash. Mr. Bennett was a man of fine, soldierly qualities, not very large but well built and very neat in appearance, seldom speaking unless spoken to, and then with few words. I cannot remember ever having seen him smile, yet he was kind and generous and brave. A flat piece of shell had struck him in the breast and killed him instantly, without cutting the skin or leaving any kind of a mark. There was also another member of the regiment killed. He was badly mutilated, and was not of our crowd.

PRIVATE JOHN A. WYETH

4TH ALABAMA CAVALRY, RUSSELL'S BRIGADE

Pictured at left as a callow cadet at La Grange Military Academy in Franklin, Alabama, John Wyeth brought his own rifle to war—a Burnside carbine that he purchased for $50 with money given to him by his married sister. The rear-guard action Wyeth describes here took place at Elk River.

Nothing so depresses an army as a retreat; no duty is so harrowing and demoralizing as that of fighting rear-guard actions day after day. South of Tullahoma, with the regular installment of rain, we stood off the aggressive Union cavalry until we cleared the half-barren post-oak and black-jack plateau, from the summit of which we descended to cross Elk River on a planked-over railroad-bridge, and at dark on July 1st found ourselves posted to oppose the enemy at the crossing of this river known as Morris' Ford.

On the morning of July 2, we were up early and were congratulating ourselves on having a short rest. It was clear, and as soon as the sun rose we turned our saddles bottom side up to dry, and while some of the men were busy getting breakfast a number of us went down to the river to indulge in the luxury of a swim. As we were finishing our simple breakfast of corn-bread and bacon the videttes left half a mile from the ford on the north side of the stream fired at a squadron of the Fourth Ohio Cavalry, which chased them into the river. As soon as the guns were heard we were ordered to rush to the ford and hold the enemy back. Some of us (sixteen in all) were fortunate enough to reach a small thicket near the crossing, where we ensconced ourselves in a gully. Others lay down behind a worm-fence, with nothing but that and the light fringe of bushes for protection.

We had barely reached our places when the Federals opened on us with a heavy fire of small arms and two pieces of artillery. This fire raked the bivouac on the open hillside behind us—excepting the small number who had already succeeded in sheltering themselves close along the bank—back over the crest of the hill fully a half-mile away. As we had no artillery, our position was not to be envied. To try to escape exposed us at close range to the fire from small arms, and to grape and canister for fully four hundred yards of open hillside. Realizing that we were in for it, we prepared for rapid loading by laying our cartridges and caps in rows on the ground and concentrated our fire on the narrow roadway which led into the stream from the other side.

After having driven everybody else away, the enemy gave their undivided attention to us, and for nearly three hours there was the liveliest firing I ever heard. They were so near we could distinctly hear every command given in an ordinary tone of voice. Those of our men who were lying behind the old fence suffered severely, and a number were killed or wounded (we could hear their groans), and long before the fight was over no resistance was offered anywhere except by our small squad of sixteen men. . . .

Being informed of our situation, General Wheeler had hurried back two Parrott guns, which at this moment were unlimbering on the crest of the ridge behind us where we could not see them, but were in plain view of the Federals. The roar of these guns, the whizzing of the shells as they passed not far above our heads, and their explosion in the timber across the river was the most welcome sound I ever heard, for the Yankees scampered away as fast as our men had earlier in the day. Then when all was clear we ventured out and rejoined our company, to be publicly commended by our good colonel for what we really couldn't help doing.

"Leaning over his saddle he spoke of the loss of Middle Tennessee and whispered: 'This is a great disaster.' "

SERGEANT AXEL H. REED
2D MINNESOTA INFANTRY, VAN DERVEER'S BRIGADE

Reed and the men of the 2d Minnesota marched south out of Tullahoma early the morning of July 2. Reed recorded in his diary that the route was littered with, among other things, "a number of Secesh wagons broken down and clothing strewn by the roadside, corn meal was scattered along the road," all abandoned by the Confederates in retreat. The day after the river crossing described here, in celebration of Independence Day and the victories at Vicksburg and Gettysburg, "a salute of 35 guns was fired by the 4th regular battery."

July 3. . . . It was a novel sight to see the troops crossing the stream which was about 6 rods wide and four feet deep, with swift current. Two ropes were stretched across for men to hang onto to keep from going downstream. Some would strip naked, do their things in a rubber blanket and string it with their accoutrements on their bayonets. Then they would make their way across, some by ropes, and others by hanging onto horses' tails. I noticed Capt. Roper, our division quartermaster, busy with his horse hauling the boys across, and he would take nearly a dozen at a time. Someone remarked that it was too many hanging on to his horse's tail when Capt. R. sais, "I'll pull them through if the tail doesn't come out." Some lost their haversacks, others their accoutrements, etc. One of the 10th Ky. was drowned. Our brigade all got across about 4 o'clock and went into bivouac about three-quarters of a mile from the ford. There was a heavy shower today until 10 o'clock, until noon. Vicksburg is reported taken, and Lee's army whipped out by Gen. Meade who superseded Hooker. We have to move slowly on account of the roads and streams and our transportation is doubtful whether we come up with the enemy before they reach Chattanooga.

Private Nathaniel Delzell of the 17th Tennessee Infantry was captured by the Federals on July 3 near Tullahoma, only six miles from his home. Declaring himself a deserter, Delzell swore an oath of allegiance to the Union and was allowed to go free six days later.

DOCTOR CHARLES T. QUINTARD

CHAPLAIN, POLK'S CORPS

The Reverend Charles Quintard's conversation with a depressed and unnerved General Bragg occurred as the Army of Tennessee was retreating from Tullahoma. Born in Stamford, Connecticut, Quintard graduated from medical school in New York City in 1847. After completing an internship at Bellevue Hospital, he traveled south, eventually settling in Tennessee, where he took up the study of theology, joining the Episcopal priesthood in 1856.

Thence I rode to Cowan, where I found General Bragg and his staff, and General Polk with his staff. I rode up to them and said to General Bragg: "My dear General, I am afraid you are thoroughly outdone."

"Yes," he said, "I am utterly broken down." And then leaning over his saddle he spoke of the loss of Middle Tennessee and whispered: "This is a great disaster."

I said to him: "General, don't be disheartened, our turn will come next."

CAPTAIN ALFRED LACEY HOUGH

STAFF, MAJOR GENERAL JAMES S. NEGLEY, ARMY OF THE CUMBERLAND

Hough describes for his wife the difficulties the Federals faced in attempting to pursue Bragg through the Cumberland Mountains. The New Jersey-born Hough was raised a Quaker but fell away from the faith. When the Civil War broke out, he gave up his business and volunteered, even though he was 35 years old and married with two children. It was the beginning of a 29-year military career.

Head-quarters, Second Division
Fourteenth Army Corps.
July 5th, 1863

My Dearest Wife:

. . . We are in camp to-day at the foot of the Cumberland Mountains, S.E. from Tullahoma. We intended to reach the top of the Mountains yesterday but after toiling all the afternoon, it was found to be impossible, the mud, rocks and fallen timber could not be overcome, so we countermarched and got into camp at the foot of the Mountain just after dark. Our pioneers are clearing the road to-day and to-morrow I suppose we shall start again. It was a fearfully hard day's work, and oh how good it is to rest to-day this Sabbath, but it still rains, coming down in torrents as I write. The rains have been the means of preventing us from entirely intercepting Hardee's Corps, which I can see now was part of our campaign. We have driven them hard all the time, but they having the start, destroyed the bridges, and the swollen streams could not be forded, we would have to wait for them to subside, and then another rain before we reached the next stream, we aimed to get into the mountains before they did, but they passed over on the 3rd of July, and will be safe in Chattanooga before we get over. If we could have had fine weather I verily believe we would have destroyed Hardee's Corps this side of the mountains. This has been the hardest work I ever experienced, and Gen. Negley says the hardest one he ever had at this season of the year. We left Murfreesboro on the 24th ult I believe and it has rained every day but two since we left. The elements obstructed us, but we pushed the enemy so hard they could do nothing to stop us except burning the bridges, until they got into the Mountains, and there they have felled trees across the passes, that will take us some time to clear away. We are still in the advance on this road, and what we will have to do when we get across I do not know, but suppose the different corps will join, and make a combined attack on Bridgeport or

Major General James S. Negley, commander of the 2d Division in Thomas' XIV Corps, stands bareheaded in front of his staff on a steep slope in the rugged Cumberland Mountains. The 36-year-old Negley served as a private in the Mexican War and commanded a militia company in his hometown of East Liberty, Pennsylvania. But his first love was botany. "When in the field of war," a journalist wrote, "his leisure hours were devoted to the study of various fruits, flowers and shrubs in which the Southern fields and woods abounded. I have known him, when on the march frequently to spring from his saddle to pluck a sensitive plant."

Chattanooga; the fall of either will carry both of these strongholds; we have been eminently successful in driving them across the Mountains, compelling them to evacuate two strongly fortified towns Shelbyville & Tullahoma (good depots for us) and opening up a large space of country in a few days with but little loss to ourselves, but at the same time we feel disappointed at not having destroyed Hardee's Corps, which was in the rear. But the more we get the more we want, when we started, there was not a man or office that I know of, but what expected we should have had two or three heavy battles with great loss on our side before getting this far, and most certainly if we had not surprised them, this would have been the case, they were not prepared for our ordnance from the direction we came on them. . . . I don't say anything about our fighting but we have had plenty of it. I have been in the front during all of our advance and have done my duty, that is all I have to say. Am looking anxiously for a letter from you. . . .

    Alfred

SECRETARY OF WAR EDWIN M. STANTON

Amid the rejoicing in the North over the great victories at Gettysburg and Vicksburg, the fall of tiny Tullahoma received scant attention. Rosecrans' nine-day campaign had been a model of planning and execution, yet it had failed to impress his superiors in Washington, who worried that he was giving up an opportunity to destroy Bragg's army by failing to pursue more vigorously.

War Department,
    Washington, July 7, 1863.
      Major-General Rosecrans,
Tullahoma, Tenn.:
We have just received official information that Vicksburg surrendered to General Grant on the 4th of July. Lee's army overthrown; Grant victorious. You and your noble army now have the chance to give the finishing blow to the rebellion. Will you neglect the chance?

    Edwin M. Stanton,
    Secretary of War.

"I beg in behalf of this army that the War Department may not overlook so great an event because it is not written in letters of blood."

MAJOR GENERAL WILLIAM S. ROSECRANS
COMMANDER, ARMY OF THE CUMBERLAND

Rosecrans had all but swept the Confederates from Tennessee at a cost of fewer than 600 casualties, and he bitterly resented Stanton's badgering telegram. His immediate and scathing reply—sarcastically laced with the secretary's own words—is printed below.

Tullahoma, *July 7,* 1863.
    Hon. E. M. Stanton:
      Just received your cheering dispatch announcing the fall of Vicksburg and confirming the defeat of Lee. You do not appear to observe the fact that this noble army has driven the rebels from Middle Tennessee, of which my dispatches advised you. I beg in behalf of this army that the War Department may not overlook so great an event because it is not written in letters of blood. I have now to repeat, that the rebel army has been forced from its strong intrenched positions at Shelbyville and Tullahoma, and driven over the Cumberland Mountains. My infantry advance is within 16 miles and my cavalry advance within 8 miles of the Alabama line. No organized rebel force within 25 miles of there, nor in this side of the Cumberland Mountains.

    W. S. Rosecrans.

Maneuvering for Battle

General Rosecrans, settling into his new Tullahoma headquarters on July 3, had good reason to move with deliberation on Chattanooga. He would be advancing into rough country, he reminded General in Chief Halleck in Washington, and needed to stockpile supplies. Besides, Rosecrans worried that Braxton Bragg's Confederates might be reinforced with troops coming from the east or west or both—a fear that was, as it turned out, well founded.

Halleck fumed as usual and on August 4 sent Rosecrans another of his rockets. "Your forces," wired Halleck, "must move forward without further delay. You will daily report the movement of each of your corps until you cross the Tennessee River." Shocked that Halleck would send such a message to a commanding general in the field, Rosecrans requested confirmation. Replied Halleck: "The orders are peremptory."

At last on August 16, after a six-week pause, Rosecrans got under way. Once started he again moved swiftly and succeeded, as at Tullahoma, in taking Bragg and his Confederates by surprise.

The most logical approach to Chattanooga was to move southeast across a rocky mass known as Walden's Ridge, then fall on the town from the north. But Rosecrans, deciding to stage another feint, sent only a modest force led by Brigadier General William B. Hazen swinging off over Walden's Ridge —three infantry brigades spearheaded by John Wilder's fast-riding horsemen.

Wilder's brigade moved swiftly, emerging from the hills across the Tennessee River from Chattanooga only five days later, on August 21. In minutes Eli Lilly had unlimbered his battery of guns and was lobbing shells into the town, causing huge consternation. General Hazen did not have the manpower to storm across the river but staged such a clever show of force that Bragg was fooled into thinking the whole Federal army was nearby and about to attack from the north or northeast.

With Bragg's attention fixed, General Rosecrans prepared his hammer blow, marching his main force—three corps of 50,000 infantry plus 9,000 cavalry—toward crossings on the Tennessee River more than 20 miles west of Chattanooga. The Federal troops crossed the river unseen by September 4, then prepared to make a sweeping left wheel, moving on Chattanooga and Bragg's army from the southwest.

The wheeling maneuver was exceedingly risky because it sent the Federal troops into rough, tangled terrain south of Chattanooga dominated by the 30-mile-long mass of Lookout Mountain. But Rosecrans counted on speed and surprise, and the expectation that Bragg, suddenly finding the entire enemy army on his flank, would be forced to evacuate Chattanooga and flee full speed into northern Georgia.

Bragg, in the dark for days, finally realized in early September that a powerful force had streamed across the river and threatened his left. At first he vacillated, shifting a few units. But then on September 7, with his vulnerable supply line in immediate danger of being cut, Bragg ordered his army to march south, abandoning the prize of Chattanooga without firing a shot.

Rosecrans fired off a triumphant message to Halleck, "Chattanooga is ours without a struggle," and ordered his army to pursue at full tilt. He dispatched General McCook and his XX Corps more than 40 miles south to cross Lookout Mountain through distant Winston's Gap and assail Bragg's rear. At the same time George Thomas and his 20,000-man XIV Corps were to march across Lookout Mountain via Stevens' Gap and hit Bragg's flank while Crittenden's XXI Corps secured Chattanooga and then sped south on Bragg's coattails. The Confederates, Rosecrans was convinced, were in complete, panic-stricken retreat. "He didn't expect to get a fight out of Bragg," wrote one of his officers, "this side of Atlanta."

But Rosecrans, as he would soon discover, had made a blunder. Bragg was not retreating in disorder. Instead he was reorganizing his army around the town of La Fayette, Georgia, 25 miles south of Chattanooga—and hefty reinforcements were beginning to pour in: 8,000 men led by Major General Simon Bolivar Buckner who had marched west from Knoxville and 11,500 more under Major Generals John C. Breckinridge and William H. T. Walker coming from the west.

Seizing the chance to trap and destroy Rosecrans' divided army one segment at a time, Bragg directed Major General Thomas C. Hindman to fall on the flank of Thomas' advance guard. This Federal division, under Major General James S. Negley's command, had pushed through Stevens' Gap into a cul-de-sac called McLemore's Cove. To finish the job, Bragg ordered Hardee's old corps, now led by Lieutenant General Daniel Harvey Hill, to smash head-on at Negley's exposed position. Once he had Negley, Bragg thought, he could roll up the rest of Thomas' corps.

Incredibly, the usually aggressive Hill failed to attack, claiming his troops were not in position; to make matters worse, Hindman also hesitated. In a fury, Bragg ordered Buckner and his new arrivals to support Hindman. But both of these generals became over-cautious, and soon Negley, suspecting a trap, pulled his Federals safely back from McLemore's Cove to rejoin Thomas.

Frustrated but still determined to destroy his tormentors, Bragg on September 12 ordered General Polk to strike northward and wipe up Crittenden's corps, elements of which had pushed south to a place called Lee and Gordon's Mills. But Polk, fearing he faced a superior force, said the attack was impossible and refused to budge.

Seeing two chances lost, Bragg paused for three days. But then, even more grimly set on smashing the enemy, he sent his entire 65,000-man army marching toward what he thought was Crittenden's isolated corps. At the same time Rosecrans, finally seeing the danger, began feverishly pulling McCook and Thomas north out of the mountains. By September 17 the two armies were both lurching up the dusty roads toward Chickamauga Creek. There, after a day of skirmishing, they would crash together in the biggest battle in the West—and the deadliest, for the numbers engaged, of the entire war.

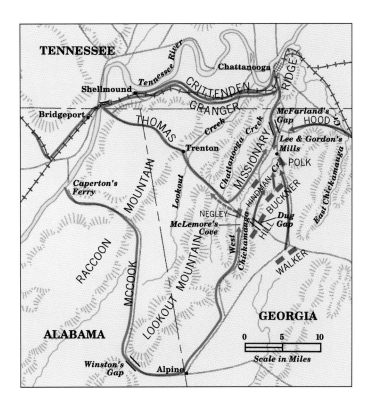

After evacuating Chattanooga, Braxton Bragg made an orderly withdrawal into Georgia, stopped near the town of La Fayette, and reorganized his forces. Then he turned to face the unsuspecting Federal columns. Bragg botched one attempt to trap Thomas' lead division under Negley in McLemore's Cove, and another effort to strike Crittenden near Lee and Gordon's Mills. After that, both sides girded for battle along Chickamauga Creek.

CAPTAIN ALFRED L. HOUGH

STAFF, MAJOR GENERAL JAMES S. NEGLEY

The duties of a staff officer were many, and sometimes included the bizarre—as Hough explains in this tongue-in-cheek letter to his wife, Mary Jane, in which he describes his concern over the prospect of frisking the wife of a Prussian who was seeking safe passage through the Federal lines. Following the war, Hough served at Nashville, New York harbor, and various posts in the West and also in Alaska. Throughout his 29-year career, Hough and his wife maintained a regular correspondence. He retired in 1890.

Dechard Tenn
July 26, 1863
My Dearest Wife: . . .

I have but little mustering to do now, but the general finds some pleasant duty to occupy me continually. I notice with satisfaction, that he selects me for any delicate or confidential duty to be performed. I yesterday had a very interesting case. A Prussian who has been living in Georgia came into our lines to proceed north, having a pass from Bragg for himself and family, wife and two children, he has a protection from his own Government, Prussia. Genl Thomas suspects that he is an emissary, and wished him examined he sent word to Genl Negley to that effect. The General directed me to attend to it with many injunctions as to the delicate nature of the business, so that no complications with his Government should arise. The joke of it is, that we only know that he is in our lines and has a pass from Bragg and his own Government's consul, he is to come here to take the cars, but we don't know

his name. I examined all suspicious persons yesterday, but my friend has not arrived. I am looking anxiously for him and am bothered somewhat about examining his wife. I can take care of him well enough, but how do I know but what Mrs. Prussian has some terrible papers sewed up in her "bustle" or some such out of the way place. I wish you were here to help me, and between us may be we could fix up any important matters of that kind. But I will be very discreet, so don't be uneasy. . . .

Good-bye,
As ever your true husband
Alfred

ANONYMOUS FARM LAD

Tennessee farm families were plundered by both sides, although the Confederates sometimes paid for the forage they took and the Federals usually tried to limit their targets to secessionist families. There were occasional reprisals; at least two of Wilder's brigade were shot as outlaws. "Our wholesale confiscation of property was looked upon by the suffered as wholesale robbery," one of Wilder's riders wrote, "and hence a very bitter feeling was entertained toward us."

The Rebel army had been in the vicinity all along befo' that, and occasionally some of the soldiers would come and take a horse—"press it into service," they said. Sometimes they'd kill a hog and skin the hams and carry 'em off, and leave the balance. We'd hardly ever see 'em kill an animal, but we'd find the carcass afterward. Their forage wagons would come around and go into our fields and take the oats, and the sheep. We had hogs, sheep, and cattle, plenty of 'em, then. Sometimes we'd git pay for the things that were taken, and sometimes we would n't. But when we did git pay it was in Confederate money which was n't of much value.

We did n't fear the regular armies as we did the guerillas. There were two bands here. One claimed to be Yankees and the other Rebels. But they were just robbers and both mean alike—that was all we could make out of 'em. The Rebel band would raid north, and the Yankee band would raid south. Sometimes they'd whip a man if they thought he belonged to the other side. They prowled around on their horses

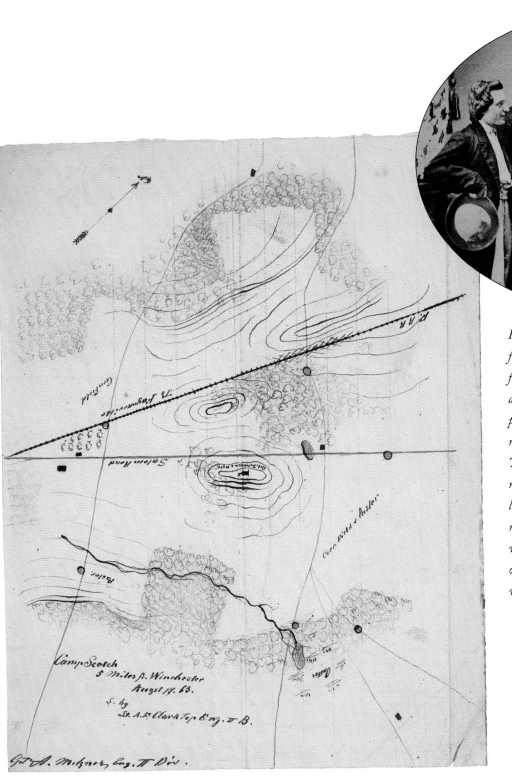

First Lieutenant Adolph Metzner (shown above in uniform, visiting with his family), the topographical engineer for Willich's brigade, drafted this map of the Federal camps around Winchester, Tennessee. In addition to his cartography, Metzner chronicled the history of his regiment through more than 100 watercolors, drawings, and field sketches. The all-German unit fought at Shiloh, Corinth, Chickamauga, Chattanooga, Missionary Ridge, and Atlanta. Its last campaign was with General William Tecumseh Sherman on the legendary march through Georgia. Metzner, who had received pharmaceutical training in Germany, opened a pharmacy and a tile-making factory after the war. He died in New Jersey on February 16, 1917.

and went in the houses and pilfered. Generally their raids were made at night.

I remember once some of 'em drove right up in our yard after we'd all gone to bed. I expect it was ten or 'leven o'clock. We all slept in the living room. There were two beds in the other room, but that room was for company. The guerillas knocked, and Mother got up and opened the door, which was fastened with a wooden button. Several men came in. They were dressed like Rebel soldiers. One of 'em with a big revolver had Paw set by the fire. Of course Paw did n't show any fight or order 'em out. He knew what they was up to. They'd been through the valley before.

We children stayed in bed. There was five of us, and we was skeered. We did n't like to see such visitors that time of night. They asked for food. We was good livers and had plenty to eat and wear—such as it was. The guerillas cooked some of our meat by the fireplace. While a few of 'em was doin' that the others looked around to see what we had that was worth carryin' off. They took some of our homespun clothing and a couple of quilts and a counterpane. They did n't find any silverware. We did n't have any those days. After they'd eaten they left.

The Yankee guerillas was commonly known as Wilder's Thieves. They taken the last horse we had. She was a little claybank filly, two years old—old enough to work pretty well. We had her grinding cane to make sorghum molasses, and they taken her right out of the harness. We asked 'em to leave an old mule we had that was about wore out, but they was kind of hardhearted and they went off with both the animals.

Befo' that, the Rebels had taken a mare and a young horse.

A Federal foraging party plunders livestock from a Tennessee farm despite angry protests in a painting by newspaper artist William D. T. Travis. Most of the foraging was done by Colonel John T. Wilder's mounted brigade, which shared its booty. Not everyone opposed the Federals. Many mountain families in eastern Tennessee welcomed them. One of Wilder's men recalled how the poor mountaineers "vied with each other in bestowing upon the boys their kindness—sweet potatoes, all kinds of vegetables, ducks, chickens, pies, cakes, honey, and applejack brandy."

PRIVATE PHILIP D. STEPHENSON
13TH ARKANSAS INFANTRY, GOVAN'S BRIGADE

Stephenson recalls the vicissitudes of finding and preparing enough to eat for an army on the march. "Cooking arrangements were crude, the vessels of the primitive kind . . . no stoves but the 'dutch oven,' skillet, frying pan, and camp kettle, and coffee pot were given out to each mess and each mess cooked its own. If cut off from the wagons for two or three days, or if we failed to get our rations cooked at the stops, we had to suffer the consequences."

On this march, it was either feast or famine. . . . . . . There was the surfeit at a little railroad station, name forgotten, where we were told to help ourselves to stores left behind by the trains and in danger of capture. In we went with a vengeance and the warehouse was soon emptied.

There was more than we could carry away. Boxes and barrels of bacon and flour and sugar and molasses and tobacco were brought out, broken open and scattered. Men loaded themselves down and still there was more! Some chose tobacco more than anything else and I myself took several plugs, although I had no use for it. Man after man marched off with a ham or side of bacon spitted on his bayonet. If the enemy had come it would have been a little awkward to have fought, but we would have done so. Would have had all the more inducement.

Further on, the tables turned again and we felt once more the pinch of hunger. It was at Dechard and Cowan Stations, just before we went up into the mountains. We stopped there several days to cook rations and rest. Although rations were given us, we had no cooking utensils. They were up ahead in the wagons or on the cars. Many were the devices to get dough and bread. The most common way was to find the biggest leaves we could, bend them into concave shape, put the flour into the hollow, pouring in water and mixing very carefully. Or, hollow out a log or stick of wood roughly. This for the dough. As to baking, we wrapped the dough around sticks or ramrods, or flattened it out on flat rocks and heated it. Of course we had no yeast or anything to make it rise. The meat problem was easily solved. All we had was bacon, and that we fried, holding it over the fire on forked sticks or on the ends of ramrods. As to coffee, sugar, or other rations, we had no trouble in the world about them—for we did not have them.

This was before we went up into the mountains. We were several days on or in the mountains, our rations failed, and we had another "hunger fest." For a day and night or more, we were almost literally without a crumb of food. Still, we marched. I do not remember a single rest on the mountains, except of course at night. Shortness of rations compelled expedition for there was nothing to be had in those barren wilds.

"Tom, have you anything to eat? I am so weak I can hardly walk."

"Nothing at all, Pheel. I am without myself," said he, holding up his haversack, but I taught him a thing or two. I had noticed as he held it up, that one corner of the haversack seemed packed and rounded out to some little extent, as though with crumbs. I thrust my hand in it to the bottom of the empty bag and sure enough it was. I had him turn it upside down and empty the crumbs out into my hands. Dirty old and musty— the accumulations of no telling how many weeks, but I ate them.

PRIVATE SAM WATKINS
1ST TENNESSEE INFANTRY, MANEY'S BRIGADE

One of the only men who enlisted in 1861 in Company H and lived to see the last major Confederate force surrender in the field on April 26, 1865, Watkins survived Shiloh, Corinth, Murfreesboro, Shelbyville, Chattanooga, Chickamauga, Missionary Ridge, the Hundred Days Battles, Atlanta, Jonesboro, Franklin, and Nashville.

The Tennessee river is about a quarter of a mile wide at Chattanooga. Right across the river was an immense corn-field. The green corn was waving with every little breeze that passed; the tassels were bowing and nodding their heads; the pollen was flying across the river like little snowdrops, and everything seemed to say, "Come hither, Johnny Reb; come hither, Johnny; come hither." The river was wide, but we were hungry. The roastingears looked tempting. We pulled off our clothes and launched into the turbid stream, and were soon on the other bank. Here was the field, and here were the roastingears; but where was the raft or canoe?

"The screaming of the men and the bellowing of the cow aroused the pickets and the sentinels, who fired their guns, the long roll was beaten, the brigade was called into line."

We thought of old Abraham and Isaac and the sacrifice: "My son, gather the roastingears, there will be a way provided."

We gathered the roastingears; we went back and gathered more roastingears, time and again. The bank was lined with green roastingears. Well, what was to be done? We began to shuck the corn. We would pull up a few shucks on one ear, and tie it to the shucks of another—first one and then another—until we had at least a hundred tied together. We put the train of corn into the river, and as it began to float off we jumped in, and taking the foremost ear in our mouth, struck out for the other bank. Well, we made the landing all correct.

CAPTAIN ROBERT P. FINDLEY
74TH OHIO INFANTRY, SIRWELL'S BRIGADE

Findley was promoted to major in the months following the Battle of Chickamauga and to lieutenant colonel on June 3, 1865, seven days before the 74th Ohio was mustered out. He sent journal excerpts to the Xenia (Ohio) Torch-Light throughout the war. This one describes his unit's march toward Chattanooga in mid-August 1863.

On the 16th of August we again took up our line of march and crossed the Cumberland Mountains. The road was narrow and precipitous, and the sun beat down unmercifully upon us. Our brigade halted for the night at the base of the mountain, our regiment camping some little distance up its side. We constructed beds of rails,

on which we spread green corn cut from the fields.

On in the night, as I lay awake, I heard a strange sound as of some large body sliding down the mountain. I sat up and looked in the direction of the noise. I soon saw what I thought to be a large bear, and it was heading directly for me. As it came nearer I discovered that it was a cow, and as the declivity was steep it was sliding down on its hind legs. It passed within a foot or so of me, and, becoming frightened by my movement, began to run along the line on which the regiment was sleeping. As it ran it stepped on the men who were lying along its track. They awoke alarmed, and that increased the fright of the beast, which ran at full speed, bellowing. The men tried to drive her away, but she was evidently following a trail usual to her, and she kept on in her mad dash. Men were knocked down by her horns and hoofs, and some were severely hurt. The screaming of the men and the bellowing of the cow aroused the pickets and the sentinels, who fired their guns, the long roll was beaten, the brigade was called into line, and not until the commanding officers were assured of the cause of the disturbance did they permit us to return to our beds. The next morning there were many amusing and strange stories related of the experiences of the night. A number of the men were willing to make oath it was a bear they had seen.

COLONEL NEWTON N. DAVIS
24TH ALABAMA INFANTRY, MANIGAULT'S BRIGADE

Contrary to Davis' expectations, the Federals did not attack Chattanooga directly. Not until early September did Bragg realize that the Union presence north of the river was a feint and that flanking moves to the west and south were endangering his supply lines. The evacuation of Chattanooga began on September 7.

The Yanks made their appearance very suddenly on the opposite side of the River and commenced shelling the town. The streets are always crowded with soldiers & citizens, men, women & children. You never saw such skidadling in all your life. Shop Keepers, Peach & apple venders, and speculators of all descriptions, both

581

HARPER'S WEEKLY.

[SEPTEMBER 12, 1863.]

VIEW OF THE CITY OF CHATTANOOGA, TENNESSEE, FROM THE NORTH SIDE OF THE TENNESSEE RIVER.—[SEE PAGE 587.]

The Second National Flag of the Confederacy flies atop one of the hills surrounding Chattanooga in this illustration from Harper's Weekly. The unnamed artist noted that "Chattanooga is one of the strong points of the Confederacy. . . . Here, as I write, are Bragg's headquarters, the army being encamped within ten miles. The pontoon-bridge has been . . . thrown over the river, which is here about 1200 feet wide. The place was formerly one of resort for Southerners. The climate is very pleasant and the country is abundantly supplied with springs."

Jews & Gentiles commenced running in every direction. The shelling was kept up nearly all day. I understand that four persons were killed and some seven or eight wounded, mostly citizens. One lady was killed and a little Girl had her thigh broken. All the floating population, camp followers, are leaving on the trains as fast as they can get off. We will have hot work here before many days I think. The Yanks are in large force on the opposite side of the River and doubtless will make a desperate effort to cross the River at some point. Every thing is in readiness to give them a warm reception whenever the attempt is made.

LIEUTENANT GENERAL DANIEL H. HILL

CORPS COMMANDER, ARMY OF TENNESSEE

President Jefferson Davis sent Hill west from Richmond to command William Hardee's corps in July 1863. Hill's humor shows in this anecdote about the sudden end to services on the official Confederate day of fasting in Chattanooga. Another time, Hill rejected a soldier's request to be transferred to the band, noting: "Respectfully forwarded, disapproved. Shooters are more needed than tooters!"

On Fast Day, August 21st, while religious services were being held in town, the enemy appeared on the opposite side of the river and began throwing shell into the houses. Rev. B. M. Palmer, D.D., of New Orleans, was in the act of prayer when a shell came hissing near the church. He went on calmly with his petition to the Great Being "who rules in the armies of heaven and among the inhabitants of earth," but at its close, the preacher, opening his eyes, noticed a perceptible diminution of his congregation.

SERGEANT BENJAMIN F. MAGEE

72D INDIANA INFANTRY, WILDER'S BRIGADE

To confuse Bragg, Rosecrans sent two infantry brigades under Brigadier General William B. Hazen, supported by Wilder's brigade, to feint toward Chattanooga from the north on August 16. Two days before the incident related here, Friday, August 21, a day set aside by Jefferson Davis for prayer and fasting, Wilder's battery in the hills across the river had pounded the city and sent the worshipers fleeing. The brigade continued its harassment for almost three weeks.

The ridge our battery occupied each day was nearly a mile from the river. Off to the right of our position, and about half way down the hill, was a little frame house. After a few days' shelling with but an occasional shot from the rebels, the thing became monotonous and our men and officers became saucy and venturesome. About the 23d, Col. Wilder and his Staff Officers, in order to get a better view of Chattanooga and surroundings, concluded to go down and get into the house. In the squad were Col. Wilder, Capt. Shields, Lieut. Crick and Lieut. Newell, of the Topographical Engineers. This was rather a bold adventure, but they succeeded in getting into the house from the back way, as they supposed unobserved. The back of the house sat on the ground, and the front part, next the river, was three or four feet from the ground. Everything was quiet about the house, but the officers saw under it a very large old sow, serenely sleeping. The Johnnies had observed all their movements and turned a 32-pounder upon the house, and just as our heroes had secured the best positions at crack and crevice with their field glasses, and had begun to survey the situation, the Johnnies let drive at them. The 32-pounder was well aimed and well timed, and came under the house "thud," literally blotting the old sow out of existence, and at the same instant exploding, and quicker than you could wink, pieces of the floor, hair, entrails, fresh pork and old iron came boiling out through the roof of the house like lava from a crater. To say that the officers rolled out of that house faster than hornets ever tumbled out of a nest, would be putting it rather mildly; and to say that they made good time up the hill would be *true*. Lieut. Newell jumped out of the window, and in just two minutes by the watch was going over the brow of the hill, when Capt. Rice hallooed "hello, Newell, what's the matter with you?" Without checking up Newell hallooed over his shoulder as he ran, "O! there's nothing the matter with me, but it was terrible hard on the old sow."

Federal troops and wagons cross a pontoon bridge spanning the Tennessee River at Caperton's Ferry, about 30 miles southwest of Chattanooga, during Rosecrans' bold attempt to outflank Bragg's army. Sand Mountain overlooks the eastern riverbank. Rosecrans is portrayed by William Travis on horseback, pointing his sword. The Union maneuver surprised Bragg: He was expecting the main push to come north of Chattanooga.

BRIGADIER GENERAL JOHN BEATTY
BRIGADE COMMANDER, ARMY OF THE CUMBERLAND

Although a prosperous banker and businessman in civilian life, Beatty identified with the volunteer soldier. He was especially suspicious of ambitious officers striving for personal advancement, like fellow Ohioan Brigadier General James A. Garfield, Rosecrans' chief of staff and future president of the United States. When Beatty himself made brigadier general, he noted that henceforth he could sign himself "B. G." which "in my case will probably stand for Big Goose."

This afternoon Colonels Stanley, Hobart, and I rode down to the Tennessee to look at the pontoon bridge which has been thrown across the river. On the way we met Generals Rosecrans, McCook, Negley, and Garfield. The former checked up, shook hands, and said: "How d'ye do?" Garfield gave us a grip which suggested "vote right, vote early." Negley smiled affably, and the cavalcade moved on. We crossed the Tennessee on the bridge of boats, and rode a few miles into the country beyond. Not a gun was fired as the bridge was being laid. Davis' division is on the south side of the river.

The Tennessee at this place is beautiful. The bridge looks like a ribbon stretched across it. The island below, the heavily-wooded banks, the bluffs and mountain, present a scene which would delight the soul of the artist. A hundred boys were frolicking in the water near the pontoons, tumbling into the stream in all sorts of ways, kicking up their heels, ducking and splashing each other, and having a glorious time generally.

A detachment from the 1st Michigan Engineers builds a log-trestle and pontoon bridge at Bridge-port, Alabama, 25 miles southwest of Chattanooga in late August 1863. The retreating Confeder-ates burned the Nashville & Chattanooga Railroad trestle (background) to slow the Yankee ad-vance. Private Amandus Silsby, 24th Wisconsin, described the destruction in a letter to his father: "Being previously tarred, it blazed up almost as soon as they set the match to it. The whole land-scape brightened up, as if lit by gas lights. Finally came a tremendous crash and all was over."

COLONEL SMITH D. ATKINS

92D ILLINOIS INFANTRY, WILDER'S BRIGADE

A lawyer in civilian life, Atkins enlisted as a private in 1861 "without a particle of military schooling." Although he was a talented soldier and rose swiftly through the ranks, Atkins never overcame his self-doubt. "I always had a larger command than I believed myself capable of handling," he wrote.

"Who will fall and who will survive, Heaven only knows."

CAPTAIN THADDEUS M. BRINDLEY

22D ALABAMA INFANTRY, DEAS' BRIGADE

In this letter to his married sister, Malvinia Brindley Hall, written when the Army of Tennessee was demoralized and in retreat, Brindley expresses his willingness to die for the Southern cause. He was one of five sons of Asa R. Brindley of Cherokee County, Alabama, who lost their lives fighting for the Confederacy, including one who died at Chickamauga. Brindley survived that bloodbath only to be killed the following summer in the fighting before Atlanta.

My regiment went to Harrison's Landing, threatening to cross at that point fifteen miles north of Chattanooga. We found the enemy in earthworks on the edge of the river on the opposite bank, with quite a heavy fort on the hills back from the river, mounting three guns en barbette. Our Spencer rifles carried over the river easily, nearly a mile wide, and the Confederates were kept closely within their rifle pits by our sharpshooters.

For a bullet from a rifle to travel a mile takes a long time. Let me illustrate that. The confederate officer of the day, with his sash across his shoulder, came riding down to the river from the Confederate fort, and was soon kneeling under a box elder tree on the bank of the river, and I said to my adjutant standing by me, "What is he doint?" but I had hardly asked the question, when a blue puff of smoke told me that he was shooting at us; Adjutant Lawyer stepped behind a tree, when the bullet from the Confederate rifle passed over my head, and through the side of the house by which I was standing, wounding one of my soldiers inside of the house, the first soldier in my regiment to be struck with rebel lead. If you see a man shooting a rifle at you a mile away, you will have abundant time to dodge before the bullet reaches you; if you can dodge behind a tree, as my Adjutant did, you will be safe; but if you are in the open you may as well stand still, for you are as liable to dodge in front of the bullet as away from it.

Camp Near Chattanooga
September 3rd, 1863
My dear Sister:—

You need not suppose from my not writing that I have forgotten you. The fact is I have had a bad chance to write and suppose that writing to Father's folks was letter to all. It is impossible for me to interest you with anything like war news as you have all and more than I have.

I look for a fight in this vicinity soon, and it will be a bloody one. I think we will hold the river and drive the enemy back. If we do and hold our own in Charleston, prospects will be brighter. There is much despondency in the army, many deserters and many others feeling whipped and ready to desert. Man in that state of feeling cannot be relied on for a good fight, and consequently it is much harder on those of us who stand firm to the end. Many valuable lives must and will be lost.

Who will fall and who will survive, Heaven only knows. I do not despair of final success. When I do I shall be willing to die the death of a martyr upon any battle field on Southern soil, subjugated, I have little desire to live, at best, and when I die I have nothing to leave Mary and Luta better than the ashes of a fallen patriot on some blood-stained battle field. If we are conquered, and I survive, I will not live under the Lincoln government. I can manage to get to Havana or some other foreign port. But we *shall not* be conquered, we cannot be. There—why

"The valley was one expanse of impenetrable darkness, except the camp-fires of advanced regiments dotting this darkness hundreds of feet below, like so many stars."

trouble you with this nonsense. Trust in God and all yet will be well.

For some time we have been moving from post to pillar and never know in the morning where we shall sleep at night. In this fix I am unable to write or do anything else.

. . . My health is tolerably good. I am a little lame, but not much. I feel old. Oh, that I could call back twenty years and be as all was then. Pardon all this nonsense. Give my love to all. Write to me. I will write again when I have a better chance and try to do better.

Your brother,
Marion

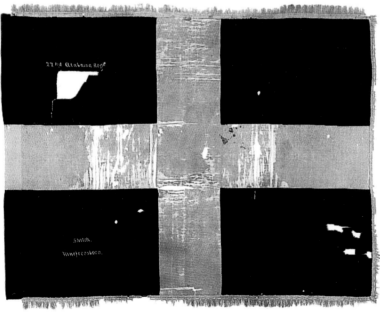

Fighting beneath this banner, the 22d Alabama lost 205 of its 371 men at Chick-amauga, including Captain Brindley's brother Mace, who was mortally wounded on September 20. The flag was captured that day by the 121st Ohio when the 22d Alabama's colorbearer fell dead a few feet from the Federal lines.

CAPTAIN FRANCIS W. PERRY
10TH WISCONSIN INFANTRY, SCRIBNER'S BRIGADE

On September 5, the 10th Wisconsin and other units in Thomas' XIV Corps camped near Spring Cove on the eastern side of the Tennessee River and contemplated the awesome task of crossing the mountain barrier that towered above them. "At first it seemed a hopeless job," Perry recalled, "but stout hearts and determined wills soon overcame every obstacle."

A road must be constructed up an inclined plane on the mountain side from foot to summit, winding around bluffs and boulders, cutting and rooting up trees, filling gullies, dislodging rocks and leveling earth until a track could be cut wide enough to permit artillery and baggage-wagons to pass up. Each brigade had been provided with shovels and picks sufficient to supply at least one regiment in each brigade. As each regiment detailed for that purpose was armed and equipped with a shovel or pick, they slung their guns over their shoulders and marched up the mountain side, taking their places at intervals, stacked their arms and, with cheers and jovial good spirits, made an attack, charging (with picks in advance) upon trees, rocks and dirt. . . .

In the space of three days' hard labor we had constructed our roads up, across and down the mountain sides into the valley beyond. I shall never forget the laborious and hazardous march as we approached the southern declivity and commenced the descent. It was the day for our brigade to march in the rear of the division. The night was dark and, as we commenced the descent, the valley was one expanse of impenetrable darkness, except the camp-fires of advanced regiments dotting this darkness hundreds of feet below, like so many stars scattered along the valley, forming a most grand and beautiful sight.

PRIVATE MATTHIAS B. COLTON

15TH PENNSYLVANIA CAVALRY, ESCORT STAFF, MAJOR GENERAL WILLIAM S. ROSECRANS, ARMY OF THE CUMBERLAND

Colton and his brother, William (right), served as escorts for General Rosecrans. They enlisted for three years or the duration of the war in August 1862. The day the boys left home, their father held family prayers for their safe return. Both survived.

CAPTAIN WILLIAM F. COLTON

15TH PENNSYLVANIA CAVALRY, ESCORT STAFF, MAJOR GENERAL WILLIAM S. ROSECRANS, ARMY OF THE CUMBERLAND

Although he was three years younger than his brother, William (age 22 in 1863) progressed further in his military career. Like Matthias, he began his service as a private, but he was quickly promoted to corporal, sergeant major, and finally to captain of a company.

At Bridgeport we crossed the Tennessee on the pontoon bridge, and then proceeded to Cave Spring, a large spring running out of a cave. Near this spring on the hillside is a very large cave. Sept. 4th four of us took candles and went into the bowels of the earth a good distance. After we had gone in some distance we met General Rosecrans and his party who were just returning from their exploration. The General was much excited and perspiring at every pore, and oh, tell it not in Gath, he was much frightened. In fact the party were lost. The General asked us if we knew the way out, we did and we turned back and piloted him out. Quite an adventure, wasn't it? He said they had been an hour trying to find their way out. It is an easy thing to get lost in this cave, there are so many different passages leading off in every direction. However, we did not get lost, and returned in safety. I got a very large stalactite, and would like to have sent it home.

Many of the men . . . visited Hill's Cave, and during a visit to this cave by General Rosecrans and staff, the General's rather bulking form became wedged in a narrow passage, and for a few minutes it was a question whether the campaign might not have to be continued under the next senior general.

MAJOR GENERAL WILLIAM S. ROSECRANS
COMMANDER, ARMY OF THE CUMBERLAND

On September 7, 1863, the Confederates abandoned Chattanooga without firing a shot and marched away on the roads heading south. Convinced that Bragg was in full retreat, an overconfident Rosecrans ordered his three widely separated corps to push over the mountains in hot pursuit. According to one officer, "He didn't expect to get a fight out of Bragg this side of Atlanta."

Trenton, Ga., *September 9, 1863*—12.30 a.m.
(Received 3.15 p.m.)
Major-General Halleck,
Commander-in-Chief, U.S. Army, Washington D.C.:
Information to-night leads to the belief that the enemy have decided not to fight us at Chattanooga. Our reconnaissances to-day show he has

"Chattanooga is ours without a struggle, and East Tennessee is free."

The model of a gallant leader, Major General William S. Rosecrans gallops through shot and shell on a song sheet that was published in his native Ohio at the height of his fame in 1863. Perhaps stung by past criticisms from Washington of his perceived lack of boldness, Rosecrans suddenly grew overly bold. Ignoring the advice of General George H. Thomas, his most trusted subordinate, to consolidate the army at Chattanooga, he sent his entire force rushing after Bragg. It would prove a fatal error.

withdrawn his pickets on Lookout Mountain opposite and below us. Our troops are moving into Stevens', Frick's, and Winston's Gaps. McCook and Stanley start to-morrow with advance to reconnoiter toward Broomtown Valley, and Crittenden to gain the summit of Lookout south of Chattanooga, with a reconnaissance in force, holding his corps ready to enter the place if practicable.

Granger closed up to Stevenson and Bridgeport with four brigades.

W. S. Rosecrans,
Major-General.

Camp near Trenton, Ga.,
September 9, 1863—8.30 p.m.
(Received 6.40 p.m., 10th.)
Maj. Gen. H. W. Halleck,
General-in-Chief:

Chattanooga is ours without a struggle, and East Tennessee is free. Our move on the enemy's flank and rear progresses, while the tail of his retreating column will not escape unmolested. Our troops from this side entered Chattanooga about noon. Those north of the river are crossing.

W. S. Rosecrans,
Major-General.

LIEUTENANT WILBUR F. HINMAN
65TH OHIO INFANTRY, HARKER'S BRIGADE

Following the Confederate withdrawal from Chattanooga, Harker's brigade and the rest of General Thomas L. Crittenden's XXI Corps marched up the Tennessee River valley into the city. Their orders were to follow Bragg's line of retreat. After the war, Hinman became a popular author of works of fiction and served as brigade historian.

We neared Lookout, but not a shot was heard. As we rounded the point of the mountain, far below the frowning cliffs, our eyes discerned, through the clouds of dust that filled the air, the spires and buildings of Chattanooga. A wave of prodigious cheers swept along the column, and this was repeated again and again. The blood which was the price paid for Chattanooga, was to be shed a few days later. But the soldiers knew not, recked not, of the future. They thought only of the present, and rejoiced with exceeding great joy in the possession, so easily gained, of the Confederate stronghold. As we

The distinctive profile of Lookout Mountain looms over Chattanooga, a sleepy river town of frame buildings and 3,500 people in 1863. At far left is the vaulted roof of the Nashville & Chattanooga Railroad depot, built before the war with slave labor. Immediately to the right of the depot are the multiple chimneys of the Crutchfield House hotel. In the middle distance at center is Academy Hill, topped with whitewashed buildings built by the Confederates and known as Bragg Hospital.

entered the town, the street was lined with people gratifying their curiosity to have a look at a crowd of real live "Yankees."

"Why," exclaimed an urchin of twelve, "you look just like we-uns! They told us you-all had horns!"

"There's a brigade right behind us that's got horns!" said ready Phil Sheridan, of Company I, Sixty-fifth. "I'd like to have a good 'horn' mesilf jist now!"

LIEUTENANT GENERAL DANIEL H. HILL
CORPS COMMANDER, ARMY OF TENNESSEE

Hill had been a messmate of Bragg's during the Mexican War, but when Hill was reunited with his old friend in Tennessee, he found a changed man. "He had grown prematurely old since I saw him last," Hill wrote, "and showed much nervousness." When Hill recommended to President Davis that he sack Bragg for incompetency, Davis refused and angrily withheld Hill's promotion papers from the Confederate Senate.

General Bragg had said petulantly a few days before the crossing into Will's Valley: "It is said to be easy to defend a mountainous country, but mountains hide your foe from you, while they are full of gaps through which he can pounce upon you at any time. A mountain is like the wall of a house full of rat-holes. The rat lies hidden at his hole, ready to pop out when no one is watching. Who can tell what lies hidden behind that wall?" said he, pointing to the Cumberland range across the river.

BRIGADIER GENERAL JOHN BEATTY
BRIGADE COMMANDER, ARMY OF THE CUMBERLAND

Beatty jotted these notes when the Army of the Cumberland was separated and vulnerable. "For nearly two weeks now, I have not had my clothes off," he wrote on September 12, "and for perhaps not more than two nights of the time have I had my boots and spurs off. I have risen at 3 o'clock in the morning and not lain down until 10 or 11 at night."

Sept. 10. Our division marched across McLemore's Cove to Pigeon mountain, found Dug Gap obstructed, and the enemy in force on the right, left, and front. The skirmishers of the advance brigade, Colonel Surwell's, were engaged somewhat, and during the night information poured in upon us, from all quarters, that the enemy, in strength, was making dispositions to surround and cut us off before reinforcements could arrive.

11. Two brigades of Baird's division joined us about 10 A.M. Five thousand of the enemy's cavalry were reported to be moving to our left and rear; soon after, his infantry appeared on our right and left, and, a little later, in our front. From the summit of Pigeon mountain, the rebels could observe all our movements, and form a good estimate of our entire force. Our immense train, swelled now by the transportation of Baird's division to near four hundred wagons, compelled us to select such positions as would enable us to protect the train, and not such as were most favorable for making an offensive or defensive fight.

It was now impossible for Brannan and Reynolds to reach us in time to render assistance. General Negley concluded, therefore, to fall back, and ordered me to move to Bailey's Cross-roads, and await the passage of the wagon train to the rear. The enemy attacked soon after, but were held in check until the transportation had time to return to Stephens' Gap.

12. We expected an attack this morning, but, reinforcements arriving, the enemy retired. This afternoon Brannan made a reconnoissance, but the result I have not ascertained; there was, however, no fighting.

"During the night information poured in upon us, from all quarters, that the enemy, in strength, was making dispositions to surround and cut us off before reinforcements could arrive."

A narrow road snakes through Raccoon Mountain at the northern edge of the Sand Mountain range near Whiteside, Georgia. The hill country around Chattanooga was a tortuous place to march, let alone fight. "Roads horrible," one division commander reported to Rosecrans, "fully as bad as anything we have had."

BRIGADIER GENERAL ARTHUR M. MANIGAULT
Brigade Commander, Army of Tennessee

On September 10 the Confederates lost a precious opportunity when Thomas C. Hindman failed to aggressively attack James S. Negley's division, which had advanced into a cul de sac between Missionary Ridge and Pigeon Mountain known locally as McLemore's Cove. The failure earned Hindman a rebuke from Bragg and the contempt of Manigault and the men in the ranks.

The enemy had now crossed the river at three points—Bridgeport, at Chattanooga (General Bragg having evacuated it), and at some other crossing higher up. Thus their different army corps were widely separated. General Hindman had under his command about 11,000 men, and he received orders to attack the enemy at as early an hour on the following morning as he could find him, with instructions to cut him off from a retreat from the way he came into the Valley, whilst General Bragg himself with a portion of Hardee's corps, already in the neighborhood of Dug Gap, would fall upon his right as soon as the action commenced. Our orders were to move at daylight, but much time was lost by General Buckner, whose corps was to move in advance. Our Division did not move until nine o'clock. My brigade was in the rear. Hours passed without our advancing more than two and a half miles. At about two o'clock we could hear that our skirmishers in front were becoming engaged. The enemy had marched into the cove, leaving the mountain and pass in their rear. The opportunity offered General Hindman for distinguishing himself and striking a terrible blow was favorable in the extreme, but he was not up to the work, it being far beyond his capacity as a general. So much time was lost in selecting his line and forming his troops, that the enemy discovered a trap laid for them to their peril, and whilst keeping up a show of resistance, rapidly retreated towards the mountain. By the time General Hindman had completed his arrangements, the Federal General had also completed his. Our advance commenced, but we soon found out that only a skirmish line and a brigade or two of infantry were in our front to resist us, who gave way easily, and the main body had secured its retreat, holding the pass, and their line strongly posted a short distance up the mountain side.

Several hundred prisoners were taken and perhaps as many killed and wounded. The whole affair proved a miserable failure, altho had there been a proper man to manage for us, I have little doubt but that a most brilliant success would have been achieved. It was one of several most favorable opportunities that offered themselves during my connection with the Western Army, not taken advantage of, and lost from incapacity on the part of the officer to profit by the error or folly of his opponent.

COLONEL JOHN T. WILDER
BRIGADE COMMANDER, ARMY OF THE CUMBERLAND

Wilder and his men had scouted almost the entire Confederate front by September 12. Rosecrans had not believed previous reports of Confederates massing to confront him, but Wilder's information began to shake his confidence. After similar reports from other quarters, Rosecrans finally acknowledged on the 13th that pulling his widely scattered forces together had become "a matter of life and death." Orders were issued, and the Federals rushed to consolidate before the Rebels could attack.

At daybreak we pushed on to Ringgold, driving the enemy before us, and while halting to give a detachment time to flank the enemy out of the gap in Taylor's Ridge, at Ringgold, was surprised at the cannonading of the enemy from the west of the place. I soon found that it was two divisions of Crittenden's Corps, that had come on from Lookout Mountain to intercept the force we were driving.

I immediately passed through the Ringgold gap, and two miles beyond, was attacked at the Stone Church. We drove them backward and they again made a stubborn stand at Bell's Farm, two miles farther on; we still drove them past Catoosa Springs and on through the village of Tunnel Hill. Here Forrest tried to get us into an ambuscade formed by Stewart and Buckner's Divisions of Infantry, coming forward to Bragg's' relief.

Forrest led a charge at my advance guard, but was repulsed and wounded in the back as he turned to flee from their fire.

I saw the glint of the bayonets of the infantry, as they deployed behind the crest of Tunnel Hill, expecting us to fall into their trap, but we halted for the night and I notified Crittenden at Ringgold of the situation. At daylight we marched back to Ringgold and had hard work to induce Crittenden to fall back to Lee & Gordon's mill behind Chickamauga River. I had reliable information that Buckner with two Divisions and a corps from LaFayette were coming up to crush Crittenden. I at once started toward LaFayette, down the old Alabama road to meet and impede the force coming from there.

At Leet's tanyard, I struck their cavalry under Pegram, and after a sharp fight, carried the hill at the Cross Roads, and found their Infantry advancing in full force from LaFayette. We held our ground and their advance swung around and took position, between us and Lee & Gordon's mill, close in our front.

I sent a decoy letter out toward Crittenden, telling him we were surrounded at Leet's tanyard and said I would fight my way back toward Ringgold at day light in the morning; and asked him to make a demonstration in our favor; but told the messenger to deliver the letter to the enemy if possible and to tell Crittenden to pay no attention to it, if he got through. He was captured and gave the letter to one of Cheatham's Staff.

At nine that night, I pushed down the valley of Peavine Creek, through the enemy's pickets, and got through without loss, and captured Bragg's mail wagons coming to him, in which there was information that Walker was coming from Jackson, Miss., with ten thousand rearmed Vicksburg prisoners, and that Longstreet was on his way from Virginia with his corps of twenty-three thousand men to aid Bragg in destroying Rosecrans' Army.

We reached Lee & Gordon's mill about 3 A.M., where Crittenden was encamped. I went to his tent to inform him of this momentous news, and found him asleep. He was awakened, but refused to be disturbed or listen to what I said. Taking a few men with me, I rode up to General Thomas, then at Pond Spring, in McLemores Cove, some twenty miles up Chickamauga Valley. I took the letters and four prisoners we had picked up, one from Longstreet and three from Walker, who had come on ahead of their commands. I reached General Thomas about sunrise just as he was preparing for breakfast and told him the situation. He asked me if Rosecrans had been informed, and I told him he had not. He called for his horse, and without waiting for breakfast, rode with me to General Rosecrans' headquarters, about a mile farther up the valley.

Rosecrans was just sitting down to breakfast as we rode up, and came out to me and warmly congratulated me on my work at Chattanooga. I immediately informed him of my movement to Tunnel Hill, and told him of the information obtained from the letters and prisoners. He assured me that I was mistaken as he had a telegram from Washington only a few moments before, saying that no troops had left Virginia or Mississippi for Bragg.

I showed him the letters and called in the prisoners, each of them told him of their commands coming to Bragg's assistance.

General Rosecrans at once gave orders for McCook, who was in the valley below LaFayette, in Bragg's rear, to come at all speed and join Thomas in McLemores Cove.

SERGEANT WILLIAM M. WOODCOCK
9TH KENTUCKY (U.S.) INFANTRY, S. BEATTY'S BRIGADE

Fresh water and pork came as a pleasant change from the trials of the past two weeks. Short of rations, constantly skirmishing, and feeling alone in the face of the Confederate army, Woodcock and his fellow Kentuckians had marched out of Chattanooga, over Lookout Mountain to the area around Ringgold, down to Lee and Gordon's Mills, back across Lookout Mountain to the Chattanooga Valley, and finally, crossing the mountain again, went into camp at Crawfish Springs.

Mon.—Thurs. 14th, 15th, 16th and 17th. Marched back in the direction from which we came on the previous day about four miles, and encamped near the celebrated Crawfish Springs. After we had stacked arms, and before we received the command to "break ranks," Colonel Cram pointed to a drove of hogs that were grunting and munching but a short distance from us, and which were very numerous, and large and fat, and remarked "I have bought all the hogs in this country, boys, but if you are mean enough to take them from me, I can't help it. Break ranks." The boys were not so dull of perception that they could not at once see that this was a hint for them to make some provisions for their empty haversacks and hungry stomachs; consequently, the last command of the Colonel was the signal for a general charge upon the unlucky representatives of the swinish population of Georgia, and they made it with a yell that would have been worthy of a much more difficult and dangerous undertaking, but which resulted in the speedy killing and dressing of a sufficient quantity of meat to feed the Regiment bountifully for some days. Some of the boys found a sufficiency of salt in a neighboring barn. Our Camp here was in a pleasant situation and the water was of the first quality, as everyone knows who has ever drank of the clear and cooling water of Crawfish Springs.

We remained at this place the next day, and finally began to hear some correct rumors as to the whereabouts of the other two Corps, but the news did not serve to satisfy us any when we were informed that Thomas was twenty, and McCook at least forty miles away, for we believe, from the actions of the enemy, that they were reinforcing heavily, and had hardly the confidence in our little Corps that it could withstand an attack from the whole Rebel army. Gen. Rosecrans came to the Springs and put up his headquarters on this evening, and this event raised our spirits to some extent.

General William Rosecrans, sitting in front of a tree, is flanked by members of his staff, including his chief of staff, Brigadier General James A. Garfield, who would be elected president of the United States in 1881 (seated, right, next to Rosecrans). One of Rosecrans' most skilled division commanders, Major General Philip H. Sheridan, sits at far right. Rosecrans and his generals worked well together. The Army of the Cumberland, one officer noted, "was singularly united and free from dissensions."

"Trusting in God and the justice of our cause, and nerved by the love of the dear ones at home, failure is impossible and victory must be ours."

GENERAL BRAXTON BRAGG
COMMANDER, ARMY OF TENNESSEE

With his army bolstered by reinforcements from Mississippi and Virginia, Bragg sensed a chance to redeem his reputation with a smashing victory. One of the most disliked generals in the Confederacy, the grim, ill-tempered North Carolinian was described by a visiting British officer as a man with "a sickly, cadaverous, haggard appearance, rather plain features, bushy black eyebrows which unite in a tuft on the top of his nose, and a stubby iron-gray beard."

General Orders, Hdqrs. Army of Tennessee No. 180. *In the Field, La Fayette, Ga., Sept.* 16, 1863. The troops will be held ready for an immediate move against the enemy. His demonstration on our flank has been thwarted, and twice has he retired before us when offered battle. We must now force him to the issue.

Soldiers, you are largely re-enforced; you must now seek the contest. In so doing I know you will be content to suffer privations and encounter hardships.

Heretofore you have never failed to respond to your general when he has asked sacrifice at your hands. Relying on your gallantry and patriotism, he asks you to add the crowning glory to the wreath you wear. Our cause is in your keeping; your enemy boasts that you are demoralized and retreating before him.

Having accomplished our object by driving back his flank movement, let us now turn on his main force and crush it in its fancied security.

Your generals will lead you; you have but to respond to assure us a glorious triumph over an insolent foe. I know what your response will be.

Trusting in God and the justice of our cause, and nerved by the love of the dear ones at home, failure is impossible and victory must be ours.

Braxton Bragg,
General, Commanding.

Clash at the River of Blood

The two armies sat south of Chattanooga within a rifle shot of each other, separated only by Chickamauga Creek. General Bragg still itched to attack, and his chances of doing so successfully were greatly boosted by the arrival in mid-September of an elite body of reinforcements. Two divisions of Lieutenant General James Longstreet's veteran corps, the cream of Lee's Army of Northern Virginia, had been detached and hurried west in a desperate gamble that their added weight would help smash the Federals and keep them from invading Georgia and splitting the Confederacy in half. Boarding trains September 9, Longstreet's 12,000 men had traveled south and then west on a bone-shaking 950-mile roundabout trip on battered railroads. By September 18 the first three brigades, led by Major General John Bell Hood, had arrived, ready to fight.

In this unfinished sketch, Colonel Robert Minty's Union troopers withdraw from Reed's Bridge on the west side of the Chickamauga on September 18. Minty reported they were demolishing the vital bridge when surprised by Confederates.

Bragg immediately ordered Hood to advance across Chickamauga Creek along with General Bushrod Johnson's division and the two corps of Generals Buckner and W. H. T. Walker. Bragg's scheme: to hit the left flank of Crittenden's XXI Corps near Lee and Gordon's Mills, drive it south, and trap it in McLemore's Cove. If the plan worked, the Confederates would destroy a third of Rosecrans' army—and cut off the rest from their line of retreat to Chattanooga.

Things did not go according to plan; they seldom did for Bragg. Johnson's men were slow in starting, then found themselves stopped cold at Reed's Bridge by the Union cavalry commanded by a hard-fighting, Irish-born colonel named Robert H. G. Minty. Walker's troops ran into trouble, too, at Alexander's Bridge, raked by wicked fire from the Spencer rifles of Wilder's Lightning Brigade.

After hours of skirmishing, Walker's Confederates, with the support of Johnson's division, managed to drive off Wilder's men and ford the creek a mile to the north. Hood, coming to Johnson's aid, helped send Colonel Minty's pesky Federals fleeing into a nearby woods. But by nightfall Bragg had only about 9,000 men across the Chickamauga and, although the bulk of his army sifted over during the night, he had lost a day. He had also alerted the Federals that the danger lay on their left.

Rosecrans, who had already ordered Crittenden to move leftward, sent General Thomas and his footsore troops marching clear around Crittenden's corps during the night of the 18th to extend the threatened flank. By dawn on September 19, two of Thomas' divisions led by Brigadier Generals John M. Brannan and Absalom Baird had reached the area of the Kelly house on the La Fayette road, more than three miles north of where Bragg estimated the Union left was located.

The fighting began almost by accident on the morning of the 19th, when General Thomas, who had been informed that an enemy brigade had crossed the creek, ordered Brannan to make a reconnaissance. Brannan soon sent a brigade of infantry under a 26-year-old Kentuckian, Colonel John Croxton, to do the job. About 8:00 a.m. Croxton's men encountered some of Nathan Bedford Forrest's cavalry and opened fire, starting a fierce melee.

With that the battle seemed to explode. As Croxton was driving Forrest back, his troops were hit hard by a division of William Walker's corps commanded by Brigadier General States Rights Gist, named to honor his father's secessionist politics. At that, Thomas sent Brannan's other two brigades forward, and into a furious fight with Gist's Confederates.

To back Brannan, Thomas sent the three brigades of Absalom Baird. Walker countered by ordering up his other division, led by Brigadier General St. John Liddell. In minutes, Liddell's Confederates had slammed into the right of Baird's troops, capturing 400 and driving many of the rest back almost two miles.

The beleaguered Thomas lacked two of his divisions, led by Generals Negley and

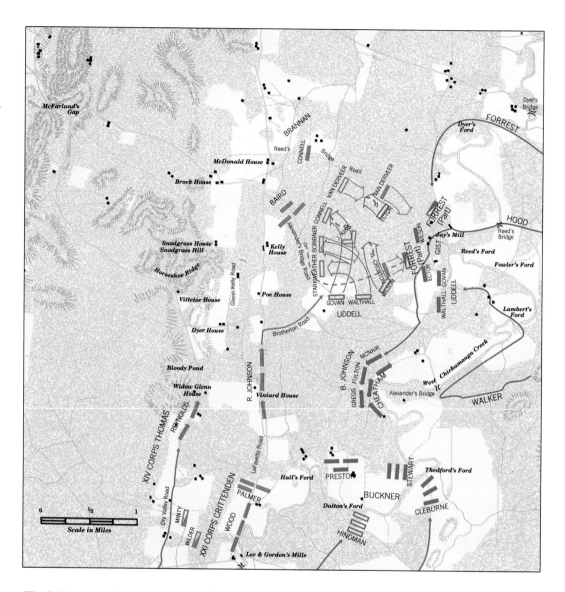

The fighting erupted on the morning of September 19, when General Thomas sent Brannan's division, followed by Baird's, to reconnoiter the Chickamauga. Brannan's Federals drove back Forrest's cavalry until the Yankees were hit hard by States Rights Gist's division from W. H. T. Walker's corps. Thomas inserted Baird's division to bolster the line, but it, too, was beaten back by Walker's other division under St. John Liddell. The seesaw battle grew furious, but neither side could gain an advantage. "The Chickamauga lived up to its name that day," later wrote Colonel Thomas Berry, one of Forrest's officers. "It ran red with blood."

Reynolds, which were still marching around Crittenden. Fearing that he might be overrun, he asked Rosecrans for help, and the commander soon sent Brigadier General Richard W. Johnson's division from McCook's corps hurrying up the La Fayette road. These fresh troops, along with some of Brannan's men, charged into Liddell's attackers and stemmed the near rout.

Now it was Walker's turn to call for aid. Soon Major General Benjamin Cheatham led his 6,000-man division forward and, shouting, "Give 'em hell, boys," sent them charging into Thomas' line. For two hours Cheatham's men pounded away at the Federals near the Brotherton road, until counterattacked by Johnson's men and Major General John M. Palmer's division, now helping to hold Thomas' right.

As more divisions were fed in, the battle took on the nature of a gigantic and vicious brawl. The air, recalled Colonel Thomas Berry of Forrest's cavalry, was full of "whistling, seething, crackling bullets, the piercing, screaming fragments of shells." On the ground "the ghastly mangled dead and the horribly wounded strewed the earth for over half a mile up and down the river banks." The whole fight, a Union brigadier general later said, was "a mad irregular battle, very much resembling guerrilla warfare on a grand scale, in which one army was bushwhacking the other."

About 2:00 p.m. Bragg, trying to take control of the battle, dispatched the division of Major General Alexander P. Stewart to help Cheatham's exhausted men. Plunging in on Cheatham's left, Stewart's men, screaming the rebel yell, almost immediately broke the Federal division led by Brigadier General Horatio Van Cleve, sending the Union troops reeling back and opening a hole between Thomas' and Crittenden's corps.

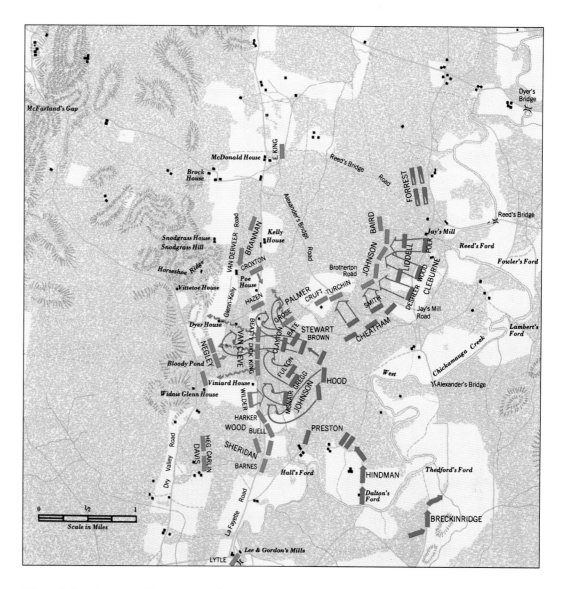

Through the afternoon of September 19, the two armies surged back and forth, roughly along the lines shown here. The Rebels launched an attack against Horatio Van Cleve's division, which had marched north to reinforce the Union line. The assault bent back the center of the Federal line, but counterattacks by the divisions of Brannan and James Negley in the center, and Philip Sheridan and Thomas Wood on the right, halted the Confederate advance. In late afternoon, Cleburne's division attacked on the Federal left but was repulsed by the divisions of Richard Johnson and Absalom Baird. Later that evening, Longstreet arrived to reinforce Bragg.

The middle of the Federal line had cracked, but the Rebels could not take advantage of the situation. Negley's and Reynolds' Federal divisions—both hurrying to join Thomas—were marching right behind Van Cleve's men when they bolted for the rear. Hastily Reynolds' troops formed a line and, with the help of General Hazen, who brought up 20 cannons, blasted Stewart's oncoming Rebels back into the cover of a dense woods.

Bragg, as if stunned by the failure of his original flanking maneuver, had yet to order a general assault and continued to throw in units piecemeal. Among those impatiently waiting for orders was John Bell Hood. Finally, at about 4:00 p.m., Hood could wait no longer and decided to attack on his own, sending Evander Law's and Bushrod Johnson's troops charging into the Federal right.

Breaking out of some woods, the six Rebel brigades smashed into the three commanded by Brigadier General Jefferson C. Davis. In minutes Hood's attack had virtually annihilated one of Davis' brigades led by Norwegian-born Colonel Hans Christian Heg, killing him and inflicting 696 casualties. Again the Union line was close to breaking.

Yet again the momentum shifted. Brigadier General Thomas Wood rushed his division of Crittenden's corps into the gap, followed by Wilder's Lightning Brigade and then Major General Philip Sheridan's division of McCook's corps. Acting fast as always, Eli Lilly set up his guns and fired into the flank of Hood's men, killing so many as they took cover in a ditch that Wilder was horrified. It seemed, he later wrote, "a pity to kill men so. They fell in heaps, and I had it in my heart to order the firing to cease, to end the awful sight."

As the sun set, firing slackened along the four-mile-long front. General Thomas began

reorganizing his lines—but he warned that another Rebel assault was possible. Indeed, it came. This time the aggressor was Cleburne's division, which Bragg had belatedly ordered to march north behind the front from its position near Lee and Gordon's Mills.

Cleburne's 5,000 men, wading the Chickamauga at twilight, exploded out of the woods west of Reed's Bridge directly at Baird's and Johnson's divisions. The Confederates captured 300 prisoners while gaining a mile of ground before it became too dark to fight.

Company H of the 44th Indiana stood its ground in the Federal center just after midday on September 19. Attacked by Clayton's Alabama brigade, the Hoosiers responded with a withering fire. One Alabamian recalled: "Did you ever note the thickness of raindrops in a tempest? Did you ever see the destruction of hail stones to growing cornfields? Did you ever witness driftwood in a squall? Such was the havoc upon Clayton."

chair, occasionally rousing himself to warn, "I would strengthen the left." It was sound advice, and later Rosecrans shifted Negley's division from the Federal center to strengthen Thomas' left flank.

At Confederate headquarters, Bragg reorganized his force, this time into two wings. Polk would be in charge of the right, leading his own corps along with Hill's and Walker's. Longstreet would attack on the left with his own troops as well as Buckner's corps.

The arrangement required much shifting of large bodies of troops, and it would cause trouble in the morning. So would the fact that not all of Longstreet's men would come up in time from the train depot a dozen miles to the south. Longstreet himself was on the scene, however. When he arrived at the Ringgold train station at 2:00 p.m., he was exasperated to find that Bragg had sent no one to meet him, and he and two aides spent the rest of the day riding through the Georgia woods to the distant sound of gunfire. It was 11:00 p.m. before they happened on Bragg's headquarters. But Longstreet's irritation at Bragg's oversight did not long endure and at daybreak he would be ready to fight. Longstreet would, as always, attack with precision and thunderous force, and almost succeed in destroying Rosecrans' army.

The first day's confused struggle had ended, but the night brought little rest. Units on both sides marched to get in position for the fighting that was sure to begin again at dawn. Pickets exchanged sharp volleys. Other troops felled trees to make breastworks.

About 11:00 p.m. Rosecrans called a council of war at his headquarters, a log house belonging to a widow named Eliza Glenn. The Army of the Cumberland would stand on the defensive, it was agreed. During the meeting, General Thomas napped in his

LIEUTENANT GENERAL JAMES LONGSTREET
COMMANDING I CORPS, ARMY OF NORTHERN VIRGINIA

Before the Battle of Chickamauga, Longstreet tried to persuade Robert E. Lee that defending the western region of the Confederacy was more important than resuming the offensive in the East. As a result Lee dispatched Longstreet and his corps to the western theater in time to play a decisive role in the Confederate victory at Chickamauga. But the widely detested Bragg retained command.

Headquarters
September 5, 1863.
. . . I do not know enough of our facilities for transporting troops, &c., west, to say what time would be consumed in moving my corps to Tennessee and back.

Your information will enable you to determine this much better than I. I believe, though, that the enemy intends to confine his great operations to the west, and that it is time that we were shaping our movements to meet him.

If this army is ready to assume offensive operations, I think that it would be better for us to remain on the defensive here, and to re-enforce the west, and take the offensive there. We can hold here with a smaller force than we would require for offensive operations; and if it should become necessary to retire as far as Richmond temporarily, I think that we could better afford to do so than we can to give up any more of our western country. I will say more; I think that it is time that we had begun to do something in the west, and I fear if it is put off any longer we shall be too late.

If my corps cannot go west, I think that we might accomplish something by giving me Jenkins', Wise's, and Cooke's brigades, and putting me in General Bragg's place, and giving him my corps. A good artillery battalion should go with these brigades. We would surely make no great risk in such a change and we might gain a great deal.

I feel that I am influenced by no personal motive in this suggestion, and will most cheerfully give up, when we have a fair prospect of holding our western country.

I doubt if General Bragg has confidence in his troops or himself either. He is not likely to do a great deal for us. . . .

I remain, most respectfully, your obedient servant,
James Longstreet,
Lieutenant-General.

MARY BOYKIN CHESNUT
CIVILIAN

Wife of a U.S. senator who resigned to become a Confederate army officer and ultimately an aide to Jefferson Davis, Mary Chesnut moved in the highest social circles of Charleston, South Carolina, and the Confederacy. The war's leading diarist, she began keeping a journal in February 1861 and maintained it until several months after Appomattox. She was 33 years old at the time of this portrait.

At Kingsville I caught a glimpse of our army. Longstreet's corps going west. God bless the gallant fellows. Not one man intoxicated—not one rude word did I hear. It was a strange sight—miles, *apparently,* of platform cars—soldiers rolled in their blankets, lying in rows, heads and all covered, fast asleep. In their gray blankets, packed in regular order, they looked like swathed mummies.

One man near where I sat was writing on his knee. He used his cap for a desk, and he was seated on a rail. I watched him, wondering to whom that letter was to go. Home, no doubt—sore hearts for him there!

A feeling of awful depression laid hold of me. All these fine fellows going to kill or be killed. Why? And a word got to beating about my head like an old song—"the unreturning brave."

CAPTAIN D. AUGUSTUS DICKERT

3D SOUTH CAROLINA INFANTRY, KERSHAW'S BRIGADE

Dickert, who left school at age 12, became a noted writer of history and fiction. He fought in Kershaw's brigade at First Manassas, Harpers Ferry, Antietam, Fredericksburg, Chancellorsville, Gettysburg, Chickamauga, the Wilderness, Spotsylvania, Cold Harbor, Petersburg, the Shenandoah Valley, and finally, against Sherman in defense of his native state. By then Dickert, though still a captain, commanded the regiment, and after the war was generally addressed as Colonel.

Long trains of box cars had been ordered up from Richmond and the troops were loaded by one company being put inside and the next on top, so one-half of the corps made the long four days' journey on the top of box cars. The cars on all railroads in which troops were transported were little more than skeleton cars; the weather being warm, the troops cut all but the frame work loose with knives and axes. They furthermore wished to see outside and witness the fine country and delightful scenery that lay along the route; nor could those inside bear the idea of being shut up in a box while their comrades on top were cheering and yelling themselves hoarse at the waving of handkerchiefs and flags in the hands of the pretty women and the hats thrown in the air by the old men and boys along the roadside as the trains sped through the towns, villages and hamlets of the Carolinas and Georgia. No, the exuberant spirits of the Southern soldier were too great to allow him to hear yelling going on and not yell himself. He yelled at everything he saw, from an ox-cart to a pretty woman. . . . The news of our coming had preceded us, and at every station and road-crossing the people of the surrounding country, without regard to sex or age, crowded to see us pass, and gave us their blessings. Our whole trip was one grand ovation.

"A feeling of awful depression laid hold of me. All these fine fellows going to kill or be killed."

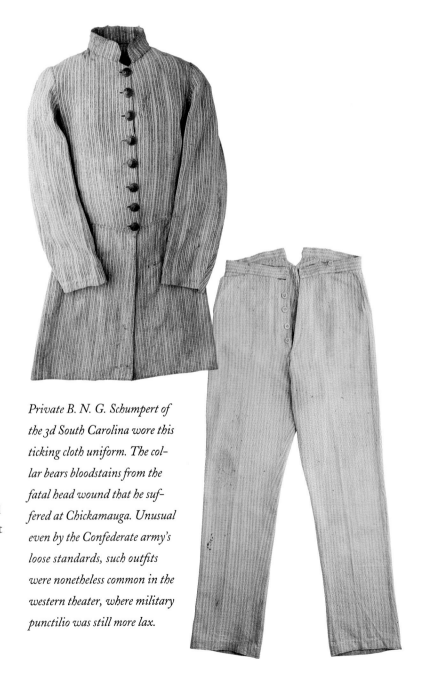

Private B. N. G. Schumpert of the 3d South Carolina wore this ticking cloth uniform. The collar bears bloodstains from the fatal head wound that he suffered at Chickamauga. Unusual even by the Confederate army's loose standards, such outfits were nonetheless common in the western theater, where military punctilio was still more lax.

PRIVATE THEODORE PETZOLDT

17TH INDIANA INFANTRY, WILDER'S BRIGADE

Only three years after arriving from his native Saxony, Petzoldt found himself at the very center of the conflict at Chickamauga, riding and fighting in the famed Lightning Brigade. The defense of Alexander's Bridge helped delay Confederate forces at Chickamauga Creek and kept them from falling with devastating force upon an unprepared Union left.

On the forenoon of the 18th we were skirmishing out toward Ringgold, when we met *Walker's* Corps with *Walthall's* Brigade in advance, a little more than 5000 strong. Seeing that we were outnumbered our brigade . . . fell back to the Chicamauga River, crossing it at Alexander Bridge.

Alexander's Bridge was one of three spans over which Confederate general Braxton Bragg intended to cross Chickamauga Creek and attack the Union forces that had been in hot pursuit of his army since forcing him to abandon Chattanooga. Unaware of Bragg's purpose, or even of where his army was, the Federals nonetheless managed to upset his plans on September 18 by fiercely defending both Alexander's Bridge and Reed's Bridge, several miles downstream, against powerful Confederate forces.

Here we made a stand. Our regiment was a few hundred yards from the river close to the old Alexander house (some farmer by that name having formerly lived there), where we were supporting Lilly's Battery. . . .

. . . We were west of the road, the 98th Illinois regiment east of the road, while the rest of the brigade were down near the bridge, the floor of which they had torn up and used to make a defense.

At 3:00 the Rebels came up and attacked us, both with artillery and small arms. Lilly's Battery replied, firing continuously into their ranks. Once I heard a Rebel cannon ball strike over to our right and turning we all tried to see what damage had been done. But from where we were we could see nothing, but the report soon came that it had struck the Adjutant, carrying away part of one of his legs. He was quickly taken in an ambulance to the rear.

The firing was continuous till about four o'clock. In the meantime

"It was dark enough so that I could see the fire stream from the muzzle of my gun every time I shot."

Colonel Wilder had sent part of our brigade to the assistance of Colonel Minty who was stationed at the Reed Bridge about two miles farther up the Chicamauga River and who had reported that he was being very hard pressed at that point. Though weakened by this yet we were able to hold the Rebels back.

At 4:00 . . . the report reached us that the Rebels had forded the Chicamauga River both above and below us and were threatening our flanks. Thereupon we mounted our horses and fell back about three miles northwest of the Alexander Bridge, swinging around in front of the Rebels who had forded the river below us at Dalton Ford. . . .

After we had fallen back we again faced the advancing army who were approaching from the east. It soon began to grow dark. Mounted infantry is supposed to do its fighting from the ground, but this time we were so hard pressed and the emergency was so great that we remained on our horses ready to fall back rapidly if the pressure became too great. We did not know at any minute when the enemy might appear at the right or left out of the darkness. My horse was not accustomed to

firing from his back and every time I would fire he would jump so that he would nearly throw me off. It was dark enough so that I could see the fire stream from the muzzle of my gun every time I shot.

We were soon joined at this point by Dick's Brigade and the 44th Indiana and the 59th Ohio regiments, and soon we had the Rebel advance checked. Then we dismounted and our horses were taken to the rear, while we laid down with our guns beside us. No one was allowed to go to sleep. Every one must be alert, ready to sieze his gun and shoot at a moment's warning.

Private Lorenzo C. Glenn heard the first shots of the Battle of Chickamauga while advancing with the 17th Tennessee Infantry, one of the lead units of Bushrod Johnson's division, as it moved to cross the creek at Reed's Bridge on the morning of September 18. Even before they reached the bridge, the Confederates encountered Union cavalry vedettes, and shooting erupted. Despite its prominent position, the 17th Tennessee suffered only one casualty the entire day.

Sergeant Isaac Skinner was a trooper in the 4th Michigan Cavalry when it stymied the opening move of Bragg's offensive by keeping Johnson's division from reaching Reed's Bridge the morning of the battle's first day. Outnumbered 6 to 1, the 4th Michigan and other regiments of Minty's brigade held up the Confederates for seven hours, fighting so stubbornly that one Yankee squadron had to swim to safety after the Confederates finally took the bridge.

MAJOR MICHAEL H. FITCH

STAFF, BRIGADIER GENERAL ABSALOM BAIRD, ARMY OF THE CUMBERLAND

Fitch found marching with Thomas' XIV Corps to be an almost mystical experience yet commented sardonically about the trials of army life. A few weeks after the battle he wrote, "I go out to the picket line occasionally and get shot at merely to keep up a healthy state of the system."

The movement did not begin until 4 P.M., of September 18th, for the reason that McCook's corps could not connect with Thomas' right with all his divisions until that date, and in such close proximity to the enemy, the lines must be kept compact, or at least within supporting distance of each other. The first division commanded by General Absalom Baird took the lead, after Negley's division, which at first was leading, dropped into line on the right of Crittenden. As General Thomas and his staff rode with us, and it was one of the most important movements made by us during the war, the main facts are quite vividly impressed on my mind. It proved to be an all night march. But the men were veterans at that time. They had crossed the Tennessee River at Bridgeport on the 3d or 4th of September, marched over two mountain chains, and were thoroughly seasoned to such service.

The enemy was not far away, and the utmost secrecy had to be exercised. McCook's corps followed us closely, so as to leave no gap in case of attack. Had the enemy discovered that we were hurrying by our left flank to get between him and Chattanooga, he would have done one of two things—either attacked us in the midst of the movement, or increased his own speed to gain the coveted point before us. Therefore, to deceive him, when darkness came on, the evening of the 18th, the troops left fires burning in their former camps, and along the line they had just occupied. In fact the night proved to be cold. Whenever a halt occurred, fires were built of fence rails, on the roadside, by the troops

to keep themselves warm, and when we reached Crawfish Springs at midnight, there was a streak of fire on each side of the road as far back as the eye could reach. The weird forms of the blue coated soldiers, with arms at right-shoulder shift in the fitful light of the blazing fires at some points, and again at others, in the shadows only of the smoldering ashes, reminded the beholder as he glanced back over his shoulder at the long line, of the ghostly march of the killed in battle of "The Soldier's Dream."

LIEUTENANT ALFRED PIRTLE

STAFF, BRIGADIER GENERAL WILLIAM H. LYTLE, ARMY OF THE CUMBERLAND

Pirtle and the rest of Lytle's brigade would hold out valiantly on September 20 after the other brigades of Sheridan's division and the rest of McCook's XX Corps had fled under the pressure of an attack by Longstreet's two corps. Pirtle survived the battle, but Lytle was struck down while rallying the brigade.

In August I had received from our sutler a gold seal ring with my initials engraved in script upon a beautiful piece of bloodstone. Though the ring was rather larger than my finger, I managed to use it, for it was then great fashion for the officers to sport seal rings.

The night of September 18th I was wearing gauntlets as I rode with Gen. Lytle at the head of the Brigade, marching half asleep along the sandy road. I put my right hand into my back right-hand pocket for some article, but as I drew it out I felt the ring drop from my finger. Instantly, in a loud voice, I gave the command "Halt." Reaching ground, I felt in my haversack for a short piece of candle which I habitually carried. The instant I had felt the ring slipping from my finger I dropped the gauntlet into the dust, and it lay before me. Every horse and man was worn out, remaining perfectly still right in their tracks where they had stopped at my order to "Halt."

I found the candle, lit it, and there in the dust shone the oval shadow of the ring, showing in the dust right by the gauntlet. I seized it, dust and all, and gave the command "Forward" and the march was resumed. Gen. Lytle asked why I so suddenly assumed the authority to stop the column, which gave me a chance to tell him the story in full, to which he said, "A man who can drop a ring in six inches of dust at the head of a column, in such a scene as this, and find it, is not going to be hit in the coming battle."

> ## "In August I had received from our sutler a gold seal ring with my initials engraved in script upon a beautiful piece of bloodstone."

COLONEL HANS CHRISTIAN HEG

BRIGADE COMMANDER, ARMY OF THE CUMBERLAND

The Norwegian-born Heg grew up in Wisconsin, became a Free Soil partisan, spent a year as a forty-niner, and later gained prominence in state politics. In 1861 he was commissioned a colonel and recruited Scandinavian immigrants into the 15th Wisconsin Infantry. He was mortally wounded the day after writing this letter.

Head Qurs 3d Brigade—
 19 miles from Chattanooga
 Sept 18th 1863

My Dear—

Once more I have an opportunity to write a few words. We have continued to march since I last wrote, and are still laying here ready at a moments notice for anything. The Rebels are in our front and we may have to fight him a Battle—if we do it will be apt to be a big one.

Do not feel uneasy for me. I am well and in good spirits—and trusting to my usual good luck. I shall use all the caution and courage I am capable of and leave the rest to take care of itself. The soldie[r]s are in tollerable good condition. Many of ours however have marched hard

and had rough time for the last two weeks and ought to have a few days rest before fighting. Our train is not with us—but I have one Head quarter waggon with me and get along well. Even has gone home I understand. . . . I got several Newspapers—some of them I see have accounts of my Brigade crossing the Tennessee River. The Rebels were here where we are camped yesterday, and got one of their Colonels killed in a skirmish. . . .

Old Roseys Head Quarters are only a few miles from here. I think, if it is true that the Rebels have not gone, that he will give them one of the biggest whippings they ever had. Burnsides Army is close by us, and can assist us any time I think. Thus far Roseys Army has gained a tremendous victory by forcing Bragg to leave Chattanooga.

I can of course say nothing about the prospects of getting home—but as soon as this present campaign is ended—I am certain of being able to come. We have had such hard work marching over these mountains that we are entitled to some rest. The *"Gen."* will call and see you the first thing you know—probably surprise you. My love to the children.

Good Bye my Darling—write often, but do not expect to hear from me very often till the campaign is over.

Your Own
Hans

Crawfish Springs fed into the Chickamauga above Lee and Gordon's Mills. Parched Union troops rushing to meet an imminent Confederate onslaught were ordered not to break ranks to drink. Said a sergeant of Crawfish Springs, "I am told they exceed anything in the Spring line that we have seen yet."

CORPORAL JAMES FENTON

19TH ILLINOIS INFANTRY, STANLEY'S BRIGADE

Fenton, whose company was placed in reserve at Crawfish Springs on September 19, describes listening to the sound of the battle. Proud of his regiment's training in "French bayonet drill," he wrote, "No regiment in the Confederate army of anywhere near equal size had any business with the 19th Illinois at close quarters."

At early dawn on the morning of the 19th of September, the advance of General Thomas's troops, after all night march and a part of the day before, reached Crawfish Springs, tired, thirsty, and all covered with dust from a road nearly shoe-top deep with a thick splurgy dust that was partially damp from a slight rain the night before. The equipment and faces of the soldiers were black with this dust, it just raised enough to cover everyone a dark color. Every soldier in that nights march knew that the confederate army was moving on the other side of the Chickamauga to gain the road that led to Chattanooga. The fences had been set on fire to give the enemy the impression we were lying in the battlefield. On reaching Crawfish Springs, the 19th Illinois, the advance of Negley's division was detached from the line, Companies I and K were deployed in the front of the Spring the rest of the regiment in reserve.

Instantly the enemy opened us with a battery from the other side of Chickamauga River. This was the opening of the great battle; almost at the same time, our cavalry and mounted infantry were heard disputing the enemy at the fords and bridges away to our left, on the battleground proper. Crawfish Springs gushes out at the foot of a small bluff, a sheet of the finest water, some 50 feet wide and over a foot in depth; being dammed up at the Lee and Gordon Mill on the Chickamauga it made a beautiful lake up to within 150 yards of the spring proper. Bridges's battery now took a position on a sloping garden in front of a fine brick house back from the spring, and replied to the Rebel battery. Our battery, on account of its exposed positions, was roughly handled and a gun dismounted and a caisson blown up and several killed and wounded. Another battery soon took its place and this duel was kept up for some time.

I have often wondered why the enemy did not depress its guns a few feet and sweep the troops that were marching around the spring to reach the battlefield; General Thomas's whole corps was moving with closed ranks, urged by the officers to their utmost speed, toward the distant sound of battle. We lying down on the skirmish line to the right of Company K, close to the road would be asked by these troops where that firing was and we pointed out to the left . . . the troops, tired, hungry, and thirsty, covered with dust were not allowed to break ranks to get water. In some regiments in spite of officers, men rushed down and waded across the sheet of water, dragging a canteen or a large cup, to get a drink.

That was the last water hundreds of them saw. . . .

Both sides rushed in troops by brigades and divisions. It was charge and countercharge, until past noon, and some of the most desperate fighting of the war was taking place. We lying on the skirmish line at Crawfish Springs listened to the roar of battle and saw the great clouds of powder smoke rising over the field, but could not see the battle. We would look at one another but not much was said. Some would say that is the Rebs charging and soon would hear our men charge, as the yells were quite different. There were probably two thoughts uppermost in our minds, lying there, and they conflicted with one another, and the average soldier just then would not care to own them. One was a secret satisfaction that we

were not in it. And yet, we knew we would be needed. It is most trying on the nerves, of even old soldiers, to be held back when the battle is on. But when he can hear a few bullets whistling near him, he inherits fighting blood it soon begins to circulate and should he take part in a successful charge, there is an exultation that makes him forget for a few moments the comrades who fell on the way.

CHAPLAIN WILLIAM W. LYLE
11TH OHIO INFANTRY, TURCHIN'S BRIGADE

A veteran of Second Bull Run, South Mountain, and Antietam, Lyle wrote that the roar of battle at Chickamauga was worse than all three of those battles combined. Below, the chaplain offers a journalist's account of a prayer before the fighting broke out.

At eight o'clock our regiment formed in line of battle and took position on the brow of a hill about two miles north of Gordon's Mills, and near the Chattanooga road. By this time the engagement had become general, and troops were rushing forward rapidly. Feeling anxious to have one more opportunity of speaking a word of encouragement to the soldiers who were about to enter into the very jaws of death, and many of whom, perhaps, would never hear words of prayer upon earth again, I rode up to Colonel Lane and asked just five minutes time to pray with them before going into action. "Certainly," was his instant reply. "I wish you would have services; I think there will be time."

Another pen must describe the scene as witnessed by others on the morning of that eventful day. Says a correspondent:

"General Turchin's brigade of Reynolds' division, Thomas' corps, consisting of the Eleventh Ohio, Colonel Lane; the Thirty-sixth Ohio, Colonel Jones; the Ninety-second Ohio, Colonel Fearing, and the Eighteenth Kentucky, Lieut. Col. Milward, took position on a low spur of the ridge near the Chattanooga road, and in the rear of [a] tannery.

Before the skirmishers were deployed, a scene occurred with the Eleventh, which, for sublimity and moving power, has been seldom surpassed. The chaplain rode up in front of the line, and the colonel gave an order which, on being executed, formed the regiment in two divisions, with the chaplain in the center. Without dismounting, he addressed the troops in a clear, loud voice that sounded strangely amid the loud explosions of the artillery and the rattle of musketry.

" 'It is but little I can do for you,' said he, 'in the hour of battle, but there is one thing I will do—I will pray for you. And there are thousands all over the land praying for you this morning, and God will hear them. You must now pray, too; for God is a hearer of prayer. And if this is the last time I shall ever speak to you, or if these are the last words of Christian comfort you will ever hear, I want to tell you, dear comrades, that God loves you. I pray God to cover your heads today in the battlestorm. I pray that he may give you brave hearts and strong hands today. Be brave, be manly! Remember the dear old flag, and what it covers. And if any of you feel uncertain as to your future, look to the Savior who died for you; and, if any of you fall this day in battle, may you not only die as brave soldiers for your country, but die as soldiers of the Lord Jesus Christ. Let us pray.'

"Instantly every head was uncovered and bowed in reverence, while hands were clasped on rifles, the bayonets on which were gleaming in the morning sun. The flag, pierced and rent on a dozen battlefields, was drooped, and, strange but glorious sound on a battlefield, the voice of prayer was heard. When the chaplain closed, he raised himself in his saddle, waved his hat two or three times around his head, exclaiming, 'God bless you today, dear comrades, and make you strong and brave. Strike for liberty and Union! Strike for God and humanity! And may our battle-torn flag lead to victory this day! God's presence be with you, comrades!'

"A low, murmuring Amen was heard from the ranks as the chaplain closed. Major-General Reynolds and staff passed along the lines during the services, but halted when they came to the Eleventh. With uncovered head the General rode up close to the regiment and remained till the conclusion of the brief services. At the moment they were concluded he uttered a hearty Amen, which had a thrilling effect. Grasping the chaplain's hand and shaking it warmly, while a tear glistened on his cheek, he was heard to exclaim, 'Sir, I am glad I was here to join with you!' and instantly rode off, followed by his staff. This acknowledgment of religious principle on the part of General Reynolds had a very happy effect."

Scarcely five minutes elapsed till the entire brigade moved forward and engaged the enemy.

CAPTAIN ISRAEL B. WEBSTER
10TH KENTUCKY (U.S.) INFANTRY, CROXTON'S BRIGADE

Although Webster almost lost a hand to a Minié ball during fighting on Horseshoe Ridge, he kept a sense of humor about the enterprise of war. When the Federals were interrupted by cannon fire while preparing breakfast at dawn on September 19, he wrote, "Many among our regiment went into the Chickamauga battle with both hands full of something to eat or drink."

We had thus advanced but a short distance when "Halt! Lie down!" came. We promptly obeyed. The brigade sent to relieve us had been routed and was making tracks to the rear at a lively gait, closely followed by the Johnnies in hot pursuit. Over our prostrate line went the blue-coats like a mob without form, in squads of from one to half a dozen. When nearly all had passed over us, "Attention!" rang out, which brought every man to his feet. The pursuing grays, seeing us come up out of the ground, as it were, stopped from their mad run and poured a volley into us. Their aim was not good, as little damage was done, but Private Richard Roaler of my company received a mortal wound just as he straightened up.

"Fix bayonets, forward, double-quick, charge!" was now the order, and away we went in full chase of the Johnnies, who, but a few moments before, were rushing over the same ground in mad pursuit of the flying "Feds." In this second race the "un-Feds" showed up well as racers, for when our commander at the proper time called a halt not a Johnny Reb could be seen. When we came to a stand-still our line presented a curious formation. The center had advanced far ahead of the flanks, making an inverted V-shaped line. "Dress on the colors" necessitated the advancing of the flanks.

While this was going on I saw, some distance in advance of us, what appeared to be a full battery. The horses were lying down, and not a

"I pray God to cover your heads today in the battlestorm."

LIEUTENANT ALBION W. TOURGEE
105TH OHIO INFANTRY, E. KING'S BRIGADE

Wounded and blinded in one eye at First Manassas, Tourgée (above, right) was captured at Murfreesboro in January 1863. Exchanged the following May, he got married before rejoining the 105th for the Tullahoma, Chickamauga, and Chattanooga campaigns. He resigned in December 1863. A Radical Republican after the war, Tourgée served six years as a superior court judge in North Carolina, and after a failed congressional race, moved to New York State, where he wrote novels.

man was to be seen around there. I immediately called Col. Hays' attention to it, and suggested that we "go for it" and take it off the field. He shook his head, but said nothing. I returned to my place. The next moment I heard a voice in front, and looking in the direction of it saw the Adjutant of the 14th Ohio sitting upon his horse a short distance in front of the line, calling attention to the battery. The 14th Ohio was formed on our left, and the Adjutant was in front of the junction of these two regiments. Col. Hays observed what was going on, and seeing a disposition on the part of the men to take that battery, he called out: "If you want it, go for it," and we were soon moving toward it.

At a proper distance we halted, and Company I was ordered to advance and deploy to cover the whole line to prevent a surprise while the guns were being hauled off to the rear. This skirmish line was many yards from the main line, and when this order was completed the skirmish-line was very thin, as the company was not numerically large and had considerable ground to cover.

When all was ready men from both regiments were detailed to do the work. As they neared the battery a cry came from away beyond— a cry of distress, an appeal for help, a boyish voice crying to be saved. It was a cry that went to the hearts of the men of the detail there present, and I said to one of them: "Go to his relief, and I will protect you with my guns."

Away he sped, closely followed by a dozen pair of eyes. Suddenly he was lost to view. For a time great uneasiness prevailed among our little squad. Each man was straining his eyes to catch a sight of the rescuer, while a deep silence reigned in our midst. At length he was seen returning, and as he neared us we observed that he had something in his arms. That something proved to be a lad, apparently some 12 or 14 years of age, who had received a wound of some kind that had crippled him, and he was unable to get off the field without help. His rescuer carried him to the rear, and as he passed me he said: "This is my boy from now henceforth," while great tears rolled down his cheeks and his voice trembled with emotion. I have never heard of this boy since, neither do I know who the rescuer was. I believe he was of the 14th Ohio.

No one seemed to know where our position was. All was doubt and uncertainty. The ground was wooded, broken with low, transverse hills and irregular knolls. The woods were open, but grown here and there with baffling stretches of dense underbrush. There were a very few small fields and indistinct roads. The ground in

In this romanticized engraving, Lieutenant George Van Pelt of Battery A, 1st Michigan Artillery, defends his guns the morning of September 19 against soldiers of Walker's corps on the Confederate right. In a desperate, seesaw clash, the Confederates of Liddell's division made the final, triumphant push, driving two Union divisions into retreat. Van Pelt refused to fall back, firing 64 rounds of canister at the enemy before he was killed and the battery taken.

our rear was elevated, in our front slightly depressed. Palmer had taken position to the eastward of a road running north and south. He guessed it to be the Chattanooga road, but did not know. Suddenly firing began away to our left. The men awoke and listened, comparing views in regard to it. It grew louder and came nearer. Turchin was hurried to the left of Palmer. Presently our brigade commander, Colonel King, rode up and in slow, deliberate tones put the brigade in motion. We moved by the double-quick around a low, wooded knoll, across an open field, faced to the right and advanced in line of battle. The One Hundred and First Indiana were on our right in the front line. The wave of battle rolled down the line toward us. There seemed to be an interval at our right; we were moved by the flank to fill it. It was the worst possible region in which to maneuver an army, being without landmarks or regular slopes, and so thickly wooded that it was impossible to preserve any alignment. Besides, there seemed to be, as we know now there was, an utter lack of fixed and definite plan, and a woeful ignorance of the field. Soldiers are quick to note such things, and one of the Thousand, seeing a group of officers in consultation, said he guessed they were "pitching pennies to decide which way the brigade should front."

There was a lull in the action. We lay in the edge of the wood. From a thicket a hundred yards away came a dropping but deadly fire. By and by, the turmoil deepened about us. There was no chance to use artillery save at close range. On our whole front there was hardly a place where a range of three hundred yards could be secured. Communication between the flanks was almost impossible. The winding roads were full of lost staff-officers. The commander of a regiment rarely saw both flanks of his command at once. Even companies became broken in the thickets, and taking different directions were lost to each other. Confusion reigned even before the battle began. It is folly to attempt to unravel the tangled web of that two days' fight. Even the part a single regiment took is almost untraceable. More than a hundred accounts of it have been prepared; hardly two of them are alike in essentials; very few of them reconcilable in details.

PRIVATE ROBERT A. JARMAN
27TH MISSISSIPPI INFANTRY, WALTHALL'S BRIGADE

Jarman recounts the 27th Mississippi's attack on Battery H, 5th U.S. Artillery—a lightning strike that overwhelmed the Union gunners. A Union round dropped a large oak limb on Walthall and his horse but caused little injury. Battery commander Burnham and 12 of his gunners were killed.

Soon we had the order to forward skirmishers double quick, through an open woods with only low post oak bushes about waist high, our objective point being a battery of eight guns in front of us. In our excitement and charge we ran through part of a line of Federal infantry in front of the guns, and I thought our time then had about come, but they surrendered to us and we pushed on to the battery that was just beginning to pay out grape and canister on the brigade that was not more than 75 yards behind us; but J. S. Thompson, Bill Wofford, Green Westbrook and myself, I think between us, killed the last gunner at the battery, when each of us bounced astride of a gun and yelled our loudest, then we turned the loaded guns on the Yankees and gave them their own grape. We could not then get the guns off the field, for all the horses were killed. All of our regiment had been well drilled in artillery, and at that time it came into good use. Every regiment capturing artillery in battle was entitled to the crossed cannon and name of battle on their regimental flag, and that was a grand inducement to get men to charge batteries where it looked like instant death. In a short while the enemy rallied and retook the battery from us then we again took it from them and finally got the most of it off the field. Near this battery that evening word was passed up our line as we were lying down that there was a Yankee sharpshooter in a certain fence, killing a man everytime he shot, and if somebody didn't kill him the line would have to move. I volunteered to try and get him, and went some forty steps in front of the skirmish line, where there were some logs lying, asking the balance of my file of four to watch close for me. At first I could not see the man but could see the smoke of his gun, but he soon exposed himself to ram his gun, that was my chance and I fired at him about 125 yards, striking him under the left shoulder blade. He lay in the same place until the next Tuesday when I was over the battle field again.

LIEUTENANT LUCIUS G. MARSHALL
CARNES' TENNESSEE BATTERY

Moving forward with the battery, Marshall observed the newly arrived men of Longstreet's corps lying at their ease on either side of the road. He was surprised at their finely turned out state of dress and could not help noticing their surprise, in turn, at the scruffiness of the westerners. "The Army of Tennessee never looked worse," he wrote, "while at the same time it was never in better fighting order."

William W. Carnes, shown in the uniform of a Confederate artillery officer, began his military career as a U.S. Naval Academy midshipman. Transferring to the Confederate navy in 1864 he rose to command of the steamer Samson. As an artilleryman he gained a reputation for deadly use of canister at close quarters. At Chickamauga he led the battery that was lost and regained at terrible cost on September 19, the day after his 22d birthday.

The order to unlimber (which was done by simply unhooking and dropping the trails without reversing the teams) and commence firing was obeyed in much less time than I take to relate it, and that too by every piece simultaneously except the right, the ammunition of whose limber-chest had become fast and for a few seconds resisted all efforts to extricate the cartridges. The limber-chest standing open, and the team not having been reversed, the white pine of the unclosed cover raised vertically attracted hundreds of hostile infantry shots, which, passing through the wood and puncturing the outside tin, made the chest resemble a huge grater. Three or four men were endeavoring to loosen the ammunition at the same time with their heads over the chest, but strangely enough not one of them was then hit. All the horses of the piece, however, except the wheel-team, were killed before the gun was discharged. The wheel-team were hit, and, springing over the roots of a large tree, turned the limber bottom upward, scattering the ammunition on the ground like a load of apples. The driver, Mathews, thinking the situation desperate, urged on the two wheel-horses, and their speed at once righted the empty limber. Mathews, with his team, escaped further casualties and crossed Alexander's bridge, thus saving the only two horses belonging to the battery that survived the battle.

Four times a minute for the first three or four minutes, at least, each gun was discharged at very short range, probably two hundred yards; but the battery was a target for the concentrated fire of both the adverse artillery and infantry, since Wright's brigade had disappeared from the right flank, though it had rallied long enough to stand one vol-

ley after the battery went into action. But now—that is, eight or ten minutes after the artillery was in line—the whole brigade was out of sight. Probably they did right to leave, for otherwise they would have been annihilated. As it was, they left the ground strewn with their wounded and dead. The battery now stood alone, with no support in sight either on the right or on the left; in fact, there had at no time been any support on the left. . . .

When all the horses had fallen except one of the teams of the right section, the Captain gave orders to limber up the right piece and get away. The team came forward under the gallant drivers in the midst of a storm of all sorts of shot, but the six horses fell in a heap, the lead-team with their heads on the trail of the piece they were going to save. The Captain then said: "We can't save the battery. Let the men leave as quick as possible."

The guns were now silent. The men were all lying on the ground, whether dead, wounded or unhurt, and occupying as little space as possible. I called to my section to rise and follow, when I mounted my horse which stood near hitched to a swinging limb. I mounted not very hastily, for the act seemed to challenge the enemy's fire. The latter, however, were intent on felling at first all the artillery-horses they could, and besides they were at the moment extending their flanking enterprise and were now somewhat in rear of the battery. These two circumstances probably saved the survivors, for it was at that time quite in the power of the enemy, without danger, to pick off every one of the battery men who left the place. Only thirty-five men followed the Captain and Lieutenants from the terrible spot. . . .

As to our battery, the enemy rushed in, chopped down the limbers and dragged the gun-carriages by hand about one hundred and fifty yards toward their line before Stewart's division, then approaching double-quick, could open fire. At the first volley, however, the enemy abandoned the guns where they were and returned to a line of works in rear of the first. To insure the early restoration of the battery, Col. Walter of Bragg's staff, a friend of Capt. Carnes, invited the General to the ground to see the evidences of the desperate fight made on the spot. Stewart's division had made a fight of perhaps three hours over the ground before it was recovered, and thus the heaps of dead were somewhat greater than were due to the battery. Bragg said he would like to sell Rosecrans some more batteries at the same price as this. His orders were positive to restore everything as the Captain desired and prescribed. As a compliment, the new guns were inscribed "Chickamauga, Sept. 19, 1863."

LIEUTENANT BROMFIELD L. RIDLEY

STAFF, MAJOR GENERAL ALEXANDER STEWART,
ARMY OF TENNESSEE

Only 18 at the time of Chickamauga, Ridley was Stewart's aide-de-camp. He was also good friends with another 18-year-old lieutenant, James D. Richardson of the 45th Tennessee. Encountering Ridley on the battlefield during the worst of the fighting on September 20, Richardson said simply, "This is hot, isn't it?"

A young staff officer of Wright's (Harris) met us with the statement that Wright's Brigade was much cut up by an enfilade fire: that Carnes's Battery had been lost and help was wanted. As quick as told, Clayton, forming Stewart's first line, was obliqued to the left and vigorously rushed to the rescue.

Did you ever note the thickness of raindrops in a tempest? Did you ever see the destruction of hail stones to growing cornfields? Did you ever witness driftwood in a squall? Such was the havoc upon Clayton. Four hundred of his little band were mown down like grain before the reaper. It was his first baptism of fire, but he stayed there until out of ammunition. J. C. Brown then went in, and was greeted like Clayton. The booming of the cannon, the thinning of the ranks, the thickness of dead men, the groaning of the dying—all were overcome to recapture that battery. Thirty-two horses of Carnes's had been shot down, and amid their writhings the close quarters had set the woods on fire. The shot and shell were raging in the tempest and ramrods flew by us, but Brown drove back the hordes and got Carnes's Battery out of the

cyclone. Another surging wave after a while brought him back upon the reef. Then Bate came into arena, and with his crack brigade and prompt movement vied with his compeers in deeds of valor. He rescued the colors of the Fifty-First Tennessee Regiment, and captured several pieces of artillery. Tennessee and Georgia and Alabama tried themselves, and from two o'clock till dark beat and battered the walls of blue, buffeting the storm clouds, charge meeting charge with sanguine success until nothing would stand before them. . . .

Stewart here penetrated the enemy's center, threatened to cut his army in two, drove Vancleve beyond Lafayette road to the tanyard and the Poe house, and carried dismay to Rosecrans, to the Widow Glenn's. Later, Hood and Johnson on our left followed it up, until from the Brotherton to the Poe field we pierced his line. Added to the horror of the galling fire, the generals and staffs encountered a number of yellow jackets' nests, and the kicking of the horses and their ungovernable actions came near breaking up one of the lines. Blue jackets in front of us, yellow jackets upon us, and death missiles around and about us—O, the fury of the battle, the fierceness of the struggle over Carnes's Battery! From two o'clock until an hour after dark it was war to the knife and a fight to the finish.

This small pond behind the house of the widow Eliza Glenn was one of the only water sources available to the fighting Federals. It became known as Bloody Pond because of the injured horses and wounded soldiers who dragged themselves to it and, while drinking, died or stained it with their blood.

LIEUTENANT GENERAL JAMES LONGSTREET

WING COMMANDER, ARMY OF TENNESSEE

When Longstreet and his staff arrived at a railroad depot near the battlefield on the 19th, no one was there to greet them. Spending hours in the saddle trying to find their way to Bragg's headquarters put them in a chilly mood. Said one officer, "Some hard words were passing" about Bragg that night.

The train upon which I rode reached Catoosa about two o'clock of the afternoon of the 19th of September. That upon which our horses were came up at four o'clock. Only part of the staff of the corps was with me, and General Alexander was with his batteries far away in South Carolina. As soon as our horses could be saddled we started, Lieutenant-Colonels Sorrel and Manning and myself, to find the head-quarters of the commanding general. We were told to follow the main road, and did so, though there were many men coming into that road from our right bearing the wounded of the day's battle; the firing was still heard off to the right, and wagons were going and coming, indicating our nearness to the field. Nothing else occurring to suggest a change of the directions given us, we followed the main road.

It was a bright moonlight night, and the woodlands on the sides of the broad highway were quite open, so that we could see and be seen. After a time we were challenged by an outlying guard, "Who comes there?" We answered, "Friends." The answer was not altogether satisfying to the guard, and after a very short parley we asked what troops they were, when the answer gave the number of the brigade and of the division. As Southern brigades were called for their commanders more than by their numbers, we concluded that these friends were the enemy. There were, too, some suspicious obstructions across the road in front of us, and altogether the situation did not look inviting. The moon was so bright that it did not seem prudent to turn and ride back

under the fire that we knew would be opened on us, so I said, loudly, so that the guard could hear, "Let us ride down a little way to find a better crossing." Riding a few rods brought us under cover and protection of large trees, sufficiently shading our retreat to enable us to ride quietly to the rear and take the road over which we had seen so many men and vehicles passing while on our first ride.

We reached General Bragg's head-quarters at eleven o'clock, reported, and received orders, which he had previously given other commanders, for attack early in the morning.

PRIVATE JOHN T. COXE

2D SOUTH CAROLINA INFANTRY, KERSHAW'S BRIGADE

Coxe, a teenager six months removed from civilian life, was thrown into the fighting of September 20 with his regiment. Later he marveled that he and his comrades could fall hungrily upon captured Union rations and then sit relaxing and chatting "while the dead and dying lay all about."

In any army, there are always plenty of men "cocked and primed" for shooting off "tongue bombs." So while getting out of the cars many not very choice expressions were heard, such as: "I'm damned hungry," "I wish Abe Lincoln was in hell," and many others of like import. I noticed a group of officers standing at a short distance, and to the surprise of all we heard the stentorian but perfectly cool voice of General Kershaw say: "That is lovely language to be coming from the mouths of South Carolina gentlemen!" And that was all he said. And it was quite enough, because after that one could have "heard a pin drop" while we were crossing that cornfield.

"It was a bright moonlight night, and the woodlands on the sides of the broad highway were quite open, so that we could see and be seen."

This drawing by Alfred R. Waud captures the arrival at Chickamauga of five brigades from Lee's Army of Northern Virginia under Longstreet's command. Longstreet so strongly felt the need for this deployment that at first he went behind Lee's back to urge the Confederate secretary of war to order the move. "The subject had not been mentioned to my commander," Longstreet stated in his memoirs, "because . . . he was opposed to having important detachments of his army so far beyond his reach."

CAPTAIN JAMES R. CARNAHAN
86TH INDIANA INFANTRY, DICK'S BRIGADE

Carnahan remembered the savage fighting of the 19th, when he and his fellow Indiana men repulsed several charges by the newly arrived troops under Longstreet. Writing in 1886, Carnahan asserted that because the Union had in the end been able to hold Chattanooga, the defeat at Chickamauga was not strategically damaging. "Had the battle been fought at Chattanooga instead of Chickamauga," he wrote, "Chattanooga would have been lost to us, and disaster overwhelming and crushing would have been the fate of the Army of the Cumberland."

Scarce had our lines been formed, when the sharp crack of the rifles along our front, and the whistling of the balls over our heads, give us warning that the advance of the enemy has begun, and in an instant the shots of the skirmishers are drowned by the shout that goes up from the charging column as it starts down in the woods. Our men are ready. The Seventh Indiana Battery—six guns—is on the right of my regiment; Battery M, Fourth United States Artillery, is on our left. The gunners and every man of those two batteries are at their posts of duty, the tightly drawn lines in their faces showing their pur-

After beginning the war as a private in the 5th New York Zouaves, Francis L. D. Russell became an artillery lieutenant and commanded the battery on the right of Dick's brigade in the fighting described on this page. Said one brigade commander of Russell and a fellow officer, "Those lieutenants, although they look like mere boys, yet for bravery and effective service are not excelled if equaled in efficiency by any artillerists in the army." Russell lost his life eight months after Chickamauga.

pose there to stand for duty or die. Officers pass the familiar command of caution along the line—"Steady, men, steady." The shout of the charging foe comes rapidly on; now they burst out of the woods and onto the road. As if touched by an electric cord, so quick and so in unison was it, the rifles leap to the shoulder along the ridge where waves the stars and stripes. Now the enemy are in plain view along the road covering our entire front; you can see them, as with cap visors drawn well over their eyes, the gun at the charge, with short, shrill shouts they come, and we see the colors of Longstreet's corps, flushed with victory, confronting us. Our men recognize the gallantry of their foe, and their pride is touched as well. All this is but the work of an instant, when, just as that long line of gray has crossed the road, quick and sharp rings out along our line the command, "Ready," "Fire!" It seems to come to infantry and artillery at the same instant, and out from the rifles of the men and the mouths of those cannons leap the death-dealing bullet and canister; again and again, with almost lightning rapidity, they pour in their deadly, merciless fire, until along that entire ridge it had become almost one continuous volley. Now that corps that had known little of defeat begins to waver; their men had fallen thick and fast about them. Again and yet again the volleys are poured into them, and the artillery on our right and left have not ceased their deadly work. No troops can long withstand such fire; their lines waver; another volley, and they are broken, and now fall back in confusion. The charge was not long in point of time, but was terrible in its results to the foe.

Along the entire line to our right and left we can hear the battle raging with increased fury. We are now on the defensive; and all can judge that the lull in our front is only the stillness that forbodes the more terrible storm that is to come. A few logs and rails are hastily gathered together to form a slight breastwork. Soon the scattering shots that be-gan to fall about us gave us warning that our foe was again moving on us. Again we are ready, now laying behind our hastily prepared works. Again we hear the shout, as on they come with more determination than before. But with even greater courage do our men determine to hold their lines. The artillery is double shotted with canister. Again the command, "Fire!" and hotter, fiercer than before, the battle rages along our front. Shout is answered with shout, shot by shots tenfold, until again our assailants break before our fire and are again forced back. But why repeat further the story of that Saturday afternoon. Again and again were those charges repeated along our line, only to be hurled back—broken and shattered. It did seem as though our men were more than human.

LIEUTENANT W. J. MCMURRAY

20TH TENNESSEE INFANTRY, BATE'S BRIGADE

Of 140 men in McMurray's regiment, 98 were killed or wounded in the fighting described here. McMurray was wounded but recovered and later became a physician. He wrote that during a battlefield tour, Jefferson Davis saw a dead horse bearing officer's trappings identified as having belonged to Bate. Farther on, the president's party spied a second dead mount, also said to have been the general's, and farther still, a third. "This man Bate must be a gallant fellow," Davis remarked.

Awakened at dawn on September 19, Orderly Sergeant James L. Cooper of the 20th Tennessee faced the terrors of the forthcoming clash with a measure of fatalistic calm. "The day was bright and beautiful," he wrote after the war, "and the world never seemed half so attractive before, now that there was a good chance for leaving it soon." Cooper got through Chickamauga untouched but was hit at Missionary Ridge two months later and again at Resaca, Georgia, the following year.

By two o'clock all of our forces were exhausted except Stewart's Division, numbering 3,800 men. We were formed in column by brigades, as an assaulting column, with Bate in front. Bate's command advanced to within about one hundred and fifty yards of the enemy's battery, and were ordered to lie down. In a few minutes afterwards Clayton, with his Alabama brigade, rushed over us and engaged the Federals at the toe of the shoe, but the gallant Alabamians could not withstand the galling fire of Palmer's veterans, so in about 30 minutes Clayton and his command came back very badly used up, and passed on to the rear. Bate was ordered to lie still and in a few minutes Clayton had gotten out of the way, and then that grand Tennessee soldier, John C. Brown, who could always ride the waves of battle as gracefully as the swan could the ripples of a lake, came with his Tennesseeans, swept right over Bate's line, heading for the point of the toe, and in a few seconds it seemed as if the earth had opened up all of her magazines, and not a man would be left to tell the tale. There was roar after roar of musketry and artillery, and rebel yells that could be heard for miles away. After a struggle of about half an hour that gallant command had to withdraw. Passing back over Bate's line, Brown soon uncovered Bate's front. At this time, everything we had was exhausted except Bate, and the point had not been driven in. We had lain there and had seen two of our best brigades go to pieces, but as soon as our front was clear I heard some one coming from my left (my regiment was the right of the brigade) on horseback, and it was Gen. Bate riding his old single-footing sorrel. I was standing near Col. Thomas Benton Smith, who commanded the Twentieth Tennessee Regiment, when Gen. Bate rode hurriedly up to him and said: "Now, Smith, now, Smith, I want you to sail on those fellows like you were a wildcat." At once Col. Smith gave the command, "Attention, Battalion! Fix bayonets! Forward! Double-quick! March!" and the whole brigade moved as one

man. In five minutes all the horrors of war that a soldier ever witnessed were there; in fifteen minutes we were in possession of every piece of artillery, had broken Palmer's line, and had driven him from the point, and cut our way so far in the Federal rear that they began to close in behind us, and we had to fall back. As we did so we met Brown and Clayton, who had rallied their men. Bate's brigade was also badly scattered. We rallied on Clayton and Brown and straightened out our scattered lines. By this time the Federals had brought up a fresh division, under Gen. Van Cleve, of three brigades. With our already thinned ranks we attacked Van Cleve, and in less than two hours he was forced back before the deadly assaults of the "Little Giant Division." We were so badly used that we were compelled to halt and straighten out our line, and by the time this was done who should we find in our front but Gen. Reynolds, with his heavy division of four brigades to swallow up this remnant of Stewart's little division? But this was not to be done easily. Stewart attacked Reynolds after five o'clock that evening, and we fought until in the night. When the fighting closed we had driven back his right wing and had his lines in bad shape. We held him there all night. As I understand, he fortified his lines that night, and was driven out next day. I can't tell you anything about the battle after the first day, as I was almost mortally wounded in the right groin and left on the field all night.

PRIVATE FRANK T. RYAN

1ST ARKANSAS MOUNTED RIFLES (DISMOUNTED),
MCNAIR'S BRIGADE

Ryan was wounded in the leg shortly after the action described below and would have died except for a coincidence. He was lying in a morphine haze when a shirker from his company appeared. The shirker tried to flee to his company, but Ryan asked him to stay. That night the woods caught fire, and only the soldier's quick action in clearing away all combustibles saved Ryan.

And it was not until about three o'clock in the afternoon that we were ordered forward, the order was given: "Rout step; arms at will; do not shoot; hold your fire; friends are in front, and we are merely going to their support." We had to descend a slight wooded declivity into a bottom, or for some distance a level piece of ground. Just as we got down into the bottom proper, my file leader, pointing his finger at an object in front of us, said: "Look! if that is a Confederate flag it is the strangest one I ever saw."

He had scarcely spoken the words when, just ahead of us, arose a perfect wall of men, and the next instant there was a deafening report, and we had received a most galling and deadly volley from the Federal muskets. It seemed that by some terrible mistake we had marched right up on an ambuscade; that we were not more than twenty feet from them when they fired into us. It was a most deadly volley; it killed instantly two men from my company and wounded severely seven, and it was about the per centage of mortality and wounded in each company throughout the regiment.

As soon as we had recovered from their staggering fire, and had somewhat composed ourselves, the order was given, "Up and at them." It was now our time, as we had reserved our fire, and most effectively did we do our work. I remember that next to me was a man, the brother of one of the men who had been instantly killed, and the sight of his dead brother seemed to stimulate him afresh, and he seemed to delight in seeing our enemies die. We drove them back and continued to follow them up, thinking that those on our right and left were doing the same, but it proved otherwise. We had merely blocked out the width of our regiment, and our forces on our right and left had failed to do likewise.

The Federals had swung around and cut us off; thus were we hemmed in; Federals in our front and rear. We had driven those in our immediate front quite a distance before we saw the predicament we were in; besides, those we had been driving had fallen back to a battery of their artillery, and it now began to play upon us with two or three guns with all their might. They were shooting solid shot at us. It looked to be the size of an ordinary rubber ball, about a two pounder, and to see it bound and ricochet over the ground made one cringe.

When we learned the dangerous situation of ourselves we halted, and began to counsel together as to the best and safest way out of it. In the mean time the troops in our rear were coming steadily towards us. We were divided in our opinions as to who they were. Some insisted that they were Longstreet's men, and therefore, our friends; others said that they could distinguish them plainly, and that they were the Federals. How such a difference of opinion could arise was owing to the fact that Longstreet's men were uniformed; wore light blue pants, grey jackets and a regular blue soldier's cap; where, on the other hand, the Western troops had no uniform at all, but wore clothes of all kind and hue; and as these troops were so far away that they could not be unmistakably seen, and the fact of them having uniforms, was why some of our men thought them to be our friends.

There being such a difference of opinion, our Colonel concluded to send back a flag of truce, and asked who would volunteer to go. A large six-footer, by the name of Page, readily said he would go; whereupon the Colonel told him to strip himself of his accoutrements and set his gun aside. Page drawing his ramrod, and the Colonel tying his white handkerchief to it, he was soon ready to start. A member of my company, by the name of Williams, said he would accompany him. Unfortunately for Williams, he did not do as Page did, but took along his gun and accoutrements. We watched them anxiously as they neared the body of approaching troops, and when we saw Williams throw up his hands, as if an act of surrender, and the next moment saw him fall to the ground, and the manner in which they acted towards Page, we soon knew who they were. At this the Colonel gave the order to retreat—adding, every man for himself; and, as we turned to leave, the battery which was in our front, but now in our rear, opened up all four guns with grape, canister and solid shot; and as one of those solid balls would ricochet by you, coming in rather too close proximity, it made one feel as if his back was twenty or more feet broad. We finally, with much disorder, escaped capture and succeeded in finding once more the body of our troops, of course losing several of our men—some wounded, some killed and others captured. Poor Page! we never heard from him afterwards; supposed that he was sent North to some of their prison pens and died from—good treatment.

The men of Company E, 8th Kansas Infantry, pose near a tepee-like Sibley tent in this 1862 photograph taken in Kansas. Organized in the fall of 1861, the 8th Kansas was originally intended for duty in New Mexico and actually set out for that location before being recalled to Fort Leavenworth. Assigned to provost duty for most of its time in service, the 8th Kansas nevertheless saw more than its share of fighting at Chickamauga. The account by Hinman on the following page indicates that it did not fare well against the Confederates.

LIEUTENANT WILBUR F. HINMAN
65TH OHIO INFANTRY, HARKER'S BRIGADE

Hinman was wounded in the battle. "A bullet plowed a furrow across the front of my body," he related, "and then went like a streak of lightning through my right elbow." He convalesced in Chattanooga, where the Union army lay under siege and rations were sparse. Hinman wrote, "Hundreds, gaunt from hunger and worn by toil and watching, gave out entirely and thronged the hospitals, whence many were daily borne to the city of the dead."

During the action the Sixty-fourth was dispatched to fill a gap in another division, caused by the giving way of a regiment— the Eighth Kansas. The gap had become so extended that both flanks were exposed, but the Sixty-fourth moved steadily forward, driving the enemy before it, until Colonel McIlvaine ordered a halt, directing the men to lie down in the dense timber which covered the field. While the regiment was in this position it was so far in advance of the Union line that a considerable body of rebels came up in its rear. Forty or fifty of them, including half a dozen officers, stumbled upon the Sixty fourth. Upon being ordered to surrender they did so and were sent to the rear. The Confederate General Gregg, with several officers of his staff, unaware of the presence there of Union troops, rode up. Refusing to surrender, they wheeled their horses and attempted to escape. They were fired upon, and General Gregg fell from his horse, severely wounded. Colonel McIlvaine obtained possession of his sword. The small detail which had been sent to the rear with the prisoners inadvertently struck the ragged edge of the enemy's line. In the melee that ensued the prisoners made their escape, and John McFarland, one of the guards, was wounded and made captive. The position of the Sixty-fourth, far in advance, with no immediate support upon either of its flanks, was one of imminent peril, and an order to fall back was gladly obeyed. . . .

During the mix-up of the Sixty-fourth and the Confederates, Robert C. McFarland, of Company E, disarmed five Mississippians, marched them from the field and delivered them to the provost-marshal of the division. One of the prisoners was about six feet and a half high. "He looked big enough to eat me up!" said McFarland in relating the incident.

Among the prisoners taken by Harker's brigade were a number from Longstreet's corps, of Lee's army, which had been sent from Virginia to reinforce Bragg. It was easy to distinguish them from the soldiers of Bragg's army by their clothing. Most of them wore the regular Confederate uniform, while the dress of the western men was a "go-as-you-please" matter, with every imaginable variety of garments and head covering. Scarcely any two of the latter were clothed alike.

"How does Longstreet like the western Yankees?" they were asked.

"You'll get enough of Longstreet before tomorrow night!" was the answer, which proved to be very close to the truth.

Brigadier General John Gregg, a former schoolteacher, lawyer, judge, and briefly, representative from Texas in the Confederate Congress, commanded a brigade in Johnson's division of Hood's corps. He had ridden out in advance of his brigade's line when he was wounded in the action described above. Gregg not only survived the wound but was soon rescued. A little over a year later, near Richmond, he was mortally wounded in the neck.

CORPORAL WILLIAM H. RECORDS
72D INDIANA INFANTRY, WILDER'S BRIGADE

Records rode and fought in the Lightning Brigade almost constantly in the weeks leading up to Chickamauga, which gave him an opportunity to judge the developing crisis and comment on it. Aware of the Confederate reinforcements arriving under Longstreet's command, he was indignant at the rumor—untrue—that "ten thousand rebels paroled by Grant at Vicksburg are now present without exchange."

Somewheres between that time and noon McCook's Corps began to arrive. They came in on the road from Chattanooga and passed down through the farm in front of us. Davis' division was the last to come in and they came on the double quick and cheering and swinging their hats, by this time it was about one oclock in the

"Davis' division was the last to come in and they came on the double quick and cheering and swinging their hats."

afternoon. The battle then burst out in all its' fury in front of us. The troops that were going on the double quick along the road in front of us now "right flanked" into line and moved toward the woods at the east side of the farm, and no sooner did they enter the woods than they were confronted by an overwhelming force of the enemy and encountered a terrible storm of lead and iron, which caused them to recoil. Our brigade was then ordered to go to their support. When we arrived at the woods we met Davis's division falling back in a demoralized condition, the bullets flying through them and us. Shells from the enemies' guns bursting over our heads in such quick succession that they could not be counted. Our presence re-assured Davis's men so that they reformed and advanced towards the foe. We were then ordered back to our works on the run, and as we went the rebels played their Artillery upon us at a lively rate. We had scarcely got settled in our places when Davis' men gave way and came back in dreadful confusion. They were generally throwing away their knapsacks, and in some instances their weapons. They ran over us like sheep, but were rallied a Short distance behind us. The enemy now moved out into the farm in front of us and formed their lines upon the road. All of the artillery that escaped from the enemy in front of us was now stationed at intervals along the line of our Brigade. There was an Ohio battery where our company lay. The force confronting us proved to be Longstreets' corps from the rebel army in Virginia. . . .

Halting only long enough to correct their alignment they began to move upon us. When our entire line from right to left opened out upon them with Artillery and small arms. The rapid firing of our seven shooters gave our line the appearance of a living sheet of fire while we knelt down in two ranks behind our works—Davises men formed in two ranks. Standing behind us and fired over our heads as fast as they could. The artillery used canister. They were massed eight deep and charging upon us with fixed bayonette intending to break our lines. Our fire was mowing them down by the hundred. They faltered, then stoped but only for a moment When they turned and fled from the field at a rapid rate. A large number of the enemy took Shelter in the ditch

that is previously mentioned and Surrendered to us. The same troops that had been so roughly handled Now moved out to try it again When the enemy turned upon them and crushed them again. When they took Shelter again behind our lines But the rebels did not press upon us as closely as they did at first having already learned what the Seven Shooters were They thought "discretion the better part of valor."

Tatters and bullet holes in this flag of the 15th South Carolina attest to the savage fighting at Chickamauga. This regiment shared in the triumph of Longstreet's surge through the divided Union line on September 20, although its heaviest fighting would come later in the day at Snodgrass Hill and Horseshoe Ridge.

This painting captures the fury of the fighting at Viniard's farm on the afternoon of September 19, depicting the moment when Union brigade commander Hans Christian Heg (on horseback, right center) was mortally struck. Under heavy attack from Henry L. Benning's brigade of Georgians, the men of Heg's old regiment, the 15th Wisconsin, suffered a fearful toll. Depleted to 176 effectives before this assault, the 15th Wisconsin came out of it with just 65. Benning's forces were then decimated. Only six of 23 officers in the 20th Georgia escaped wounding or death.

SERGEANT BENJAMIN F. MAGEE

72D INDIANA INFANTRY, WILDER'S BRIGADE

For Magee, the terrors of the battle took second place to the horror of witnessing the suffering of the wounded. In battle, he wrote, "manly courage bore us up; in this storm of groans and cries for help that come on the black night air, manly sympathy for comrades and enemy makes our hearts bleed." But for Magee, war's bleak face was occasionally brightened by spots of humor, one of which he relates here.

It is now about 3 p.m. and the rebels have been throwing shell, grape and canister into us for half an hour. We hear a commotion to our right-rear, and looking around we see Gen. Sheridan on his black horse coming, and in front of him a staff officer, or orderly, carrying the General's battle flag, and as he approaches the rear of our regiment he calls out, "Make way for Sheridan! Make way for Sheridan!"

Of course we gladly open ranks and let the General and his staff pass through. He moves down in the field some 200 yards in front of us, and halts, while his division undertake to perform substantially the same movement that Davis had attempted and failed in two hours before. The division swing round as if on dress parade and move over the brow of the hill in splendid style. For a short time all is still in our front, and with eager hearts we await the result. Are the rebels gone? Sheridan's lines are entering the woods and hark! that rebel yell and the infernal din and roar startle the air. In two minutes Sheridan's men come pouring back over the ridge in confusion—a marked contrast to the order in which they charged upon the woods a few minutes before—the rebels pressing hard upon their heels. When Sheridan sees his men retreating he turns and comes back—having exposed his person in a fool-hardy manner. As he approaches our line we begin to shout, with a spike of irony, "make way for Sheridan!—make way for Sheridan!"

CAPTAIN ISRAEL B. WEBSTER
10TH KENTUCKY (U.S.) INFANTRY, CROXTON'S BRIGADE

Webster's unit was one of 13 infantry regiments, four cavalry regiments, and one artillery battery from Kentucky that fought for the Union at Chickamauga. But Kentucky, a border state where sentiments were divided, also had five infantry regiments, one cavalry regiment, and one artillery battery on the Confederate side. Despite being admitted to the Confederacy, Kentucky never seceded from the Union, so its units in the Confederate army received no support from their home state.

I discovered on the right of us a fallen tree, in the lap of which was our Surgeon, Dr. Stocking, dressing the wound of a soldier. I notified him that I was the last of our troops off the field and it would be well enough for him to take note of it, and I passed along. The next time I saw the Surgeon he told me I had saved him, as he had not been thinking of anything except what he was doing at that time and he made a narrow escape from capture. He expressed his gratitude to me for calling his attention to the danger of his position.

Dr. Charles H. Stocking (left) helped tend the wounded amid the perils of the Chickamauga battlefield. By the close of the fighting on September 19, the men treated by Stocking and other regimental surgeons could only be transported to the Union hospital four miles distant at Crawfish Springs by a single road. The medical director of the Army of the Cumberland, surgeon Glover Perrin, estimated Union wounded for the day at 4,500.

LIEUTENANT JAMES F. MELINE
6TH OHIO INFANTRY, GROSE'S BRIGADE

Lieutenant Meline recounts his regiment's desperate but belated effort to save a battery of the 19th Indiana Artillery—an action that resulted in the Ohio regiment being outflanked by Confederate attackers and suffering heavy casualties. By the end of the day's fighting, the Confederates had broken the center of the Union line. But it had no fresh regiments or ranking generals on the scene to turn success into victory.

*G*eneral Reynolds was at the battery, and, as Colonel Anderson moved our regiment to re-occupy its original position, he asked the colonel to remain and support it, but Anderson replied that his orders required him to report again to General Palmer, and we kept on. Reynolds said he feared he would lose the battery as it was entirely unsupported, and all his own regiments were in action. We had just entered the woods on our way back to the first line when we saw our troops giving way; and one of Reynolds' aides just then galloping up to the colonel and begging him to come and save the battery, the regiment was about-faced and double-quicked back. Before we got fairly into position, the battery became engaged, and I saw the rebels

General John M. Palmer, division commander in Crittenden's XXI Corps, was outraged when, after the battle, the government hailed Crittenden before a court of inquiry for his role in the Federal rout. Palmer submitted his resignation, stating, "Slander is dignified into history, and henceforth refutation is impossible." The army accepted the resignation but then reinstated Palmer. He succeeded Thomas as commander of the XIV Corps.

advancing upon it in four columns. The men at the guns worked well, but fired somewhat too high. I watched the cannoneers and horses fall, picked off one by one by the unerring shots of rebel sharpshooters, and saw that, as the regiments on our right were broken, there was nothing to prevent us from being flanked. The last round of shot was fired and we heard the command, "Limber to the front!" but still we lay there, determined to save those guns. The rebels had nearly surrounded us, but the battery—all except one piece—was safely retreating, when we received the order to raise and fire. We did so, and checked the charging enemy for a short minute, and then "changed front to the rear on the tenth company," and fired a volley in that direction. We were now flanked on both sides, while the rebels were bearing down upon us in front. Things looked desperate, and I began to think of Libby [Prison]. Reynolds, who still remained with us, had his horse shot under him, and at last ordered us to retreat double-quick.

As soon as we got out of this box we reformed behind a rail fence, and soon afterward were joined by the Ninth Indiana, a splendid fighting regiment, from our own division. Reynolds then ordered us forward, and forward we went in fine style, assisted by the Ninth Indiana. Our advance was short, however, for we no sooner cleared a little stretch of woodland than we were met by a most murderous fire from both flank and front, and were obliged to fall back in some confusion. Rallying, however, as soon as we could, we fell back slowly, firing at every step. Here our loss was heavy—many privates killed and wounded, Colonel Anderson, Captain Tinker (my captain) and Captain Montagnier wounded, and Lieutenant Holmes captured. It was now nearly dark. We were relieved by Jeff. C. Davis' division, received General Reynolds' thanks for what we had done, and by his orders then reported to our own division, which we found badly used up.

The men of Company C, 9th Indiana Infantry, pose for the camera during a peaceful moment in camp. During the clash at Brotherton's farm on September 19, the 9th Indiana was badly chewed up when it joined with the 6th Ohio in the fighting described above. The next day, the 9th Indiana was one of the last Federal units to leave the Chickamauga battlefield after covering the withdrawal of Thomas' corps.

"Some of the neighbors sang at the grave, and there we buried my brother while the battle was still goin' on."

ANONYMOUS PLANTATION BOY

Written 50 years after the battle, this account tells of Chickamauga as seen through the eyes of a 12-year-old left at his family's home with his mother and two sisters when the action began. The boy's father had fled south with "four or five hundred slaves" and livestock, and his three brothers were in the army.

The battle hadn't been going long when one of my brothers was brought to the house wounded. A few hours later another brother who had been hurt in the fight was brought there. The first one stayed with us several months, got well, and went back to the army. The other had been hit in the body by a grape shot, and I don't believe he ever spoke. He came in an ambulance, and he died as the men took him out. They brought the body right into the dining-room and left it there. The next morning we had the neighbors come and make a coffin and put the body into it. Then they lifted the coffin into a spring wagon. There were a number of other wagons, and we all rode to the cemetery, five miles away. Some of the neighbors sang at the grave, and there we buried my brother while the battle was still goin' on.

PRIVATE WILLIAM J. OLIPHANT
6TH TEXAS INFANTRY, DESHLER'S BRIGADE

Oliphant recorded in his memoirs that he was "severely" wounded in this clash, having been hit in the right arm, left hand, and mouth, the last wound breaking his jaw, and that he had been "carefully nursed back from the grave" by "the kind ladies of Georgia." Despite his dire condition, he was back in fighting trim scarcely two months later at Missionary Ridge, where he helped his regiment carry out two countercharges down Tunnel Hill against attacking Federal forces.

Patrick Cleburne, from Ireland, had studied to be an apothecary and served in the British army. In Arkansas he was a druggist and a lawyer. He organized a military unit and took the Little Rock Arsenal even before the state seceded. Commissioned a captain, he became a major general and division commander by late 1862.

Late in the afternoon a mounted officer galloped up to General Deshler, hurriedly spoke a few words and dashed away. The bugle immediately sounded attention and then came the sharp commands "right face, forward, double quick march." Away we went dashing through the Chickamauga River waist deep, and double quicked to the front.

On arriving at the edge of the battle we were quickly thrown into line and ordered to charge. The Texas yell was raised and into the smoke of battle we dashed passing through lines of Confederates who had been driven back by the enemy, and over the dead and wounded lying thick on the ground. Just at dusk we broke the Federal line and drove the enemy back in confusion.

After reforming our lines and resting a short time, we were again ordered forward, the enemy giving way as we advanced. It was now quite dark but just ahead of us was a brilliant light. A field was burning and we were ordered to charge through it. A battery had been stationed in the field and it was still there. It had been captured and recaptured and, then abandoned. The firing of the guns had set fire to the high sedge grass of the field. The fence was on fire and the tall dead trees in the field were blazing high in the air. Dead and wounded men were lying there in great danger of being consumed and the federals occupying the opposite side of the field were pouring a deadly shower of shot and shell through the smoke and flames. Bowing our heads and grasping our guns firmly we plunged into this vortex of hell. On emerging from the fire and smoke, yelling like demons, we dashed at the federals and soon had them flying. It was a fearful place. The heartrending appeals of the wounded, some of whom were scorching, the hissing bullets and screeching shells, made it an experience never to be forgotten.

ANONYMOUS CONFEDERATE
2D TENNESSEE INFANTRY, POLK'S BRIGADE

Although the 2d Tennessee, advancing as part of Cleburne's division, triumphed in this engagement, during the next day's fighting the regiment was decimated. Attacking impregnable and well-hidden Union breastworks that swept Polk's forces with a crossfire of artillery and musketry, one company of the 2d Tennessee lost 33 of its 44 men in just a few minutes.

At sunset the contest had lulled from exhaustion with the advantage to the Federals, who had proceeded to kindle fires and prepare for the night's rest. The air was quite chill, and Cleburne's men, who had waded the Chickamauga, built little brush fires in spite of orders to the contrary, supposing that no further movement was intended that night. As soon as the lights disclosed their position, several shots were fired from a Federal battery, one of which struck the fifth wheel of a caison in the immediate vicinity of General Cleburne. Skirmishers were thrown out in front of Ector's Division, which was lying a little distance in front, and at dusk Cleburne's Division was ordered forward over it, seemingly for the purpose of relieving it for the night; but the command "Forward" ran along the line, and at the next instant the enemy's skirmishers opened a lively fusilade. This was followed briefly by a burst of artillery and a flash of rifles along the front, and the Division, before it was aware, found itself in the midst of one of the most memorable and thrilling scenes of the war. A short halt was made, to deliver a few rounds, when the right of Polk's Brigade advanced steadily onward, firing occasionally, as the enemy's position was disclosed. The First Arkansas, on the left, never slackened its fire as it advanced, and, consequently, received a larger share of the enemy's attention. The general alignment was remarkably well kept, and no confusion seemed to exist at any time. The enemy retreated in such disorder that the Seventy-ninth Pennsylvania regiment, U.S.A., with its Lieutenant-Colonel, fell into the hands of the Second Tennessee skirmishers, while wandering around in the darkness. Colonel Robison, of the Second Tennessee, received this officer's sword and wore it in the engagement the next day. The plate of the belt was very large and heavy, and in the progress of the fight at the breastworks it was struck by a bullet with such force that the Colonel was unhorsed, but sustained no serious injury. . . .

When the line halted for the night, a mile and a half of ground had been recovered—a matter of vital importance to the Confederates, pushed, as they were at sunset, back among the breaks of the Chickamauga.

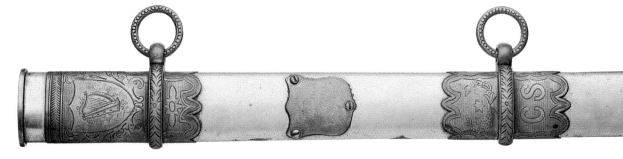

This sword and scabbard were presented to Patrick Cleburne by the men of the 15th Arkansas Infantry, his first command before being promoted to major general in December 1862 and taking over the 2d Division, which he led first in Hardee's corps at Stones River and then in Hill's corps at Chickamauga. Among other symbols, the scabbard bears the harp of Ireland in honor of Cleburne's native land.

PRIVATE ROBERT H. HANNAFORD

93D OHIO INFANTRY, BALDWIN'S BRIGADE

Hannaford was turned away, with other wounded Yankee prisoners, from several Confederate hospitals before being set on the ground at the field hospital of Cheatham's division, where he lay untreated for 12 days and nights. Hannaford summed up his feelings toward his captors, saying, "I thought I would live if possible, just to spite them."

We then prepared to meet the enemy again. We strengthened the breast works with everything we could find. I filled my cartridge box and put some in my pocket and I then intended to clean my gun and as I had no wiper of my own, I had to borrow one of a fellow named Bill Craig in our Co. I had the ramrod out and the wiper nearly screwed on when I turned my head to the left and looked down through the woods and saw them coming. I unscrewed the wiper and handed it back and said "they are coming" to Bill. I got down behind and commenced firing at them I had fired about eight or ten rounds when all at once I felt something strike me. I thought I was shot through the foot because it pained me so, it felt as if some person had throwed a log on it or something to bruise it but as soon as I straightened my leg I saw and felt I was shot above the knee for I could feel the blood running down my thigh. I then crawled off about ten feet and laid down behind a log and in front of the Orderly Sergent, his name was L. L. Sadler. I lay there a little while and groaned once or twice but I soon got ashamed of myself. I then commenced talking to Sadler I told him to pour it in to them, I could not do anything more but I wanted him to give it to them, his share and mine. I asked him if they would leave me there for I was confident they would have to fall back, he did not answer me I might have known that they would not take me back. He did not fire more than two or three rounds before they all got up and fell back leaving me there between two fires. . . . I never felt so bad in my life as I did that time. I stood pretty good chance of getting killed, and if I lived I would be a prisoner, most a

charming prospect to lay there wounded and helpless was not very nice. After laying there about a half an hour under a most terrible fire and narrowly escaping being shot I was taken prisoner as the Rebels advanced up the hill and soon as they passed I crawled over to the other side and laid down behind a large log. I was treated pretty well by them fellows as I lay there I could see the skulkers coming and I thought I would give away my canteen and coffee as I could see that was what they most desired. I did give it away and they promised to come back and help to carry me back to the rear, but they never came. While I lay there one fellow out of our company that was not wounded found Lieut Kellys hat, he brought it to me and said "Bob here is Lieut Kelley's hat." I told him to give it to me as it was better than mine which he did, it was about dark and a Reb and him carried me off a few feet and then left me. They put a shelter tent over me but the night was very cold and I lay there shivering and shaking until about nine o'clock when they carried me a little farther and laid me down by a fire as soon as they saw my hat one of them took it off and looked at it and proposed to trade, I did not like to but I thought it would be no use to refuse because they would take it anyhow. Therefore I very graciously told him to take it, which he did and handed me one about one size smaller than an umbrella, but I was forced to be satisfied, it was that or none. Oh what a miserable night that was to me, I lay there thinking of all my friends and those I loved and I never likely to see them again, I was wounded, tired, hungry, cold and dirty and worst of all a prisoner. I did not care so much about my wound as I did about being a prisoner.

This bullet-pocked plate from a Union soldier's cartridge pouch was found on the battlefield at Chickamauga. It is not known whether it saved the wearer from harm or instead bears mute witness to the soldier's fate.

"I was wounded, tired, hungry, cold and dirty and worst of all a prisoner."

This sketch by Alfred Waud shows soldiers of General Patrick Cleburne's division advancing against the Union lines at twilight on the evening of September 19. Although generally successful, the attack proved to be a prelude to disaster the following morning, when General Polk launched an uncoordinated assault against strong breastworks on the Federal left. Some Confederate regiments lost more than 50 percent of their men, while the Yankees suffered a mere handful of casualties.

PRIVATE
W. W. HEARTSILL

15th Texas Cavalry
(Dismounted),
Deshler's Brigade

*Heartsill's regiment, taking part
in Cleburne's futile assault on
Union breastworks the morning of
September 20, was raked by a
murderous crossfire as it advanced
and had to dig in behind a low
crest under heavy fire until the
survivors were finally pulled back
to the safety of the woods.*

The fight is now ringing on our right; it now reaches our Brigade and until nine o'clk in the night we are in the midst of burning woods, dead and dying men, while shells, grape shot and minie balls are handed around profusely. At one time the entire line of our skirmishers in front of Gillespies Regiment were captured, about this time Gen Preston Smith (who was in front of the right of our Brigade, his Brigade being on our right, in the darkness he got in front of our right.) challenged some troops in our front and demanded "whose troops are those." answer "the 77th Pennsylvania" and immediately fired a tremendious volley directly at our line killing Gen Smith and two of his staff, our Brigade immediately charged the enemy and captured 250 and recaptured our skirmishers that were taken a few moments before, we also got their flag which is a beautiful one. This last brush ended the contest for the night and now at 10 o'clk all is quiet, we are in the front lines. So far; I have seen seven captured Yankee flags and about one thousand prisoners, as to how the fight terminated on our left; at Lee & Gordon's mill; we have no reliable information, but we are satisfied that Longstreet will attend to his part of the fight, Breckenridge and Cheatham have done nobly on the right; while "old *reliable*" (Hardee) has given the enemy "bringer" in the center. . . . One o'clk (night) there is still considerable confusion about our lines and some doubt as to the position of the enemy; as the fight was carried on so long in the night, our commanders are at a loss where to establish our lines, we maneuver all night at 3 o'clk we are allowed to make fires

and take rest; and as the morning; as well as all last night is uncomfortably cold and all our clothes are wet from wadeing the Chickamauga last evening; the fire is thankfully received. We have literally walked on dead men all night, and now while camp fires are casting their flickering rays over the battle field, the scene looks horrible, hundreds of ghastly corpse mangled and torn; are scatrered around us, I can sit here by my little glimmering light and count a score of Federals; dead and dying. . . . It is now nearly day-light and I have not had a particle of sleep; nor do I want any while this bloody work is going on.

When some of Deshler's men retreated into his lines on the 19th, brigade commander Preston Smith rode forward to urge them back to their duty. Unaware that Deshler then shifted his brigade sideways and left Smith's front uncovered, Smith again advanced to exhort what seemed another line of stragglers. But this time he rode into a company of Pennsylvanians and was shot dead in the saddle.

CORPORAL WILLIAM B. MILLER
75TH INDIANA INFANTRY, E. KING'S BRIGADE

Although wounded in both legs and losing blood, Miller determined not to be captured as Union lines were pushed back on September 20. He hobbled toward Chattanooga until finally picked up by an ambulance. He later learned that he had been reported as wounded and captured. "What will my friends and especially my wife think when she sees that," he wrote in his diary. "Only a short time ago she burried our babe and now she thinks I am gone I know she will feel terrible."

The battle raged all day without ceasing until about five o'clock when I was struck by a Minnie Ball passing through my right thigh and lodging in my left one. It did not fracture the bone or knock me down but disabled me so I could not walk. When it first struck me I did not think I was seriously hurt. I was in the act of stepping when I was struck. I fired the charge from my gun and loaded it again and our line fell back and I undertook to follow but my left leg refused to carry me and I inserted the tompion into my gun and used it as a crutch. I managed to get back and Surgeon Dixon of the 1st Kentucky dressed it and ordered me off the field. I hobbled back and kept from being captured. . . . Our men kept falling back as the Rebels pressed them and finally came out into the open field and from where I was I could see the battle. The Rebels seemed to be desperate. Some say they are drunk and they made one charge after another and our men made terrible havoc in their ranks. They kept up the fight until darkness put a stop to it. There was heavy firing to our left until nine o'clock tonight. . . . This has been a terrible day to the American Nation and many bitter tears will be shed North and South for the dead of Chickamauga. There are thousands of men in the prime of life who this morning thought they were destined to live to a ripe old age who tonight are lying on the battlefield stark and stiff and who will be covered where they fell with a few shovels full of dirt and left to rot with nothing to mark the place where a hero perished for his country and that the government might live. They will not answer to the Roll Call in their respective companies any more and the report will be "Killed at Chickamauga Sept. 19, 1863" and how anxious will our friends scan the columns of the Newspapers to see who is among the missing.

"There are thousands of men in the prime of life who this morning thought they were destined to live to a ripe old age."

LIEUTENANT WILSON J. VANCE
21ST OHIO INFANTRY, SIRWELL'S BRIGADE

Vance reckoned himself the youngest commissioned officer in the Union army at Chickamauga, having enlisted in 1861 at age 17 and having been promoted from private to second lieutenant in January 1863. Even after he took command of Company D when its captain was mortally wounded the morning of September 20, Vance was often called Boy by the officers and men alike. During the desperate battles of that day, his company dwindled from 65 effectives to four.

The ground upon which we lay had been well fought over during the day, and as things became quiet we heard the moans and groans of the wounded, which told us that between us and the enemy were lying human beings, torn and mangled, and in agony.

One in particular was determined to have relief if making a noise would bring it. The others, perhaps worse hurt, merely tore our hearts with their piteous, stifled moans, but this fellow had strength enough to call for what he wanted. He was undoubtedly badly hurt, and his shrieks and groans grew momentarily more clamorous and insistent, mingled with bitter curses and imprecations from those who could but would not help him—for he well knew that within earshot lay hundreds, if not thousands, of human beings.

His speech plainly proclaimed him a Confederate, and for a long time we waited for his comrades to help him; but as, time going on, we found that for some reason they were not disposed to do so, the men of the 21st determined to go upon the merciful errand, at all risks. Taking a blanket to serve as a stretcher, they cautiously made their way to the sufferer, guided by his voice, which was now continuous in reproach, till at last, in spite of the shots that were fired at them, they brought

"Many, many, many a soldier asked himself the question, what is all this about?"

Private Simon Pressler, seen here sporting a six-barrel pepper-box revolver, survived the action at Chickamauga but was killed near Resaca, Georgia, in May 1864. Seven companies in his regiment, the 21st Ohio Infantry, were issued rapid-firing Colt revolving rifles before the Chickamauga campaign. One D Company officer described the reaction of charging Rebels when they first encountered the Colt and were raked by four volleys in the time they expected only one. "When, on a dead run for home base, the fifth one singing about their ears," he wrote, "they began to think that certainly the devil was in it all!"

him safely off to the rear of our lines.

Here they were unable, it being too dark to see where his hurts were, to do him much good; but what they could, they did. He was wounded in several places, and in spite of all their attempts at careful handling, they could not help hurting him. He was evidently suffering intense pain.

But the matter of the remarks he had to offer upon things of immediate interest was most extraordinary. He talked between groaning paroxysms and by agonized jerks, and with the most fluent profanity.

"It war good of you all to come out after me, —— —— —— let go my laig, stranger, you're a-killin' of me! Water, for God's sake! D'ye want-ter see me die? Thanky. I'll never forgit ye for this, Yanks! You've done me a good turn, an' I'll never forgit ye for it. Oh my God! I wish I could die! Why in —— don't this yer misery kill me? It oughtter!

"God in heaven, my friend, what do you mean? *Don't tech me!* You all got the best of it to-day, but by the jumping —— —— there won't be a corp'ril's gyard of you left by to-morrow night! Longstreet's done come, ye —— —— shad-bellies! Got hyar to-day, and we all's gwine to whip —— outen ye to-morrow! Water—water—why don't ye gimme water?"

And so on, mingling abuse and prophecies of our coming disaster with gratitude, curses, and prayers, in a manner as ludicrously grotesque as it was horrible. Our fellows gathered around him, ministering to him as best they could, in their rude, rough way, and taking no offence, but rather admiring his grit, and laughing as they understood that while he was by no means ungrateful, he could not help glorifying over the defeat he saw in store for us. At last, they carried him back to the field hospital, where he was cared for, and, it is to be hoped, set on the road to recovery.

LIEUTENANT ROBERT M. COLLINS

15TH TEXAS CAVALRY (DISMOUNTED), DESHLER'S BRIGADE

Collins' memoirs, often quite eloquent, are strangely matter of fact concerning the death of the brigade's much loved commander. During the storm of shot and shell that greeted the 15th Texas on September 20, Collins had been dispatched to inform General Deshler that the regiment was almost out of ammunition. "When we were in about ten feet of him and before we had delivered the order a bomb shell struck and killed him instantly," Collins wrote. "We reported the fact at once to Col. Mills and he took command of the brigade."

We lay in line of battle all night; the ground we occupied had been fought over several times during the day; the dead and wounded were all about us all night we could hear the wounded between ours and the Federal lines calling some of their comrades by name and begging for water. The night was cold and crisp, and the dense woodland was dark and gloomy; the bright stars above us and flickering light from some old dead pine trees that were burning in an old field on our left and in front, giving every thing a weird, ghostly appearance. . . . The Federal line was about four hundred yards from ours, and all night long we could hear them felling the big poplar and pine trees, from behind which they would fight us the next day. Our line was changed several times during the night, and notwithstanding we had slept but little, and had been on the march for the last fourteen days and nights, sleep seemed to have gone from our eyes, and slumber from our eyelids, and as we lay there with our faces turned up towards the heavens watching the bright stars and listening to the twitter of the little birds in their nests in the wildwood, many, many, many a soldier asked himself the question, what is all this about? Why is it that one hundred and twenty thousand men of one blood and one tongue, believing as one man in the fatherhood of God and the universal brotherhood of man should in the blaze of the civilization of the nineteenth century of the Christian era, be thus armed with all the improved appliances of modern warfare and seeking each other's lives? The truth of the matter is just this, many a soldier on both sides said to himself and his next friend, if you will pick out the man or men that I have to whip or kill if this thing goes on, we can settle the matters of differences by compromising, and all be at home in ten days.

Brigadier General James Deshler lost his life in the holocaust of Union fire on September 20. His next in command, Colonel Mills, wrote, "He was struck by a shell in the chest and his heart literally torn from his bosom." Private W. W. Heartsill of the 15th Texas Cavalry said, "At 9 oclock Gen Deshler is killed by shell it is usless to pass eulogies upon Gen D. for to know him was to love him and evry man in his Brigade regrets his death."

Found on the Chickamauga battlefield, this tin drum-style canteen probably belonged to a Confederate. Union soldiers were more likely to have been issued ones of an oblate spheroidal shape, a drum types that harked back to prewar militias.

Longstreet's Breakthrough

General Bragg ordered virtually the same plan of attack for September 20 that had produced the bloody stalemate on the day before. Leonidas Polk's divisions would again hammer at the Union left, going in one after another in sequence. When these attacks were well under way, General Longstreet would move forward, throwing his wing of six divisions at the Federal center and right.

As usual with Bragg's army, there were delays, caused in large measure by the general's own confusing reorganization of the night before. The irascible D. H. Hill claimed he had not received proper orders and refused to move until he did, thus stalling Polk's entire assault. Polk himself, never prone to hasty action, was found calmly reading a newspaper over breakfast hours after dawn, the planned time of attack.

It was not until about 9:30 that the fighting erupted—with the same deafening violence as the day before.

Breckinridge's division charged first, driving around the far left flank of General

On the night of September 19, the commanders of both armies made plans for the next day's fighting. Rosecrans chose to defend with Thomas on the left, McCook on the right, and Crittenden in reserve. Bragg reshaped his army into two wings, Polk's on the right and Longstreet's on the left. Repeating the original plan of striking the Union left with Polk's command, Breckinridge's division of Walker's corps attacked at 9:30 a.m. on September 20, attempting to flank Thomas and seize the La Fayette road. Within 45 minutes, the Federals had driven back the Rebel attack. Meanwhile, Cleburne attacked at about 10:00 a.m., but his men were also repulsed. At 11:00 a.m., the Federals also turned back additional assaults by two of Liddell's brigades. Later James B. Steedman's two brigades stopped a flanking attempt by Forrest's cavalry.

Thomas' position. In minutes a brigade of Negley's division had been bent back on itself—until troops from Brannan's and Van Cleve's divisions rushed to Negley's aid and forced the Confederates to retire.

Cleburne's division, next down the line, attacked about 10:00 a.m., rushing through a pine forest. But the first ranks were shot to pieces by furious fire from Federal troops dug in behind log breastworks they had hastily built during the night. While Cleburne's men reorganized, Polk sent in Cheatham's division, then Walker's, which were also stopped by rifle fire and scything blasts of canister from Federal guns.

His entire line under assault, General Thomas asked Rosecrans, as he had several times the day before, to order up reinforcements from the Union right. This Rosecrans did—and in the process made a fatal error.

While units were shifting about, a staff officer riding behind the lines mistakenly thought he saw a large gap near the Federal center. Thomas informed Rosecrans, who

At 11:30 a.m. Longstreet launched a juggernaut of 16,000 men of Johnson's, Law's, and Kershaw's divisions against the Federal right. Just as this Rebel attack got under way, Rosecrans shifted several units, including Wood's division, to the north to reinforce Thomas. To obey orders, Wood had to withdraw from the line and move to the rear of Brannan. In doing so he left a gaping hole in the Union line through which the Confederates poured. To the south, Hindman routed Sheridan and Davis, completing the collapse of the Federal right. Despite Wilder's flanking attempt to stop the Rebel onslaught, Rosecrans' troops began streaming to the rear.

immediately ordered Brigadier General Thomas Wood to move his brigades left and close up on General Reynolds' division. Wood knew there was no gap—Brannan's troops were there, hidden in the trees. But Wood had been severely reprimanded earlier by Rosecrans for apparently ignoring another order and now he obeyed.

As he moved rearward to get around Brannan, Wood in fact created a yawning quarter-mile hole in the Union center—made all the worse because two nearby divisions, Sheridan's and Davis', were also in motion, sidling north. At that moment most of Longstreet's wing charged straight into the gap. No man to attack one division at a time like Bragg, Longstreet had massed his force for a single ferocious, concentrated blow. Now he sent Hood's and Johnson's divisions smashing ahead in tandem with Brigadier General Joseph Kershaw's division just behind them and Hindman's on the left.

The effect on the Union line was catastrophic. As more than 16,000 yelling Confederates raced through the gap and past their exposed flanks, the astonished and terrified Federals fled in panic. By 12:15 most of McCook's corps and Crittenden's were in headlong flight—men, wagons, guns, horses all racing toward the nearest avenue of escape, McFarland's Gap, which cut through Missionary Ridge.

With them went Rosecrans himself, chased from his headquarters near the Dyer farmhouse with his entire staff, including Brigadier General (and future U.S. president) James A. Garfield. Rosecrans, confused and desperate, was finally persuaded by Garfield

to head for Chattanooga and organize a last-ditch defense. Garfield himself rode off to find General Thomas, hoping he was still fighting and could save the fleeing army.

Thomas was, in fact, fighting hard. Drawing together Brannan's and Palmer's divisions along with individual brigades from the scattered commands of Wood, Reynolds, Negley, and others, Thomas had organized a masterly defense with a strong southeast-facing line positioned on a wooded rise known as Snodgrass Hill and along a nearby curving piece of high ground that came to be called Horseshoe Ridge.

With murderous volleys, the Federals on Snodgrass Hill threw back a first furious charge by Kershaw's division of Longstreet's wing, which had wheeled to attack from the south. The Union troops then beat off more headlong rushes by Hindman's and Bushrod Johnson's divisions. In late afternoon General Polk also attacked, sending his five divisions against the beleaguered Federals defending Horseshoe Ridge.

There, too, the Union troops in some ferocious fighting repulsed the attackers. Soon, however, the Federals were virtually out of ammunition. At this critical moment help arrived: Major General Gordon Granger bringing two brigades from his Reserve Corps that had been guarding roads to the north—and 95,000 heaven-sent rounds for the defenders' rifles.

Through all the desperate fighting, General Thomas, calm and massive as a great bear, had gone from one unit to another, encouraging the men to hold on. He was, Garfield said, "standing like a rock"—bestowing

on Thomas the name he would have ever after, the Rock of Chickamauga.

But Thomas knew that, with the rest of the army in flight, he also had to retreat. As dusk came on he began a superbly managed withdrawal, sending his hard-pressed units one by one toward McFarland's Gap until only a few of Brannan's men were left as a rear guard. "Like magic," Longstreet later wrote, "the Union army had melted away in our presence."

Thomas collected his battered units at the town of Rossville and formed lines to hold off the expected Confederate pursuit. But Bragg, to the bitter disgust of Longstreet, Forrest, and many of his other officers, refused to go after the Federals. Pursuit, Bragg said, was out of the question. "Here is two fifths of my army left on the field, and my artillery is without horses." So the Federals slipped away to the north, toward Chattanooga, and Bragg had squandered another opportunity.

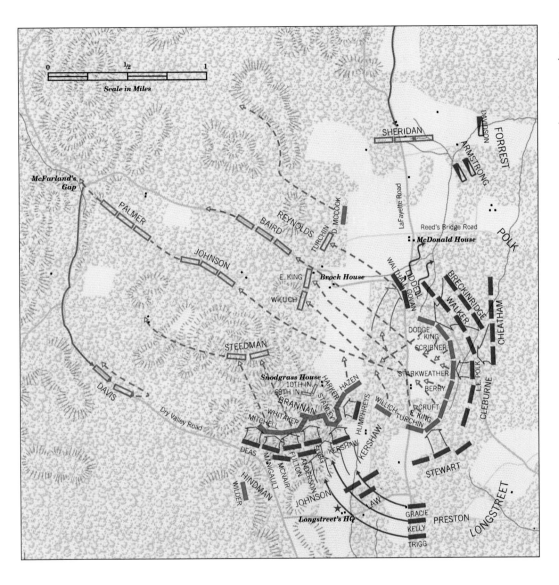

After the Federal army's right fell apart, Thomas formed a defensive line on Snodgrass Hill and along adjacent high ground called Horseshoe Ridge. Against the right of this line, Longstreet hurled the four divisions of Joseph Kershaw, Thomas Hindman, Bushrod Johnson, and, finally, William Preston. All afternoon the troops defending these two heights, bolstered by the remnants of other Federal units, repulsed attack after attack. The arrival of Steedman's reserve division on the Federal right was crucial to stopping Johnson's many assaults. While roughly half of the Union army retreated from the field, Thomas and his force prevented a total rout. On the night of the 20th, with the support of elements of Sheridan's and Davis' commands, Thomas began an orderly withdrawal. Bragg declined to actively pursue.

awaiting the attack, when some of them were peering over the top of a log which composed the upper portion of the defenses looking in the direction of the enemy, trying to discover their position. Everything was as still as death, when an enemy's bullet struck the log, knocking off a large splinter and sending it whizzing through the air. The General, seeing what happened, cried out, "Down with your head, my man, you have got only one head and you may want to use that in a minute." In an instant several more bullets came over, passing through the folds of the General's pants. One of the boys seeing what took place looked at the General and said: "General, down with your legs, you have only one pair of them and you may want to use them in a minute." In an instant all was confusion, and the bullets were coming over almost as thick as hail, and I think there was use for heads and legs.

LIEUTENANT JOSEPH A. CHALARON

SLOCOMB'S BATTERY, WASHINGTON ARTILLERY OF NEW ORLEANS

Of Major Rice E. Graves, whose death he so movingly describes below, Chalaron wrote, "No finer soldier served the Confederacy, no braver soul ever offered himself up a sacrifice on a country's altar."

PRIVATE HENRY H. EBY

7TH ILLINOIS CAVALRY, STAFF, MAJOR GENERAL JOHN PALMER, ARMY OF THE CUMBERLAND

Palmer's division was hard hit by Polk's attack but held its own in the fighting around the Kelly field. Captured and sent to Libby and Belle Isle prisons in Richmond and then to Danville, Virginia, Eby escaped in January 1864. Recaptured, he was exchanged in March, rejoining his regiment at Memphis in late May.

During the night of Sept. 19, 1863, a line of temporary defenses was constructed with old logs, trees and stones, or anything that would answer the purpose. These breastworks were from two to three feet in height, making very good protection for the infantry while they were lying down.

During the morning, when the battle was momentarily expected to open, Gen. Palmer was standing in rear of the temporary defenses, inspecting them, and the infantry were lying on the ground behind them

The enemy's batteries from in and beyond the woods still kept up their fire at us, to which no reply could be made on account of our troops between us. Their shrapnel was continually bursting over us. One of these exploded in our midst where Major Graves and Capt. Slocomb stood mounted, side by side. We saw them clasp each other, and totter in their saddles. The nearest men rushed up, arriving in time to catch them before they fell, for Slocomb's horse was sinking to the ground, mortally wounded, and Graves was leaning over on Slo-

Throughout the day of September 20, vicious fighting swirled around the Kelly house and cornfield, viewed here from the La Fayette road. As the troops of both sides massed for battle, Elijah Kelly and his family, like those of other area farmers, hid out in a heavily wooded ravine northwest of the farm. Camped outside for more than a week, they foraged during the day for whatever food the two armies had left behind, and at night they bunched together around a large fire for warmth.

comb from his horse that was untouched. Slocomb had escaped injury, but Graves was pierced by a shrapnel bullet from side to side through the bowels. He was borne to a hollow close in rear of our guns, and laid in the shade of its only tree by the spring that bubbled from under its roots. Officers and men crowded around. I opened his coat and cloth—a shrapnel bullet falling from them as they were raised. We all felt that our dear major was mortally wounded. Word had been sent to Gen. Breckenridge, and he soon rode up at a gallop. He knelt by the side of Major Graves and showed emotion such as a father alone could feel for his child. From this touching scene our attention was called by evidences of disaster to Adams' brigade in our front. The crash of battle in the woods had been incessant, stirring the echoes of their recesses with deep reverberations that ominously struck our ears. Now, with hanging bridles and frantic strides, the riderless horses of Gen. Adams and his adjutant, Guilet, came tearing to the rear from out those woods, towards and past our guns. Gen. Breckenridge immediately ordered that Major Graves should be sent to the field hospital, for the battle was

evidently going against us at this point. Bidding Graves a touching farewell the general rode off, after ordering Slocomb to hold the position at all costs until he could bring up Liddell's division. Officers and men immediately sought Major Graves' side to get a last look at him, to grasp his hand once more, to say a last farewell. With implements in hand, with faces blackened by powder and by smoke, with moistened eyes, and many with traces of tears on their besmeared cheeks, they came, each taking his hand. He gave to all, by word or by look, some sign of recognition. What a striking scene for an artist. How pathetic those eternal partings of heroic men from their gallant and beloved commander. The raging battle around, the limping wounded streaming past, the hurrying ambulances, the retreating squads from our overwhelmed brigade, the bursting shells and shrapnel rending heaven and earth, the hissing bullets, the crash of musketry rolling from the woods in front, rising into that grand roar of battle, which, once heard, is never forgotten, made a spectacle and impression that haunts me still.

"Our regiment captured General Adams, yet there are no less than six regiments who claim the honor of having captured him."

CAPTAIN BORDEN M. HICKS
11TH MICHIGAN INFANTRY, STANLEY'S BRIGADE

During one of the morning attacks around Kelly's field, Hicks' company was routed and in a near panic headed for the rear. Hicks wrote later that "it was my duty as Company Commander, to run as fast as possible, and get ahead of the men, so as to allay their fears. I overtook one of my men and chided him for running from the enemy, he looked up at me very inocently, and says Captain what are you running for?"

We took up a new position in Kelley's field, just to the left of the road, where we concealed ourselves in the underbrush, and awaited the oncoming of the Confederates, who were now flushed with victories. When within two or three rods of our line, we opened fire on them, their front rank went down, the rear rank was nearly put out of business, and we captured nearly all of the balance, including General D. W. Adams who was in command of the rebel forces making this charge—our regiment captured General Adams, yet there are no less than six regiments who claim the honor of having captured him, but as the best proof would say that I had his sword, other members of our regiment had his field glasses and revolvers, belt and so forth. I carried his sword on the charge we now made to the McDonald field, going into this charge with a sword in each hand, and looking as savage as a meat ax.

Confederate general Benjamin Hardin Helm, seen in a portrait painted by his daughter, was a graduate of West Point and Harvard, and was Mary Todd Lincoln's brother-in-law. Mortally wounded in Breckinridge's early assault on the Union left, Helm as he lay dying uttered over and over the single word "victory."

SERGEANT MAJOR JOHN W. GREEN
9TH KENTUCKY (C.S.) INFANTRY, HELM'S (ORPHAN) BRIGADE

Green had had a similar experience to the one recounted here at the Battle of Shiloh. Hit just over the heart, he fell to the ground stunned, fearing the worst. Feeling for the wound he found only two bullet fragments. The bullet had split when it hit his gun. One piece had penetrated his clothing but had done no damage, the other had "buried itself in a little testament" in his jacket pocket.

Finally at about 9:30 the order was given to advance & attack the enemy. Soon we were up with our skirmish line. They fell into their position with the regiment & the fighting began. We were in range of the enemys small arms, the artilery was sending a regular hail of shot & shell at us. We had been ordered to reserve our fire until we were in close range. A perfect shower of grape shot tore through our ranks. The enemy were pouring a voley of minnie balls upon us; we fired a volley & rushed upon them; they were posted behind breast works made of [logs] & there was so much undergrowth in the woods we were charging through that our artillery could not get in position to fire upon them.

On the left of our line the Confederate forces had not come up, so the enemy to our left poured their fire into us as did those directly in our front. We would load our guns as we advanced & fire but our men were falling fast. . . .

About this time it seemed to me a bushel of grape shot from a battery just in front of us came pouring down upon me, cutting down the bushes & tearing up the ground all around. I was running towards the enemy, as was our whole line, a grape shot struck me in the groin; it in some manner whirled me clear around & threw me flat of my back. I thought my entire leg was torn off, but I looked down & saw my leg was not gone. I felt with my hands & found no blood, but there was a grape shot in my pocket. It had force enough to tear through my pants, but struck the steel clasp of a pocket book which I had in the pocket of my pants & this stopped it. The clasp was doubled around the ball. I found I could limp along & soon caught up with the regiment which was now within thirty yards of the enemy's breast works giving & taking death blows which could last but a few minutes without utter annihilation.

CAPTAIN WILBUR F. GOODSPEED
BATTERY A, 1ST OHIO LIGHT INFANTRY, WILLICH'S BRIGADE

In the artillery duels that took place near the Kelly farm, opposing batteries were so close at times that they fired canister at each other. "My heartfelt thanks are due to the non-commissioned officers and men of my battery," Goodspeed wrote, "for the . . . coolness they preserved under the hottest fire."

At about 10 a.m. one of the enemy's batteries opened on me from the left in front. I changed front and replied with three pieces, throwing shells, soon silencing the enemy. At about 11 o'clock a heavy column of the enemy was discovered about 1,000 yards from my position. Crossing the road, I immediately changed front. At this time the Fifteenth Ohio Volunteers came up, and was ordered to the left of my battery. A few minutes later the enemy charged on us, and got up to within 50 yards. My battery then opened, double-shotted with canister, and, being gallantly supported by the Fifteenth Ohio Volunteers, we succeeded in routing the enemy, and driving him back with great slaughter. The enemy having disappeared from my front and showing himself in the rear, my battery, with the Fifteenth Ohio Volunteers, moved to the small log houses which were temporarily used as hospitals, and was faced to the rear. At about half past 1 p.m., the rest of the brigade having formed near my position, the enemy opened on me in my new front with artillery. I replied with about 50 rounds, when he ceased firing. My battery remained in this position until nearly dark, when a general retreat began. The troops on our left giving way, the enemy threw shell and canister into the position of the brigade from that side. I answered with the same projectiles.

After the other troops had passed us, General Willich ordered the brigade to fall back. I attached the prolonges to my pieces and retreated firing. The enemy closed in from three sides, and his batteries came so near that we fired at each other with canister. Under orders I limbered up and moved back to a hill in the rear, where I awaited the arrival of the brigade. Here General Willich ordered me to move on to the Rossville road, and follow the other troops. My battery arrived at Rossville at 12 p.m. and went into camp.

I brought into camp my battery complete. In the engagements of the two days my battery sustained the following loss:

Officer wounded, 1; enlisted men killed, 2; enlisted men wounded, 13; enlisted men missing, 4, supposed to be wounded. Horses wounded, 15, and, in consequence of not unharnessing for six days and the hardship they have undergone, I will lose 25 more horses.

LIEUTENANT WILSON J. VANCE
21ST OHIO INFANTRY, SIRWELL'S BRIGADE

Vance had distinguished himself at the Battle of Stones River in January 1863, an action for which he would receive the Congressional Medal of Honor. In March 1864 he resigned his commission to attend school. He did return to military service, however. Just before the war ended, he served as a first lieutenant and adjutant of the 14th U.S. Colored Troops.

The fighting had been going on for two or three hours, when I suddenly missed one of my best men—a great, tall, strong fellow, whose absence made an ominous hole in the ranks. He was a man of perhaps forty-five, sober, steady, and reliable as the sun. In all our battles and skirmishes he had borne himself coolly and with excellent judgment—a "regular old stand-by" for a company commander, and an example for the rest of the men. Inquiring and looking about for him, I at last found him lying prone upon his face, behind a tree, about ten feet in the rear of the line.

"Why, Blank, what is the matter with you?"

He raised his face; it was pallid and sickening as he looked at me with a wild, almost crazed expression.

"I'm wounded—I'm wounded," he chattered.

"Where?"

"Right here—here—here!" beating a tattoo with nervous fingers on his forehead, where the skin was not only not broken, but free from any bruise or discoloration.

"What do you mean by telling me such a lie? You're not wounded; you're not hurt—get back to your place, sir!"

"I am! I am! I tell you I am!"

"Come, come! I'll have no more of this nonsense! I'm ashamed of you! An old soldier with a record like yours! Get back to your place!"

"But I can't, lieutenant, I can't. I tell you I'm wounded—right here—right here—right here!"

Brigadier General August Willich, shown here in an Adolph Metzner sketch, commanded five regiments and Goodspeed's battery in the bloody defense of Kelly's field. Willich served through the Chattanooga campaign and was severely wounded at Resaca the following May. Brevetted major general in October 1865, he mustered out the following January.

Confederates load and fire their rifles in the tangled woodland along Chickamauga Creek. In many places the heavily thicketed terrain, noted a Union officer, made for a "mad, irregular battle, very much resembling guerrilla warfare on a vast scale, in which one army was bushwhacking the other."

There was only one thing to do. The man was unhurt, he was there to fight, and it was my business to see that he did fight. I struck him again and again with my sword—he was old enough to be my father, and could have picked me up and thrown me down the hill at the enemy—till I beat him to his feet. And so I drove him slowly back to his place, the men looking on wonderingly, as he cried out with every step:—

"Oh, lieutenant, for God's sake, don't, for God's sake, don't! I'm wounded,—I'm wounded!"

"Get to work, sir, and let me hear no more of your crazy notions!"

The order was obeyed, and Blank, with a look so full of utter despair that it might have broken a heart of stone, fell to work again, loading and firing calmly and effectively, and speaking no word, while I went about my duty with a queer sinking of the heart.

Ten minutes later I went to the head of the company line, and in my heedless haste stumbled over a dead body. Looking down, the stony, staring gaze of a dead man's eyes met mine. It was poor Blank! He was dead—shot through the forehead!

As I knelt by the body and searched his pockets for the little trinkets that should be sent to his family, and found there the pictures of the wife and the chubby children, and the locks of hair and soiled and worn letters from home, I felt like a murderer. The scene swam before my eyes, and I fairly reeled. How I got through the rest of the day, God knows. To this day I can feel the horror of the situation.

"It came with a wild yell and a storm of shot and shell which made noise enough to scare the birds to death, and shake the leaves off of the trees."

PRIVATE LEVI WAGNER
1ST OHIO INFANTRY, BALDWIN'S BRIGADE

Wagner continued to serve with the 1st Ohio until May 1864, when he was wounded in the Atlanta campaign near Dallas, Georgia. Of the wound, surgeon S. M. Smith reported that the "ball struck posterior left thigh. Wound followed by extensive inflammation, gangrene & sloughing. Adhesion of muscles with impaired power." Wagner was discharged from a Louisville hospital in August 1864.

We advanced out into the timber about thirty rods and there halted to await the coming of the enemy. The morning was very foggy, making it necessary for an army to move very slowly, consequently it was at least nine in the forenoon before the Rebel advance showed up. As we were posted behind trees and were constantly watching for them, we had some advantage over them. Their advance consisted of a heavy skirmish line, which is the only way for an army to advance through heavy timber. As they came within good firing distance, our line opened fire, and their movement showed that they had learned their lesson well.

. . . We held them in check for some time until their main line of battle approached near enough to pour a volley of musketry among us, though it was harmless as concerning Co. A. We were then recalled and took our places in the front line, behind the works we had helped build in the early morning, and as they had been improved and strengthened while we were out in front, we now felt able to hold our own against any force that might approach from the front. No sooner had we gained our position and braced ourselves for the attack, when it came with a wild yell and a storm of shot and shell which made noise enough to scare the birds to death, and shake the leaves off of the trees. But it failed to have that effect on us, we had got used to the Rebel yell and always expected it, and we had good bullet-proof works in front of us, and over these we could pour such a steady, destructive storm of bullets as no force could long endure. Our enemy surely showed a wonderful degree of courage and recklessness, as is seldom found equaled anywhere. Although the Northern and Southern soldiers were equally brave, there was a great difference in their mode of attack. The Southerner comes in at the start with a whirl and a rush, yelling like demons, expecting to overwhelm and confuse like a mighty storm. Indeed their impulsive onslaught was enough to intimidate anything but a cold blooded Yankey. It was that cold, undemonstrative nature of the north that made them superior to all other soldiers. He goes into battle in a cool, calculating, self-confident manner. When the rush comes he plants himself like a rock, pours in his deadly fire and then advances, encounters the enemy, plants himself again, and then onward in a way that nothing could resist.

PRIVATE WILLIAM J. OLIPHANT

6TH TEXAS INFANTRY, DESHLER'S BRIGADE

Oliphant describes being wounded during Cleburne's morning attack through the woods north toward Kelly's field. "The enemy's fire was terrific; besides the infantry fire, eighteen large cannon poured a deadly fire of grape and cannister into our ranks as we advanced. Half our brigade went down before that terrible rain of missles, but victory perched upon our banners and cheer after cheer rolled along our lines as the Federals turned and fled."

I was severely wounded at about eleven o'clock on Sunday morning, September 20, and lay on the field until sometime in the afternoon when I was taken to the field hospital.

The field hospital, located in an old field, consisted of a few hastily constructed brush arbors and a large quantity of straw spread on the ground. Hundreds of blood covered men were lying on the straw, and the number constantly increased as the ambulance and litter bearers arrived from the battle field.

Many of the wounded were groaning, a few were crying out in their agony, while others were quietly dying.

Assistant surgeons and attendants were moving rapidly among the men giving relief as fast as possible. The head surgeons, with bared arms, and wearing long blood stained aprons, were busy, with knives and saws, amputating shattered limbs, and cooly tossing them to a large pile of severed arms and legs which grew in size until it was so large that it would have more than filled the body of a large two horse wagon.

To me the place was horrible, even more so than the battle field itself, for the enthusiasm and excitement of battle were missing, although the thunder of cannon filled the air and the continued rattle of musketry seemed quite near, while at times that weird, thrilling yell, which had become so famous, could be distinctly heard.

CORPORAL JOHN ELY

88TH ILLINOIS INFANTRY, LYTLE'S BRIGADE

Ely and his regiment retreated into Chattanooga, having lost about 100 men in the fighting. He went on to fight around Chattanooga in November 1863 and was promoted to sergeant in March 1864. Wounded near Atlanta the following July, he spent several months in a Nashville hospital and was deemed unfit for field duty. Ely was assigned to military-police duty in Nashville, where he remained until being mustered out in May 1865.

*W*oods Div was now ordered from our left to reinforce Thomas, this left a space of a mile or more between Thomases right and our left Our Div was now ordered to move by the left flank and close up this gap. this was at about eleven oclock a.m. At this moment occured one of those little incidents or freaks of fortune . . . which so often in a large battle sudenly turned victory into defeat, and sometimes a rout. For at the same moment that Woods Div was ordered to reinforce Thomas, and we ordered to move by the left flank and close the gape thus formed, the enemy made a furious charge on our right, we were attacked by Longstreets famous corps, just fresh from their fields of triumph on the Potomac they had as yet never known defeat. We double quicked to gain a ridge and form our line to meet the shock but to late the bullets began to whiz and the men commenced falling long before we could reach the desired point. The second and third brigade first met the shock but were quickly forced back. Our brigade now wheeled into line. As we advanced up the hill, we met the second brig comeing back in confusion. Gen Sheridan spoke cheerfuly telling us to keep cool and we would surely check them but I am almost ashamed to own that I thought far different, for the second brigade was the best and largest in our Div composed entirely of old troops which had fought at Pea Ridge, Perryville & Stone River and untill then had never been repulsed. The rebs were flushed with success, we gained the crest of the hill and layed down. On come the Rebs yelling like demons, we received them coolly and our fire soon checked them in front. But soon a more serious difficulty arose they were flanking us and we had nothing to oppose to them. Slowly we fell back to the foot of the hill, we then rallied and charged up the hill but were again flanked and forced by the mear power of numbers to fall back. This time they planted their collors on a line in rear of our regt. Six times in succession did our regt rally and charge up the hill and was as often compelled to fall back by their flanking us. Oh if we had but a single Div to protect our flanks we could hold them. We find no trouble in forceing them back in our front. When we were rallying the sixth time Old Rossie, McCook & Sheridan road up in our rear and Rosecrans said charge them once for Old Rossie boys, but it was of no use we had done all that could be done without support. And they now began to get their artylery in position on the hill and the grape and canister began to fly thick about us. But that was not our greatest danger. They had pushed a strong column of troops forward on our left, and had completely cut Davis and our Div of from the rest of the Army, there was no course left but to retreat or be taken prisoners.

SERGEANT VALERIUS CINCINNATUS GILES
4TH TEXAS INFANTRY, ROBERTSON'S BRIGADE

As Giles' name suggests, his father was a lover of the classics. Even the family dogs bore classical monikers. Giles' unit had seen bloody action at Gettysburg before being shipped west with Longstreet's command. At Chickamauga, the Texans took part in Hood's headlong attack through the hole in the Federal lines.

There was an officer in my regiment who had a beautiful sweetheart in Texas. They kept up a regular correspondence and he cherished those letters above everything else and carried them with him wherever he went. With a blue ribbon tied around them he placed them in a black morocco notebook, securely fastened in the inside pocket of his uniform coat.

When the Texas Brigade made a desperate attempt to cross the old field and capture the batteries that were decimating our ranks, the Lieutenant was at his post, his coat buttoned up to his chin, although the afternoon was blazing hot. He urged the men forward and exposed himself recklessly, for he was a proud fellow, full of courage, and such men make the finest soldiers in the world. A Minié ball struck him on the left breast above the heart. His sword flew from his hand and he fell heavily to the ground, apparently dead.

But he was not killed. The bullet never entered his body, but embedded itself in his bundle of love letters. When the battle was over he took pride in showing his mutilated letters to his intimate friends, prouder of them than ever because they had saved his life. The bullet passed through eight or ten of them, and they were big, fat ones, too! The bullet lodged against the last one received. He was the merriest soldier in that weary army. He wrote home to his sweetheart, telling her of his miraculous escape, how her dear missives had checked the deadly missile, how the bullet had passed through more than fifty folds of paper without touching her sweet name.

Condemned by some for blindly obeying an order by Rosecrans that opened a massive hole in the Union line, Brigadier General Thomas J. Wood nonetheless was a highly regarded officer whose personal courage was so marked that Sherman once said he was worth 20,000 men. While Rosecrans was eventually relieved of command, Wood, who had been U. S. Grant's first West Point roommate, continued to serve; his troops were the first over the Confederate defenses on Missionary Ridge in November 1863.

"Hello! I said to myself, if the general is crossing himself, we are in a desperate situation."

CHARLES A. DANA
ASSISTANT U.S. SECRETARY OF WAR

After Dana was fired from Horace Greeley's New York Tribune for defending Edwin Stanton, Secretary of War Stanton named Dana assistant secretary. Sent west to confer with Rosecrans, Dana was regarded with suspicion. Colonel Smith D. Atkins called him an "interloper, a marplot, a spy upon rival generals."

About half past eight or nine o'clock the battle began on the left, where Thomas was. At that time Rosecrans, with whom I always remained, was on the right, directing the movements of the troops there. Just after the cannon began I remember that a ten-pound shell came crashing through our staff, but hurting nobody. I had not slept much for two nights, and, as it was warm, I dismounted about noon and, giving my horse to my orderly, lay down on the grass and went to sleep. I was awakened by the most infernal noise I ever heard. Never in any battle I had witnessed was there such a discharge of cannon and musketry. I sat up on the grass, and the first thing I saw was General Rosecrans crossing himself—he was a very devout Catholic. "Hello!" I said to myself, "if the general is crossing himself, we are in a desperate situation."

LIEUTENANT GENERAL JAMES LONGSTREET
WING COMMANDER, ARMY OF TENNESSEE

Shortly before the events he describes here, Longstreet's wing had split the Union lines by exploiting the gap left when Wood moved his brigade out of line. Longstreet lunched as some of his troops regrouped and rested briefly before turning their attention to Thomas' Federal forces still offering stiff resistance near the Snodgrass house and at Kelly's field.

It was after one o'clock, and the hot and dry and dusty day made work fatiguing. My lunch was called up and ordered spread at some convenient point while I rode with General Buckner and the staffs to view the changed conditions of the battle. I could see but little of the enemy's line, and only knew of it by the occasional exchange of fire between the lines of skirmishers, until we approached the angle of the lines. I passed the right of our skirmishers, and, thinking I had passed the enemy's, rode forward to be accurately assured, when I suddenly found myself under near fire of his sharpshooters concealed behind the trees and under the brush. I saw enough, however, to mark the ground line of his field-works as they were spread along the front of the right wing, and found that I was very fortunate in having the forest to cover the ride back until out of reach of their fire. . . . I rode away to enjoy my spread of Nassau bacon and Georgia sweet potatoes. We were not accustomed to potatoes of any kind in Virginia, and thought we had a luxury, but it was very dry, as the river was a mile and more from us, and other liquids were over the border. Then, before we had half finished, our pleasures were interrupted by a fragment of shell that came tearing through the woods, passed through a book in the hands of a courier who sat on his horse hard by reading, and struck down our chief of ordnance, Colonel P. T. Manning, gasping, as was supposed, in the struggles of death. Friends sprang forward to look for the wound and to give some aid and relief. In his hurry to enjoy and finish his lunch he had just taken a large bite of sweet potato, which seemed to be suffocating him. I suggested that it would be well to first relieve him of the potato and give him a chance to breathe. This done, he revived, his breath came freer, and he was soon on his feet ready to be conveyed to the hospital. In a few days he was again on duty.

LIEUTENANT ALFRED PIRTLE
STAFF, BRIGADIER GENERAL WILLIAM H. LYTLE, ARMY OF THE CUMBERLAND

As the events recalled here unfolded, Pirtle and the men he was trying to rally were overwhelmed by Confederates. Pirtle said of an enemy squad near him: "I have always thought that seventeen fired at me. There may not have been so many, but I thought there was, for one ball clipped the mane in front of my left hand, another's wind was felt by my left leg, and third cut hairs from the horse in front of my legs."

Major General Simon Bolivar Buckner appears in a pleated fatigue jacket originally designed for the Kentucky State Guard but widely copied by other states. Of this jacket General Leonidas Polk once said, "I like it, sir, it looks comfortable, it looks soldierly, in fact, sir, it looks rebellious."

The line was in front of us as we sat on our horses, but it was thin and losing men momentarily, giving our commander increasing anxiety. He sent one of his staff to urge the colonel of a regiment still at the foot of the slight rise to bring up his men. He directed another to bring up a section of the Battery, and place it by hand in the line. This was done, diminishing the fire at once in our front, which had been bad enough—the men only being held in their alignment by the presence of Gen'l Lytle; for if he could stay, they were ashamed to retreat. I have heard that a moment before the fire opened on the men who first formed the line on the ridge, he had said: "Men, we must make a stand right here. We can die but once. Let us die right here." It would seem, if this was true, and I did not hear it, that he felt someone had "blundered," and it was their duty to hold on. Every man must have felt as I did, that we were fighting desperate odds. And yet those men stayed as if every man had grasped the meaning of their General.

The fire reopened, and looking at one of us he said, "For God's sake, bring up another regiment." I thought he was looking at Lieut. Boal, but Boal must not have heard him, and he looked at me, near him. He had just a moment before said to me, as he leaned towards me, "Pirtle, I am hit."

"Are you hit hard, General?" My heart was in my mouth, and I was hardly able to speak.

"I saw the big sorrel horse the General had been seated on, rush riderless down the slope."

"In the spine. If I have to leave here, you stay and see that all goes right."

I answered, "I will."

Then came his call for another regiment, as I have said. . . . I looked at the General and, saluting with my sword, galloped down the hill where Col. Silas Miller of the 36th Illinois was trying very hard while on foot to rally his men, in order to lead them up the slope to reinforce the line there. . . .

Doing all I could to help Col. Miller, I held my horse's bridle in my left hand, urging the soldiers forward by all arguments at my disposal. Amid the increasing confusion, timed shells exploded almost simultaneously by my horse's side, making him frantic, perhaps wounding him, because he reared and broke loose from me, and galloped out of sight in the melee. Just at this instant I saw the big sorrel horse the General had been seated on, rush riderless down the slope, and I knew the General had fallen from him and was dead. I started towards the spot where I had left him, making my ascent in that direction, but the men gave way in a crowd and carried me along with them, so that I knew my commander was gone.

Brigadier General William H. Lytle had been wounded twice before his fatal wounding at Chickamauga. A lawyer, Mexican War veteran, and Ohio state legislator, Lytle was a prolific writer, perhaps best known for his poetry, including "Anthony and Cleopatra" with its opening line: "I am dying, Egypt, dying."

MAJOR GENERAL JOHN B. HOOD
CORPS COMMANDER, ARMY OF TENNESSEE

The blond, six-foot-two-inch-tall, "Gallant Hood" had risen quickly in the ranks from first lieutenant to major general in less than 18 months. He was wounded at Gettysburg, losing the use of his left arm. He recuperated in time to command a corps and three divisions at Chickamauga. His troops were the ones that exploited the gap in the Union lines on September 20, when he was wounded again.

With a shout along my entire front, the Confederates rushed forward, penetrated into the wood, over and beyond the enemy's breastworks, and thus achieved another glorious victory for our arms. About this time I was pierced with a Minie ball in the upper third of the right leg; I turned from my horse upon the side of the crushed limb and fell—strange to say, since I was commanding five divisions—into the arms of some of the troops of my old brigade, which

With his useless left arm in a sling, Major General John Bell Hood reels in the saddle as his right thigh is pierced by a Minié ball while he rallies troops of the Texas Brigade. Although the leg was amputated, Hood returned to command his corps, riding strapped to his saddle. Eventually he would replace General Joseph Johnston as commander of the entire Army of Tennessee in the Atlanta campaign.

I had directed so long a period, and upon so many fields of battle. . . .

The members of this heroic band were possessed of a streak of superstition, as in fact I believe all men to be; and it may here prove of interest to cite an instance thereof. I had a favorite roan horse, named by them "Jeff Davis"; whenever he was in condition I rode him in battle, and, remarkable as it may seem, he generally received the bullets and bore me unscathed. In this battle he was severely wounded on Saturday; the following day, I was forced to resort to a valuable mare in my possession, and late in the afternoon was shot from the saddle. At Gettysburg I had been unable to mount him on the field, in consequence of lameness; in this engagement I had also been shot from the saddle. Thus the belief among the men became nigh general that, when mounted on old Jeff, the bullets could not find me. This spirited and fearless animal performed his duty throughout the war, and after which he received tender care from General Jefferson and family of Seguin, Texas, until death, when he was buried with appropriate honors.

"He concluded that the next stand must be made at Chattanooga."

LIEUTENANT COLONEL GATES P. THRUSTON

STAFF, MAJOR GENERAL ALEXANDER MCCOOK, ARMY OF THE CUMBERLAND

Thruston rode to inform Thomas of the disaster recounted here and was sent to bring Davis and Sheridan back. Asking where they were as he passed fleeing soldiers, he recalled, "One old trudger in the ranks called out, 'We'll talk to you, my son, when we get to the Ohio River!'"

The order to advance came at last. The deep Confederate lines suddenly appeared. The woods in our front seemed alive. On they came like an angry flood. They struck McCook's three remaining brigades, the remnants of the Federal right. Under the daring personal exertions of McCook and Davis, they made a gallant but vain resistance. The massed lines of the enemy swarmed around their flanks. Pouring through the opening made by Wood's withdrawal, they struck his last brigade as it was leaving the line. It was slammed back like a door, and shattered. Brannan, on Wood's left, was struck in front and flank. His right was flung back; his left stood fast. Sheridan, hastening to the left with two brigades, was called back, and rushed to the rescue. His little force stayed the storm for a time. Wave after wave of Confederates came on; resistance only increased the multitude. Brannan's artillery, attacked in flank, rushed to the rear for clearer ground, and, with the Confederates at their heels, suddenly plunged into Van Cleve marching to the aid of Thomas. Disorder ensued; effective resistance was lost. The Reserve Artillery of the center, well posted in rear, unable to manoeuvre in the undergrowth, hedged around by infantry a half hour before, was now without immediate support. The sudden rush of Longstreet's compact column through the forest had foiled all plans. The astonished artillerists were swept from their guns. General Negley, with one of his brigades isolated in rear, shared the general fate of the right.

When Longstreet struck the right, Rosecrans was near McCook and Crittenden. Seeing our line swept back, he hurried to Sheridan's force for aid. With staff and escort he recklessly strove to stem the tide. They attempted to pass to the left through a storm of canister and musketry, but were driven back.

All became confusion. No order could be heard above the tempest of battle. With a wild yell the Confederates swept on far to their left. They seemed everywhere victorious. Rosecrans was borne back in the retreat. Fugitives, wounded, caissons, escort, ambulances, thronged the narrow pathways. He concluded that our whole line had given way, that the day was lost, that the next stand must be made at Chattanooga.

COLONEL JOHN T. WILDER
BRIGADE COMMANDER, ARMY OF THE CUMBERLAND

Just after noon, with orders from General McCook's headquarters to cover Sheridan's retreat on the Union right, Wilder's men held off two furious Confederate assaults near the Widow Glenn's house. Wilder's brigade prepared to launch a counterattack when they were interrupted by the arrival of a frightened Charles A. Dana, United States assistant secretary of war.

For the past hour there had been no heavy firing near us. The battle was now raging at some distance to the north, and I started forward, determined to cut through the line of the enemy and reach our forces beyond. We moved forward . . . and had advanced about a hundred yards, when a hatless, red-headed man, coming rapidly on horseback from the direction of Chattanooga to me at the front of my force, and excitedly asked me what command we had. I told him it was the 1st Brigade, 4th Division, of the 14th Corps, Wilder's Brigade of mounted Infantry on foot.

He immediately announced himself as Chas. A. Dana, Assistant Secretary of War. I had halted the command on his first arrival, and I told him in a few words that I knew him and also what I intended doing and asked him the whereabouts of General Rosecrans and how the battle was going. He again stated that he was Chas. A. Dana, Assistant Secretary of War, said he had been with Rosecrans and that the enemy had run over them and that General Rosecrans was either killed or captured, and the army badly routed, as bad, if not worse than at Bull Run, and that my Brigade was the only portion of the army left intact. He then said I must take him at once to Chattanooga to enable him to telegraph the situation to Washington. I told him he had been going in the opposite direction of Chattanooga and would have been in Bragg's

lines before he had gone much farther, also that the heavy firing to the north had not changed position for an hour. With a scared look, he insisted that it was the enemy pursuing, and killing Thomas' men, and again asserting that he was Assistant Secretary of War, directed me to move with my command, escorting him to Chattanooga, that he might communicate with Washington at once. I told him I had scouts who knew the country to Chattanooga, and that they could guide him there in as little time as it would take me to get up my lead horses and mount my men. He agreed to go with the scouts and again directed me to fall back to Chattanooga as quickly as possible and place my command on Lookout Mountain and hold in at all hazards, and to send my transportation across the Tennessee River, and then left in the direction of Chattanooga with the scouts.

The most desperate fighting of the day raged around the log Snodgrass house on the slope of Snodgrass Hill. The owner of the property, 60-year-old George Washington Snodgrass, lived there with his third wife and seven of his nine children. He had waited until the afternoon of September 19 to take his family to hide out in a nearby ravine with other local people. The scrawled commentary is probably by the sketch's unknown artist.

The Snodgrass house on the battle field of Chickamauga — near here Genl Thomas repulsed the last charge made by the confederate army — It was once said by a Confed. General, that "Here, at Snodgrass house, fell the southern Confederacy"

PRIVATE JOHN T. COXE
2D SOUTH CAROLINA INFANTRY, KERSHAW'S BRIGADE

According to Coxe, after the Federals reached their first position on Snodgrass Hill they "rallied and reformed at the edge of the woods on the top of the knob and waved their flags at us as if to say, 'Come on.'" Kershaw's brigade, with the 2d South Carolina on its left, charged the taunting enemy but was soon driven back.

It was about noon when we flanked into the field and heard from a party of jubilant officers that the center and right wing of the Federal army had been smashed and driven from the field. Although our throats were parched, we raised a great Rebel shout. But when we got well into the field and faced north, we saw something that looked ugly. There, facing us, was a Federal line of battle much longer than our own line. We could see no other Confederate troops near us, although we knew Humphrey's brigade of our division was somewhere to our right in the woods. But we lost no time. Kershaw gave immediate orders to advance and attack the Federals in our front, and the whole brigade did so enthusiastically. After one volley, the Federals gave way and fell back up a sort of knob, which was the north end of the field. The top of this knob was covered by dense woods, which went back a short distance to a depression, on the bottom of which an old road ran east and west. From the north side of the old road another and higher wooded hill rose up, and this we learned afterwards was called "Snodgrass Hill," famous as being the scene of the hardest, longest, and most bloody part of the battle of Chickamauga.

CAPTAIN ISRAEL B. WEBSTER

10TH KENTUCKY (U.S.) INFANTRY, CROXTON'S BRIGADE

Webster had a close call in the heavy fighting on Horseshoe Ridge in the late afternoon. "A single bullet went singing along and struck some object with a thud," he recalled. "Suddenly a soldier standing at my side threw up his right hand, and the sight which met the eyes was sickening. The ball had struck the back of the hand, passing through it and destroying it. His hand and mine were nearly touching each other at the time, and my escape was very close."

Gen. Thomas sat upon his horse about half way up the hill behind which we were, intently watching the events as they occurred. Several attempts were made by the Confederates to take this hill, but failed. Staff officers were constantly reporting to Gen. Thomas from other portions of the field. In doing so, they were obliged to ride up the hill through a space about 20 yards wide in full range of the enemy's sharpshooters. We knew they were there because we heard the music of the little missiles as they passed harmlessly by. Gen. Thomas seemed to know about their presence, or he bore a charmed life, as he just kept out of the range; but these staff officers, as they rode up to him, had to pass over the ground covered by them. Many a blanched face did I see cross this dangerous ground.

After several attempts of the rebs to take this hill it seems they had determined to have it, for they came again with an increased force, and apparently were on the verge of success. Our artillery support gave way

General George H. Thomas, pointing with binoculars in this engraving from Frank Leslie's Illustrated Newspaper, oversees the fighting the afternoon of September 20. His mere presence had a calming effect on the troops and raised their morale. One Ohio soldier recalled that when Thomas ordered the men to " 'give them cold steel,' how it thrilled us! That command of 'Pap' Thomas seemed to transform men into whole platoons."

and came scampering down on our side of the hill. Gen. Thomas had not ceased his vigilance. He saw it all, and in a moment he drew his sword, rose in his stirrups and rode among his men, shouting to them: "Go back! Go back! This hill must be held at all hazards!"

Riding on up to the top with his sword flashing in the light, and his face expressive of determination, his words acted like magic. The men turned again to the front and with shouts regained their positions. Like an avalanche they swept down upon the advancing and almost victorious enemy, and drove them back. Thus this important position was saved. I was told that the infantry supporting the battery was composed of stragglers, men who had become separated from their commands during the day. They were unofficered and strangers to each other, and while they respected officers in general, there was no one who would wade in deep except for "Pap" Thomas. It was he, and he alone, who saved that point at that time.

This battle flag flew over Captain Stouten H. Dent's Alabama battery as it supported the Confederate attack on Horseshoe Ridge. For several hours the struggle continued, until darkness came and the Federals slipped away.

BRIGADIER GENERAL ARTHUR M. MANIGAULT
BRIGADE COMMANDER, ARMY OF TENNESSEE

Chickamauga was Manigault's first big battle after his promotion to brigadier general in April. In the fierce fighting on September 20 against Thomas' forces at Snodgrass Hill, Manigault's brigade lost 656 out of 2,025 engaged. Claiming after the war that it was the most hotly contested action of his career, he estimated that in one three-minute period 300 of his men were mowed down.

Our men at the word of command, at 3 o'clock, went boldly forward, descending a hill into the gorge and advancing up the one opposite, Dent's Battery, 6 Napoleon guns, opening behind and above us on the enemy. A steady and rapid fire assailed us as we advanced, both artillery and infantry. After an unavailing effort we were driven back, the enemy in turn charged us, and the battery for a moment or two was in great danger. But the gunners served their pieces like veterans, and their gallant captain set an example worthy of emulation. Our men who had been charged when in a state of some confusion, and it was an equal chance whether they would stand or run, rallied and drove their assailants back with heavy loss. Taking advantage of the disorder in their ranks, the brigade charged in turn, and gained some distance. Again moving forward, they were driven back a space, and the

enemy repeating their first maneuver, but with less success, laid themselves open to another attack. The first ridge was carried, but on a second just as strong, the enemy again rallied and showed fight. From this one they were driven to a third, the fight resembling and being of the same character as that at the first hill. There was no more obstinately contested ground anywhere on that day than at this point. The blood of the men seemed to be up, and there was but little flinching. On several occasions the colors of two of the regiments fell into the enemy's hands, their bearers killed or wounded, but were quickly recovered. For two hours this contest lasted. Our ammunition was expended again and again in many instances, but the men supplied themselves from their dead or wounded comrades, or those of the Yankees, and when it did not suit their own weapons, threw them away and seized their arms. Towards the latter part of the fight, there was scarcely any order preserved, and no defined line. Regiments and companies were inextricably mixed up, and it resembled more a skirmish on a grand scale than the conflict of a line of battle. Officers and men never before or after behaved better, or showed more indomitable pluck.

MAJOR JOSEPH S. FULLERTON

STAFF, MAJOR GENERAL GORDON GRANGER,
ARMY OF THE CUMBERLAND

As Granger itched to get into the fray, Confederate troops were attempting to outflank the Union right. When Thomas asked if Granger's men could stop them, Granger replied, "Yes. My men are . . . just the fellows for that work. They are raw troops, they don't know any better than to charge up there."

Shortly before 10 o'clock, calling my attention to a great column of dust moving from our front toward the point from which came the sound of battle, he said, "They are concentrating over there. That is where we ought to be." The corps flag marked his headquarters in an open field near the Ringgold road. He walked up and down in front of his flag, nervously pulling his beard. Once stopping, he said, "Why the —— does Rosecrans keep me here! There is nothing in front of us now. There is the battle"—pointing in the direction of Thomas. Every moment the sounds of battle grew louder, while the many columns of dust rolling together here mingled with the smoke that hung over the scene.

At 11 o'clock, with Granger, I climbed a high hayrick near by. We sat there for ten minutes listening and watching. Then Granger jumped up, thrust his glass into its case, and exclaimed with an oath:

"I am going to Thomas, orders or no orders!"

"And if you go," I replied, "it may bring disaster to the army and you to a court-martial."

"There's nothing in our front now but ragtag, bobtail cavalry," he replied. "Don't you see Bragg is piling his whole army on Thomas? I am going to his assistance."

We quickly climbed down the rick, and, going to Steedman, Granger ordered him to move his command "over there," pointing toward the place from which came the sounds of battle. . . . Before half-past 11 o'clock Steedman's command was in motion. Granger, with his staff and escort, rode in advance. Steedman, after accompanying them a short distance, rode back to the head of his column.

Thomas was nearly four miles away. The day had now grown very warm, yet the troops marched rapidly over the narrow road, which was covered ankle-deep with dust that rose in suffocating clouds. Completely enveloped in it, the moving column swept along like a desert sandstorm. Two miles from the point of starting, and three-quarters of a mile to the left of the road, the enemy's skirmishers and a section of artillery opened fire on us from an open wood. This force had worked round Thomas's left, and was then partly in his rear. Granger halted to feel them. Soon becoming convinced that it was only a large party of observation, he again started his column and pushed rapidly forward. . . .

A little farther on we were met by a staff-officer sent by General Thomas to discover whether we were friends or enemies; he did not know whence friends could be coming, and the enemy appeared to be approaching from all directions. All of this shattered Army of the Cumberland left on the field was with Thomas; but not more than one-fourth of the men of the army who went into battle at the opening were there. Thomas's loss in killed and wounded during the two days had been dreadful. As his men dropped out his line was contracted to half its length. Now its flanks were bent back, conforming to ridges shaped like a horse-shoe.

Known as a strict disciplinarian, Major General Gordon Granger (left) commanded the Reserve Corps throughout the Tullahoma and Chickamauga campaigns. Acting without orders, he marched Steedman's division to assist the beleaguered Thomas on Horseshoe Ridge and thereby contributed greatly to saving Rosecrans' Army of the Cumberland from total disaster. The two brigades of his Reserve Corps taking part in the fighting suffered 44 percent casualties in less than two hours.

"What I saw was the shimmer of sunlight on metal: lines of troops were coming in behind us!"

LIEUTENANT AMBROSE BIERCE

STAFF, BRIGADIER GENERAL WILLIAM B. HAZEN, ARMY OF THE CUMBERLAND

A veteran of Shiloh, Corinth, and Stones River, Bierce was commissioned a first lieutenant in February 1863 and assigned to Hazen's brigade headquarters as a topographical engineer. The account of Granger's arrival to aid Thomas is from "A Little about Chickamauga," one of many war-related pieces that later made Bierce famous.

Unable to find my brigade, I reported to General Thomas, who directed me to remain with him. He had assumed command of all the forces still intact and was pretty closely beset. The battle was fierce and continuous, the enemy extending his lines farther and farther around our right, toward our line of retreat. We could not meet the extension otherwise than by "refusing" our right flank and letting him inclose us; which but for gallant Gordon Granger he would inevitably have done.

This was the way of it. Looking across the fields in our rear (rather longingly) I had the happy distinction of a discoverer. What I saw was the shimmer of sunlight on metal: lines of troops were coming in behind us! The distance was too great, the atmosphere too hazy to distinguish the color of their uniform, even with a glass. Reporting my momentous "find" I was directed by the general to go and see who they were. Galloping toward them until near enough to see that they were of our kidney I hastened back with the glad tidings and was sent again, to guide them to the general's position.

It was General Granger with two strong brigades of the reserve, moving soldier-like toward the sound of heavy firing. Meeting him and his staff I directed him to Thomas, and unable to think of anything better to do decided to go visiting. I knew I had a brother in that gang—an officer of an Ohio battery. I soon found him near the head of a column, and as we moved forward we had a comfortable chat amongst such of the enemy's bullets as had inconsiderately been fired too high. The incident was a trifle marred by one of them unhorsing another officer of the battery, whom we propped against a tree and left. A few moments later Granger's force was put in on the right and the fighting was terrific!

Brigadier General James B. Steedman was considered a great fighter, if not a very likable person. A subordinate said of Steedman, "He had no idea of the needs of his men. . . . His devotion to cards and whiskey and women filled the measure of his delight except when under fire, and then he was a lion."

SERGEANT MAJOR LEVI A. ROSS

86TH ILLINOIS INFANTRY, MCCOOK'S BRIGADE

Shown here at war's end as a captain, Ross, named acting sergeant major on September 20, wrote, "I saw veteran soldiers who had survived the storms of Donelson, Shiloh, Fort Henry, Corinth, Perryville and Stone River, and all said this Sunday at Chickamauga was the hottest and bloodiest of all. After listening all day to the roar of cannon and the incessant and most terrific rattle and roll of musketry, it is a wonder that every man in both armies is not in eternity."

time to stop, not even to give a drop of water to our dying comrades. A half mile from the Hospital we entered an open field, which was covered with old logs, brush and full grown grass.

These had been fired by bursting shells which had spread in flame and smoke over hundreds of acres. But the passage in this volcano of blinding smoke must be made. Just beyond our beloved flag is in danger of going down, and we must get a position to drive back the advancing enemy or we are lost. "Forward" McCook commands and the 2nd Brig. dashes into flame and smoke. Soon we became blinded and choked to an almost intolerable degree, but we stay not on the order of our going, but push on. Bang go the rebel guns and whiz and screech go the shells over and around us. . . . We ran through a field up a hill and took position in the edge of the woods on the very crest of the hill. All this time the bomb shells were bursting all around among us and many were the casualties.

The smoke so utterly obscured us from the Enemy that he could not aim with any precision, otherwise we would have suffered much more, as there was a battery and infantry support immediately in our front.

The fire spread rapidly and we had to stack arms, cut brush and fight fire for a time, instead of rebels. 'Tis now 4 P.M. Since 8 A.M. the great battle of Chickamauga has been fought with stubborn and deadly re-

At 2 P.M. . . . we were ordered to march for the battlefield about two miles distant. The fierce struggle has been heard by us all day. There has been an incessant roll of musketry and boom of cannon. We quickly marched to the terrible field where the overwhelming avalanche of Confederates were driving McCook and cutting him up badly. The 86th was in advance and presently we could distinctly see the smoke of the cannon as they belched forth their missiles of death and destruction. Here on our left is a Field Hospital where we see the melancholy realities of war in hundreds of bleeding, groaning, dying victims. Not a very inspiring scene for a soldier just as he is about to be thrown into the gaps caused by the fall of these heroes we see bleeding before us. Here and there are piles of arms and legs yet warm and blood stained from these brave fellows. Many had died in the act or after amputation, and lay stretched out in everlasting sleep. We had no

Colonel Daniel McCook Jr. commanded the Reserve Corps brigade left behind on the Ringgold road when Granger went to support Thomas. He was one of Ohio's 17 fighting McCooks, all of whom played some role in the Civil War. Four of the tribe were officers who fought at Chickamauga. Daniel's brother, Alexander McDowell McCook, commanded the XX Corps, and his first cousin, Edward Moody McCook, led a division of Stanley's Cavalry Corps. Another cousin, Anson George McCook, commanded the 2d Ohio Infantry.

sistance. The boom of cannon and terrible roll of small arms has been incessant. On the rebels come, driving and almost annihilating whole divisions of McCook's corps. Whang go a half dozen guns at once, and whiz come the shells over our heads. The enemy has discovered the position of the 2nd Brigade, and open a battery upon us. Hark! Barnett's Ill. Battery is giving an emphatic response. Once more the smoke rises, but it is not necessary to fire again at that battery. Two rounds from our battery silenced their guns and the gunners are driven away by the 18th Ky. Inftry, which just cut its way through the rebel lines which had surrounded them killing and capturing all but a hand full. These Kentucky boys took the guns and were rolling them away by hand when a whole brigade of rebels charged them, yelling like so many demons from hell, retaking the battery and some more prisoners.

We were too far away to give timely assistance. The rebels soon had these guns turned on us again, but their range was bad, while our guns did effective execution to both men and horses. Pretty soon another battery, further to our left, commenced playing on us. The 86th was in an exposed position between the two fighting batteries. This artillery duel was continued until about 5:30 when the infantry charged us with a regular rebel yell. We lay close to the ground until they had approached to a distance when our fire would be most deadly, and then the Col. shouted: "Up boys, give them hell!" Up we sprang and poured into them such a terrible volley of minnie balls that the living turned and ran in great haste and disorder.

The artillery fight continued louder and fiercer than ever, and we lay in support of our battery until 8 o'clock, the while shot and shell whizzing around us. All soldiers say that this is the most trying position in an engagement. Though not so destructive of life as infantry fire or a bayonet charge, yet it is more trying to the nerves, from the fact that one must lie exposed to danger without an opportunity to retaliate as in an infantry fight. Yet I would prefer to lie under bursting shells than to face the silent but fatal minnie balls. . . . At 9 P.M. we silently withdrew from the sanguinary field of Chickamauga, leaving our dead and wounded in the hands of the enemy.

"I would prefer to lie under bursting shells than to face the silent but fatal minnie balls."

SERGEANT MAJOR JOHN W. GREEN
9TH KENTUCKY (C.S.) INFANTRY, HELM'S (ORPHAN) BRIGADE

"Johnny" Green enlisted in October 1861 and missed only one of his brigade's engagements because he was sick in the hospital. Disappointed after failing to receive a commission by the end of the war, he discarded his sword, a rash act he later regretted.

Reinforcements were now brought up & Genls Gist & Ector with their two brigades advanced against the breast works which we had unsuccesfully assaulted. They soon found that they could not move the enemy, who had reinforced this position which was already defended by two lines of battle behind breast works. They halted & we were then ordered up & passed over them as they laid down. We rushed against the enemy but their batteries had full play upon us, while our batteries could not fire for fear of fireing into our own line. Their several lines of infantry poured volley after volley into us & again we were forced to retire.

We fell back to about the same point we had previously taken to re-form & when our lines were again mended Genl Breckinridge & Genl Cheatham & Genl Polk rode along our front & stopped to tell us that Longstreet & Buckner were driving the Yankees before them on our left. Genl Cheatham said, "Now boys, soon you will up & at 'em & give em Hell." Genl Polk, who commanded our wing of the army, said, "Boys! You are going at them again. Now when the command forward is given, go at them & give what Cheatham said." Genl Breckinridge now called us to attention, told us to fix bayonetts, hold our fire, rush upon them until within ten yards of them, then fire & rushing on them give them the bayonett.

The very air soon became full of shot & shell. Here Flying cloud (our Mohawk Indian Chief), who enlisted in Co H of our regiment, had the half of his face shot away & Mick Clary (for that was the only name by which he was known in the regiment) was fatally shot in the forhead with a minnie ball & Jim Hunter, the wit of the regiment, was shot through the heart. Dick Taylor was shot on top of the enemies breast works. John Fightmaster, Nat Hedger, & Benj F. Butler were all killed almost at my elbow & here Norborne Gray, Lute Collins, Lieutenant Wagoner, Thos Ellis, Jim Ford, Jim Yonts & many others were wounded.

The struggle was to the death but our bayonetts were fixed & our onslaught was irresistable. Cleyburn had carried their works on our left & their line broke & fled precipitately; many seeing escape was impossible surrendered. We persued the others about half a mile & shot down many as they ran.

> "We rose up as one man and poured into them such a volley from our faithful Enfields as to make many of them bite the dust for the last time."

PRIVATE JOHN T. COXE
2D SOUTH CAROLINA INFANTRY, KERSHAW'S BRIGADE

The clash described here—part of a contest between Kershaw's brigade and Harker's Federal brigade of Crittenden's corps—was one of a series of charges and countercharges up and down Snodgrass Hill that left the dead and dying of both sides scattered on the slope. The fight petered out in a duel of sharpshooters, one victim of which was Lieutenant Colonel Dwella Stoughton, commanding the 21st Ohio, who had stayed on horseback even after realizing that he was a particular target.

eanwhile the battle was raging to right and left, and for awhile we enjoyed a nice breeze passing through the woods, now and then blowing from the trees bunches of yellow leaves, which gently sailed down and settled on the ground among us. . . . in mind I compared these falling leaves to the falling men on that battle field. But we did not enjoy the protection of that depressed old road for long, because the Federals launched a charge down the hill against, or rather upon us. But we had sufficient notice of their coming to be ready for them. Our officers commanded us to hold our fire till they got in short range and then "give it to them." Here they came armed with Colt repeating rifles and a shout. They were allowed to get within twenty yards of our position in the thick undergrowth along the road, then, before they visualized our presence, we rose up as one man and poured into them such a volley from our faithful Enfields as to make many of them bite the dust for the last time, while many more fell badly wounded. The remnant staggered back up the hill as we closely pursued them with the hope of breaking up and capturing their line at the top. But we were met by such a terrific fire of grape, canister, and spherical case from their cannon and bullets from their quick-firing rifles from behind log fortifications, that we ourselves were compelled to fall back over the brow of the hill for protection, though we didn't go back all the way to the old road. Neither did the Federals dare sally out from their works any more.

This view of the action on Snodgrass Hill on September 20 shows Steedman's 3,900-strong division of Granger's Reserve Corps arriving (far right) on the field. Steedman's mission was to shore up the hard-pressed line of Brannan's division against four Confederate divisions thrown at them by Longstreet.

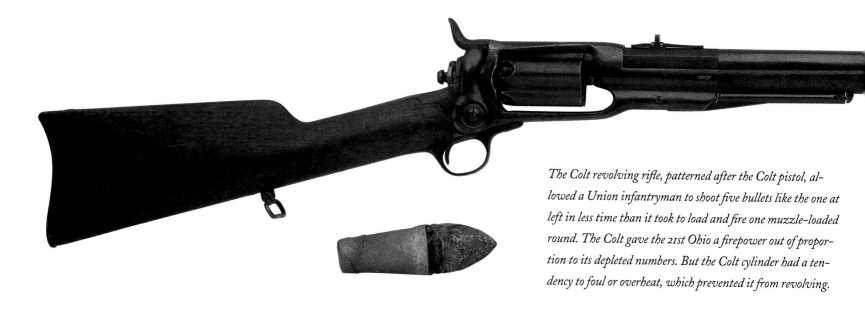

The Colt revolving rifle, patterned after the Colt pistol, allowed a Union infantryman to shoot five bullets like the one at left in less time than it took to load and fire one muzzle-loaded round. The Colt gave the 21st Ohio a firepower out of proportion to its depleted numbers. But the Colt cylinder had a tendency to foul or overheat, which prevented it from revolving.

LIEUTENANT WILSON J. VANCE

21ST OHIO INFANTRY, SIRWELL'S BRIGADE

Although the companies in Vance's regiment using the Colt rifle were among the first to run short of ammunition, the problem plagued troops of Thomas' entire corps the afternoon of the 20th. Many of the corps' ammunition wagons had been lost or scattered in the retreat before Longstreet's attack on the Federal line earlier. Despite the arrival of 95,000 rounds with Steedman's division, Thomas' forces could keep fighting only by taking bullets from the dead and wounded.

But there were all the elements of Providence . . . in the regiment; and cool men went back for cartridges from time to time, and returned in order, with the little, heavy, lead-colored boxes on their shoulders. The peculiar ammunition belonging to the revolving rifles was, of course, soon exhausted; for of course again, some fool who had lost his wits at the time the right wing of the army was stampeded, had taken it upon himself to order the wagons back. But it was soon found that, although the ball made for the Enfields was a trifle large, yet it could be made to serve in the revolvers, and it was accordingly so used. Only, in less time than it takes to write it, the men found that in using the Enfield cartridge the bayonet must be kept on the revolver, else it would split at the muzzle. And the men armed with Enfields exchanged them for the more formidable weapon, as the sad casualties of the day gave them opportunity.

CAPTAIN J. B. BRIGGS

4TH TENNESSEE CAVALRY, DIBRELL'S BRIGADE

An 1885 article credited Briggs with being the only officer to command black troops on the Confederate side during the war. Although the enlistment of slaves was proposed several times to ease the Rebel army's manpower shortage, advocates could not overcome objections to arming slaves and granting them freedom in exchange for their service. In the last few months of the war the Confederate Congress authorized a levy of 300,000 slaves, but the companies formed never saw action.

The Fourth Tennessee Cavalry was dismounted to fight as infantry, every fourth man being told off to hold horses. These horse-holders, and also all of the colored servants, were kept in the rear. The colored men numbered about 40, and having been in service a long time, had gradually armed themselves. Some of them were even better equipped than their masters, for on successful raids and battles they could follow in the rear and pick up those things that the soldiers had no time to secure; so that these colored servants could each boast of one or two revolvers and a fine carbine or repeating rifle.

During all of the early part of the battle of Chickamauga, the Fourth Tennessee Cavalry had been fighting as infantry, and as it became evident that a victory was to be won, Col. McLemore, commanding, ordered Captain Briggs to return to the horse-holders, and after placing the horses, teams, etc., under charge of the servants, to bring up the

quarter of the regiment in charge of the horses so that they might take part in the final triumph. Capt. Briggs, on reaching the horses, was surprised to find the colored men organized and equipped, under Daniel McLemore, colored (servant to the Colonel of the regiment), and demanding the right to go into the fight. After trying to dissuade them from this, Capt. Briggs led them up to the line of battle which was just then preparing to assault Gen. Thomas's position. Thinking they would be of service in caring for the wounded, Capt. Briggs held them close up the line, but when the advance was ordered the negro company became enthused as well as their masters, and filled a portion of the line of advance as well as any company of the regiment.

While they had no guidon or muster roll, the burial after the battle of four of their number and the care of seven wounded at the hospital, told the tale of how well they fought that day.

George G. Dibrell, who commanded a brigade in Forrest's corps, was a man of contradictions. Poorly educated, he became a wealthy merchant, financier, and congressman after the war. Opposed to secession, he enlisted in a Confederate regiment and was elected lieutenant colonel. At Chickamauga his brigade was one of the first to be seriously engaged, taking heavy casualties in the fighting against Brannan's division on the extreme Union left on September 19.

PRIVATE JACOB H. ALLSPAUGH

31st Ohio Infantry, Connell's Brigade

The anecdote related here was one of the 31st Ohio's worst moments at Chickamauga. The regiment performed well as part of Brannan's stand against Bushrod Johnson's brigade the morning of September 19, but fled the next day from its position at the center of Longstreet's massive attack. A few hours later, some of the men rallied to the Union defensive position being established on Horseshoe Ridge.

At points in the wood the fighting had almost been hand to hand, yet was but a prelude to the struggle that awaited us for the possession of the barricades on Horse Shoe Ridge that long, eventful Sabbath afternoon. But this place of close work was not destitute of its amusing scenes.

At one point, in a countercharge, we occupied a position held a few moments before by the enemy, which brought their skulkers and killed and wounded in the rear of or mixed up with our irregular line. Seeing a fine-looking young soldier dressed in a neat suit of dark blue, unarmed, and standing behind a tree for protection, a pompous Colonel inquired why he was not firing like the others.

"Why, I'm a color-bearer," said the soldier, hugging the tree still closer and exhibiting his color-belt.

"Well, then, where is your flag?" said the Colonel, who liked to carry a point.

"I lost it in that close work back there," said the soldier.

"Well, pick up a gun and go to work like the other men," said the officer, thinking he had added one more soldier to our depleted ranks.

"Why, Colonel," said the soldier with a kind of foolish look getting possession of his face. "I belong on the other side." And sure enough it was one of Lonstreet's men . . . that the Colonel had been trying to force into our ranks. Just then was no time to care for straggling prisoners, and as the enemy occupied the ground a short time after, the young color-bearer probably rejoined his regiment.

PRIVATE ROBERT A. JARMAN
27TH MISSISSIPPI INFANTRY, WALTHALL'S BRIGADE

Jarman's history of his unit, Company K of the 27th Mississippi, contains this humble and honest apology: "The reason there is so much of self in this, is the impossibility for one man to see all that occurred on a skirmish line from 75 to 150 yards long when he had so much to attract his attention in his immediate front."

Towards the middle of the evening . . . Company K was again deployed as skirmishers and the line advanced across the road leading to Chattanooga, where we were as hotly pressed as at any time during the battle.

The enemy struck our line on the left flank and engaged only one regiment or part of regiment at a time, and from our position on the skirmish line, nearly three hundred yards in front, we could see the brigade beaten back regiment at a time. We held our position until our regiment broke to the colors, when began a race with us only equaled by horses on some famous race course, we were so hotly pursued. When we crossed the road all pursuit seemed to stop, for the Yankees were fighting for a road to escape on. Here it was Gen. Walthall was rallying his men, and here it was that the root was cut that was presented to Gen. Walthall, so full of shot from the battle field of Chickamauga.

Found on the battlefield, these shot-ridden tree limbs, like the fragment of root mentioned in the account above, testify to the intensity of the firing at Chickamauga.

MAJOR WILLIAM M. OWEN
CHIEF OF ARTILLERY, PRESTON'S DIVISION

In August 1863 Owen was a lieutenant serving in the Army of Northern Virginia at Richmond, where he moved in social circles that included Jefferson Davis. Preston offered him promotion to major and transfer to southwestern Virginia. Owen acceded on Longstreet's advice and ended up in the thick of the fighting at Chickamauga.

During the heat of this battle Gen. Benning, of Georgia, one of the bravest men that ever lived, came charging up to Gen. Longstreet in great agitation. He was riding an artillery horse, and was using a rope trace for a whip. His hat was gone, and he was much disordered. "General," he said, "my brigade is utterly destroyed and scattered." Gen. Longstreet approached him, and said quietly, "Don't you think you could find *one* man, General?"—"One man?" he said, with astonishment. "I suppose I could. What do you want with him?"—"Go and get him," Longstreet said very quietly, laying his hand upon his arm, "and bring him here; then you and I and he will charge together. This is the sacred soil of Georgia, General, and we may as well die here as anywhere." He looked at Gen. Longstreet curiously a moment, then laughed, and, with an oath, lashed his horse with his rope trace, and was off like a flash.

In a few moments he swept by at the head of a command that he had gathered together somehow or other, and he was in the fight again.

Gen. Longstreet does not think it necessary to swear at the men, to whoop 'em up as it were; he always adopts the demeanor of quiet assurance and confidence, which is always better than strong oaths.

LIEUTENANT EDWARD S. SCOTT

89TH OHIO INFANTRY, WHITAKER'S BRIGADE

The fighting described here culminated in most of the remnants of the 21st Ohio, the 22d Michigan, and the 89th Ohio being captured on Horseshoe Ridge. Scott was sent to Libby prison in Richmond but escaped the following February. After the war he wrote that his regiment had been sacrificed to cover the withdrawal of Thomas' corps because it had no one to speak up for it, having earlier been shifted from its regular command to Granger's Reserve Corps. The 21st Ohio, however, which did belong to Thomas' corps, suffered the same fate.

It was a trying time for our Regt when the line in front fell back over it, but it stood nobly. After a short time of quiet, firing commenced again on our right. It was tremendous, almost deafening. The roar of musketry was incessant and at intervals of two or three seconds it was increased by the roar of cannon. The conflict here was terrific; first one side driving then the other. At last the rebels began to get the advantage and slowly drove our men back. As the line on our right gave way, they began to come on us and at last came on us with full force. Our Regt was lying rather too far back on the crest of the hill, I think, so that we could not see them till they were pretty near on to us. Their first onset was so impetuous and our line on the right falling back enabled them to come in on our right and pour in an enfilading fire so that our Regt gave way a little and the right had to swing around to meet the enfilading fire. We stood here for some time when the rebels came on with such force that we were obliged to retire; we fell back slowly till we reached a sort of hollow which ran up and down the hill. The 22d Michigan was on our left, more toward the top of the hill. Here we stopped and from which we made charge after charge, but were driven back to it each time by superior numbers. The question was now anxiously asked by every one, "Why don't we get reinforcements?"

The 89th & 21st Ohio, and 22d Mich. seemed to have been forgotten and left without support or assistance, and I don't suppose our whole force amounted to 500 men. In our Regiment our men were nearly half killed or wounded and our ammunition nearly gone; in some of the companies, entirely gone, and they were taking the cartridges out of the boxes of the killed and wounded. It was a fearful place; the musketry fire was terrible. We were exposed to very little cannonading. In our last charge they fired one round of grape at us. Those who had been in several heavy fights say that they never saw the musketry so heavy as it was here.

We had now been in the fight some three hours. Our men were becoming discouraged & disheartened, and night or reinforcements were more than anxiously looked and prayed for; the more so as it was pretty generally thought that we were surrounded.

"Then the Major gave orders to fix bayonets, which was promptly obeyed, but when the order was given to 'forward march,' not a man moved."

CAPTAIN ISAAC CUSAC
21ST OHIO INFANTRY, SIRWELL'S BRIGADE

A high-ranking officer gave Cusac the peremptory and terrible order related here. When Cusac protested, he was joined by Lieutenant J. S. Mahoney of the 21st Ohio's Company K. By the time the officer repeated the order to Major McMahon, his manner had so changed that McMahon later said he was "not imperious, but kind and encouraging."

We had been on the ridge but a short time when the enemy made a desperate attack on us, but was repulsed. Again and again did they attempt to drive us from the ridge, but we were not to be moved by lead or demon-like yells, but we lay close to the ground and with our Colt Revolving Rifles repelled and repulsed every attack. About one o'clock p.m. some troops came in on our right, and the 22d Michigan charged over us as we lay on the ground, but only remained in front of us a short time when they fell back over us. The enemy then followed up and made a desperate effort to break through our lines. The enemy's loss must have been very heavy as they came near us, and we kept up a constant and terrific fire on them, compelling them to fall back. About this time a regiment formed on our left and did some good work, but later in the day they disappeared. . . .

The 21st held position amidst showers of bullets, shot and shell, until sundown, when we were out of ammunition and could not get any. The regiment then moved to the rear a few rods into a hollow, where we were then secure from the fire of the enemy. While in this position I was standing in front of the regiment, when a Colonel (whom I was unable to recognize) rode up to me somewhat excited, saying to me, "Move those men up on the line." I said to him, "Colonel, we have no more ammunition." His reply to me was, "It does not make a God damn bit of difference. Have the men fix bayonets and hold that line."

The language and the manner that the command was given in stirred up my "Irish" blood, and I said to him, "Go and talk with the officer in command." He then rode to the rear of the regiment where Major McMahon was, and gave him the same orders, though not in the same language. Then the Major gave orders to fix bayonets, which was promptly obeyed, but when the order was given to "forward march," not a man moved. About that time some of the men on our right shouted, "Boys, do not leave us!" and when the second command was given, every man moved forward on double quick, and was met by a most murderous fire which killed and wounded many of our men, myself being wounded in my left hand.

When we reached the line on the ridge a short distance to the right of where we were at sundown, we fell to the ground and remained in that position until dark. The enemy could have undoubtedly driven us from the ridge at any time after sundown, as the three regiments that held that part of the line were all out of ammunition. But they had a better thing on us by lying still in front, while a part of their forces swung around to the rear of us, shutting us in. This they did in good shape, taking in the 22d Michigan, the 89th Ohio and the 21st Ohio, all except a few on the left of the 21st.

LIEUTENANT WILSON J. VANCE
21ST OHIO INFANTRY, SIRWELL'S BRIGADE

The 21st Ohio had stood up to the Rebels on Horseshoe Ridge for six hours. Its experience had ranged from the triumph of repelling superior forces with its rapid-firing Colt rifles to the hopeless assignment of charging a brigade of Floridians with empty rifles. Finally, while the last of Thomas' corps was leaving the field, the regiment suffered the ignominy of seeing its colors and surviving men captured.

Filing in through the depths of the great ravine on our right and below us, came a long line of soldiers, carrying their muskets at a right-shoulder-shift, marching "left in front," and making no noise. The rising mist distorted them somewhat and blurred their outlines, but they seemed to be in dark uniforms, and came from the direction in which Steedman's brigades had gone. As they slowly moved along and finally came to a front, facing us, they showed up a full brigade in strength.

Our fellows regarded them with a curiosity that was almost listless, and calmly debated as to who they were, some maintaining that they were Confederates who, acting with those who had just taken the crest of the hill, were about to assault us in flank, while others, arguing from the color of their uniforms and the direction from which they came, were as strongly impressed that they were Union troops. . . .

Wrapped in the fog, they looked like so many phantoms out on a ghostly brigade drill, and it gave one a creepy sensation to look at them, as it does to recall the incident.

At last Captain Alban made up his mind to know who they were. It was imperative that we should know, and yet it was plainly evident that the man who undertook to investigate would do so at the risk of his life. . . . Without hesitation, the captain plunged down the hill, and was soon lost to view. . . .

Presently, hearing nothing from the captain, a sergeant of my company approached and saluted. Be it known that, as the most juvenile member of the regiment, and the youngest commissioned officer in the Army of the Cumberland, I was generally addressed and referred to as "the Boy."

"Boy," said the sergeant, "I think I will go and see who they are. . . ."

I reluctantly gave my consent, and shouldering his rifle, the brave young fellow stepped blithely off, for all the world as if he were going squirrel-hunting in his native Putnam county woods. And from that day

to this, I have never laid eyes on him. He was soon lost to view, and from neither him nor Captain Alban came back so much as a word or a cry.

The suspense was growing unendurable. At last one of our men called out sharply:—

"What troops are you?"

The reply came back promptly:—

"Jeff. Davis's troops!"

We all heaved a sigh of relief, feeling, for a brief moment, that it was all right. The Union general, Jeff. C. Davis, had been, in the early part of the day, on the right with his division, and our first impression was that this was his command approaching us; and our fellows lapsed again into quiet, but in no wise relaxed their eager watchfulness. . . .

Suddenly came the command, from our own ranks, ringing out sharp and clear:—

"Fire!"

Now, who it was that gave the command, or why he should have done so, I have never found out—there was not a cartridge among us all—but the order had a prompt and most decided effect, for instantly the approaching column lay down—seemed to melt and disappear, like "the baseless fabric" of a dream.

For an instant it seemed as if the face of the earth had been suddenly cleared of them; then, with a shrill yell, which went far to dispelling even the fog itself, and rent the very heavens, they rose and "came for" us. A crashing volley tore great holes in our huddled mass of eager watchers, and in the winking of a gnat's eyebrow, they were upon us.

It was quick work. At least one-third of our numbers were killed, wounded, or captured—and with them, worst of all, our colors. . . . they, too, were gone! We were like a family of children bereft of our mother!

PRIVATE JAMES M. WEISER
54TH VIRGINIA INFANTRY, TRIGG'S BRIGADE

As darkness fell on Horseshoe Ridge, the three regiments of Trigg's brigade out-flanked the Union right and surprised and captured the Federals nearest them. Private Weiser relates a suspenseful moment when Rebel and Yankee soldiers stood face to face with their weapons aimed and cocked.

We were called upon late in the afternoon of the 20th to attack the Federal line, which had stood firmly up to that time against the assaults of Longstreet. As we passed over his line, one of his men remarked: "Boys, you're going to catch hell now." He spoke truly, as the loss in our own regiment, the 54th Virginia, of over one hundred men proved, but we gave more than we caught and swept on in a magnificent charge carrying everything before us till we were halted suddenly just as we were about to take possession of a battery which had no defenders left, all either shot down or put to flight.

Without orders, we began fixing bayonets. Colonel Trigg came riding along the front. "Let us go get that battery," we were shouting. It was already ours, but we wished to demonstrate our ownership by laying our paws on it. But we were astonished by the order, "About face!" Then we saw in our rear a line of blue closing up the gap in the Federal line which we had made in our impetuous charge. Colonel Trigg rode a hundred yards in front of his advancing line, where he could easily have been riddled with bullets, and in a stentorian voice, but clear as a silver bell, which made itself clearly heard above the then subsiding din of battle, shouted: "Stack your arms and lie down, or I'll cut you all to pieces!"

The boys in blue, who had not yet closed the line behind us, lay down, but did not stack their loaded and bayonetted rifles, but awaited our advance with orders, as they afterwards told us, to wait for the command to fire and then use the bayonet. But Colonel Trigg wheeled his left wing so as to enfilade the end of the incompleted Federal line, and we steadily advanced, guns loaded, bayonets fixed, fingers on triggers, and thumbs ready to cock our guns in a fraction of a second.

When perhaps fifteen or twenty feet from the enemy, a nervous Confederate inconsiderately, or accidentally, discharged his musket. Instantly came the deadliest, most menacing sound I have ever heard—the click of cocking locks of both lines—while the boys in blue jumped up and, with guns at their shoulders and fingers pressing triggers, awaited the command to fire, which was not given, their officers realizing the futility of the slaughter which would have followed. We advanced slowly, repeating "Surrender, boys, we've got you." Our opponents finally began lowering their guns, which we took and threw behind us. Then at once we became friends and began a frenzied trading of tobacco for coffee.

Colonel Robert C. Trigg, a graduate of Virginia Military Institute, led a company of the 4th Virginia of Stonewall's Brigade at First Manassas and then joined the 54th Virginia. Elevated to brigade command just before Chickamauga, he acquitted himself so well that Generals Preston and Buckner recommended that he be promoted to brigadier general. Preston and Buckner were two of Bragg's biggest critics, so Trigg was passed over.

Colonel Heber Le Favour (seated far left) and the other staff officers of the 22d Michigan shown here were among the regiment's 261 members taken captive by the Confederates on Horseshoe Ridge. Le Favour, paroled in May 1864, had commanded a mixed force from his own regiment and the 89th Ohio that repulsed several enemy attacks before being over-run at dark by Trigg's Confederate brigade. Five colorbearers were among the 135 dead and wounded Michiganders left on the field.

LIEUTENANT KELLAR ANDERSON
5TH KENTUCKY (C.S.) INFANTRY, KELLY'S BRIGADE

Anderson's brother had been killed on the first day of the battle as he carried the colors in the charge that claimed the life of General Benjamin Helm. The wound Anderson mentions was but one of three he received during the war—all in the left shoulder and arm. One flattened ball remained lodged in his forearm, discernible to the touch, for the rest of his life.

The last rays of the setting sun had kissed the autumn foliage when we stepped into open ground. . . . The boom of artillery increases. The rattle of musketry is steady—aye, incessant and deadly. The sulphurous smoke has increased until almost stifling. Only fifty yards of space separates us from the gallant Mississippians, we are there to support. They have clung to the ridge with a death-like grip, but their last cartridge has been fired at the enemy, and their support being at hand these sturdy soldiers of Longstreet's corps are ordered to retire.

Simultaneously the support was ordered forward. As the Mississippians retired, the deep-volumed shouts of the enemy told us plainer than could words that the enemy thought they had routed them. Oh, how differently we regarded the situation! If they could have seen them as we—halting, kneeling, lying down, ranging themselves in columns of files behind the large trees to enable us to get at the enemy with an unbroken front, each man as we passed throwing cap high into the overhanging foliage in honor of our presence—then I imagine their shouts would have been suppressed. "Steady in the center! Hold your fire! Hold the colors back!" The center advanced too rapidly. We are clear of our friends now, only the enemy in front, and we meet face to face on a spur of Mission Ridge, which extends through the Snodgrass farm, and we are separated by eighty yards. Thud! and down goes Private Robertson. He turned, smiled and died. Thud! Corporal Gray shot through the neck. "Get to the rear!" said I. Thud! Thud! Thud! Wolf, Michael, the gallant Thompson. Thud! Thud! Thud! Courageous Oxley, the knightly Desha, and duty-loving Cummings. And thus it goes. The fallen increase, and are to be counted by the hundreds. The pressure is fearful, but the "sand-digger" is there to stay. "Forward! Forward!" rang out along the line. We move slowly to the front.

There is now sixty yards between us. The enemy scorn to fly; he gives back a few paces; he retires a little more, but still faces us, and loads as he backs away. We are now in the midst of his dead and dying, but he stands as do the sturdy oaks about him. We have all that is possible for human to bear; our losses are fearful, and each moment some comrade passes to the unknown. At last Humphries' Mississippians have replenished boxes and are working around our right. Trigg's Virginians are uncovering to our left. I feel a shock about my left breast, spin like a top in the air, and come down in a heap. I know not how long before came the sounds "Forward! Forward! Forward!" I rise on my elbow. Look! Look! There they go, all at breakneck speed, the bayonet at charge. The firing appears to suddenly cease for about five seconds. Then arose that do-or-die expression, that maniacal maelstrom of sound; that penetrating, rasping, shrieking, blood-curdling noise, that could be heard for miles on earth, and whose volumes reached the heavens; such an expression as never yet came from the throats of sane men, but from men whom the seething blast of an imaginary hell would not check while the sound lasted.

The battle of Chickamauga is won.

Covering the Union withdrawal toward Chattanooga, troops of Absalom Baird's division stand fast before the Kelly house in the late afternoon of September 20. "We held our position, yielding not an inch," wrote Baird. "To fall back was more difficult than to remain." Baird retreated as night came on, and Thomas' forces at Snodgrass Hill began to leave the field. Only the 21st and 89th Ohio and the 22d Michigan remained to resist the Confederate assaults. Out of ammunition, they fixed bayonets and countercharged, only to be overwhelmed and captured. Thus the battle ended.

Chattanooga under Siege

By September 22, two days after the battle, Rosecrans' surviving ranks had retreated safely within the defenses of Chattanooga. That same day Bragg followed, proclaiming that he now had Rosecrans precisely where he wanted him. It only remained to besiege the Federal army in Chattanooga and starve it into submission. Apparently lost on General Bragg was the irony of his costly victory at Chickamauga actually driving the Federals into the city, rather than away from it, as intended.

For the moment, however, Bragg's course was clear. He marched his troops north and seized the commanding height of Missionary Ridge that loomed over Chattanooga and the Union trenches defending it. On the 24th, when a demoralized Rosecrans unaccountably pulled a Union brigade off Lookout Mountain to the west, Bragg quickly sent Longstreet to seize that strategic height as well.

....

Union soldiers pose among their tents in besieged Chattanooga. Yankee troops dismantled many of the city's houses and used the scavenged boards for firewood or for erecting camp structures, such as the makeshift plank fence in the foreground.

This spelled trouble for the Federals. Confederate cannons on Lookout Mountain could easily hit boats and barges on a nearby bend in the Tennessee River and the tracks of the Nashville & Chattanooga Railroad, effectively severing Rosecrans' main supply routes.

The Federals were forced to improvise a new supply line—and a very poor substitute it turned out to be. The troops had to unload the supplies shipped from Nashville at the rail depot in Bridgeport, Alabama, and pile the freight onto wagons. Then they had to get the mule-drawn wagons up a dirt track to Anderson's Crossroads and from there across Walden's Ridge on a rough, twisting trail that finally descended to the north bank of the Tennessee and a bridge spanning the river into Chattanooga. A trip on the old rail route from Bridgeport had taken about an hour. The new route, 60 miles long, took at least eight days—and often took about 20.

The first wagon trains making the long haul could barely bring in enough food to keep Rosecrans' troops from starving, and the situation soon became worse as autumn rains made the route all but impassable. The track, said a Union officer, was "the muddiest and the roughest and steepest of ascent and descent ever crossed by army wagons and mules." The overworked mules soon became exhausted and, lacking fodder, died off by the hundreds; eventually a total of 10,000 perished.

The result was persistent, gnawing hunger in Chattanooga, for the army, now reduced to 35,000 men, and for the civilian population as well. Famished troops demanded "crackers"—issues of the normally despised hardtack—and could often be seen, an observer reported, scrabbling in the gutters for "crumbs of bread, coffee, rice etc., which were wasted from the boxes and sacks by the rattling of the wagons over the stones."

Making conditions worse, the soldiers before long had all but dismantled the town, tearing apart the houses for firewood and for lumber to build shacks for themselves. The residents were reduced to living in wretched shanties—until a large proportion of them fled northward to find succor in other towns.

Meanwhile Confederate cavalry leader Joe Wheeler hammered at the rickety supply system, crossing the Tennessee in late September with 5,000 troopers and spreading havoc in the Federal rear. Wheeler wrecked Union depots and in a single raid on Anderson's Crossroads burned more than 300 wagons. Finally

Federal cavalry chased Wheeler back across the Tennessee on October 9.

Through all the misery, Rosecrans walked about as if in a daze, half insensible to his army's troubles—and the far worse misery that would ensue if Bragg attacked his weakened force. Rosecrans, President Lincoln said on being told of the general's behavior, was acting "stunned and confused, like a duck hit on the head."

Bragg, for his part, was clearer of mind but as usual in an exceedingly ill temper. Following the battle he angrily relieved Polk of command, sent Hindman packing, and tried to get rid of D. H. Hill as well. The generals—all disgusted by Bragg's continued refusal to attack the battered Federals—countered by sending a petition to President Davis saying the army was "stricken with a complete paralysis" and that Bragg was unfit for command.

In response, Davis hurried westward by train and convened a meeting of the disgruntled officers on October 9. Nothing came of it but a shuffling of assignments. Bragg stayed on, to the dismay of virtually all his subordinates.

A far more significant shuffling took place on the Federal side. In the second week of October, Secretary of War Edwin Stanton took a train to Indianapolis and there met Major

General Ulysses S. Grant, summoned east from Vicksburg. Grant, Stanton said, would immediately assume overall command of no fewer than three armies—Rosecrans' Army of the Cumberland, Ambrose E. Burnside's Army of the Ohio, and the Army of the Tennessee led by Grant's right-hand man in the Vicksburg campaign, William Tecumseh Sherman.

The first question was what to do with Old Rosy. Grant was given his choice and opted to relieve the shaken Rosecrans and replace him with George Thomas. Grant quickly sent General Thomas a telegram ordering him to "hold Chattanooga at all hazards." The blunt Thomas wired back, "We will hold the town till we starve."

Grant then sped to the railroad junction at Stevenson, Alabama, where he met Rosecrans, who was on his way home to Cincinnati. The meeting was friendly, Grant recalled, and Rosecrans both "described very clearly the situations at Chattanooga" and "made some excellent suggestions about what should be done." The wonder, Grant added, "was that he had not carried them out."

Going on to Bridgeport, Grant then rode over the treacherous, muddy Federal supply route into Chattanooga, getting a firsthand look at "the debris of broken wagons and the carcasses of dead mules and horses that strewed the trail."

Once in Chattanooga, the new commander quickly adopted a plan already set in motion by General Thomas and an old West Point friend of Grant's, Brigadier General William F. "Baldy" Smith, to shorten the execrable supply line. The solution was to drive Confederate detachments away from key points on the Tennessee River, then throw pontoon bridges across at places well beyond range of the enemy guns on Lookout Mountain.

Grant conducted a series of sharp attacks—beginning with a daring nighttime assault that involved floating 1,500 men noiselessly down the river in pontoons and flatboats past the Confederate pickets. By October 28, a week after Grant's arrival, 20,000 Union troops were south of the Tennessee, safeguarding a new supply route with an easy eight-mile overland haul that the troops, now getting their hardtack, quickly dubbed the Cracker Line.

In his adroit little campaign to push the Confederates back from the river, Grant used troops drawn from reinforcements shipped west by train from Virginia—two entire corps totaling 20,000 men from the Army of the Potomac under the command of Major General Joseph Hooker. And more reinforcements soon arrived; General Sherman reached Bridgeport on November 13 with advance elements of four divisions after an arduous trek from Vicksburg and Memphis.

Grant now had the manpower to attack and lift the siege. A few days after Sherman arrived, the two generals, surveying the Confederate lines in the distance along Missionary Ridge, began to formulate a scheme to lever Bragg's force out of its formidable defensive lines.

By the end of November all was ready. Attacking from the west, Hooker's troops took mist-shrouded Lookout Mountain with surprising ease in a fight soon to become famous as the Battle above the Clouds.

Then General Thomas' 20,000 veterans, many screaming "Chickamauga" as they charged, scrambled straight up the face of Missionary Ridge and flung the Confederates from the heights. By November 28 Bragg's defeated army was fleeing south, past the Chickamauga battlefield and down the roads into Georgia—precisely what Rosecrans had had in mind months before.

BATTLE OF CHICKAMAUGA CASUALTIES

FEDERAL

Killed	1,657
Wounded	9,756
Missing	4,757
Total	16,170

CONFEDERATE

Killed	2,312
Wounded	14,678
Missing	1,468
Total	18,458

PRIVATE JOHN E. MAGEE
STANFORD'S (MISSISSIPPI) BATTERY, CHEATHAM'S DIVISION

Magee and his battery saw some of the hottest action on the 19th but were held in reserve on the 20th. They rose early on the 21st with plenty of fight left in them but without orders to pursue the fleeing Federals. The inaction left a disgusted Magee, among many other Confederates, to ponder why the enemy was allowed to slip away without a fight.

Monday, Sept 21, 1863. Up and stirring early. Our Brigade moved forward 600 yards to the right and front, and took a position in an old field. Genl Polk ordered out heavy skirmishers, who soon brought the news that there was nothing in our front for over 3 miles. We laid in position nearly all day. I went over on the left, where the hard fighting was yesterday, and looked over the field; hundreds of dead strewed the ground, and the canon shot and minie balls had riddled the timber. The fighting here was long and desperate—positions and batteries were taken and retaken several times; but the invincible will of the Southerners, fighting for all mankind holds dear, could not be withstood by the hirelings of a tyrant however well trained, and yesterday's work has taught them a lesson they will not soon forget. They had been told the "rebels" were nothing but a rabble, utterly demoralized and disheartened, and would run at the first fire, but they have found out the contrary to their own dear cost. The victory is glorious, but dearly bought, and why the enemy have been allowed to get away so easily I am at a loss to know. That they are not in front is positive, and that they should be allowed to quietly withdraw at night is a shame to our arms.

LIEUTENANT ROBERT M. COLLINS
15TH TEXAS CAVALRY (DISMOUNTED), DESHLER'S BRIGADE

In some of the fiercest fighting of the war, the two-day battle along the Chickamauga exacted a stiff price from both sides. Federal casualties numbered more than 16,000, and the Confederates counted some 18,000 killed, wounded, and missing. In the early hours of the 21st, Collins rode over the battlefield to survey the carnage the battle had wrought.

We saw men cold and stiff in death, and yet holding on to their gun; some with the ramrod yet in their hand; some with paper yet between their teeth, just as they had bitten it from the cartridge for loading, and the cartridge yet held by their thumb, middle and forefinger as if in the act of emptying the powder into their gun. On that part of the field where the Tennessee troops had such a terrific battle with Michigan troops, supporting a steel battery of twelve guns, we found many things to wonder at. A Federal had been wounded in the knee, had crawled behind a log, was sitting with back to it, and was binding up his wound, when he was shot in the head; his head dropped over on his shoulder; he remained sitting with his hands yet holding to the linen he was trying to bind his wound with. Hard by him we found a very fine looking dog riddled with bullets. Just across the road we found a Confederate, still in death, yet sitting with his back against a tree, his eyes blared wide open. We found several dead rabbits and birds. We found one man with his brains between his feet, a cannon ball had struck him so as to lift his entire head off, and as he fell his brains fell between his feet; the lining or covering for them was not broken. We

Lieutenant Colonel William D. Gale, a volunteer aide to his father-in-law, General Leonidas Polk, decried Bragg's inaction on the 21st and blamed him for squandering the Confederate initiative after the hard-fought battle. Later, summing up thoughts shared by many fellow officers, Gale would write: "I can forgive Mr. Davis for all the blunders he made & persisted in during the war— except the infernal sin he committed in placing Bragg at the head of the army of Tenn & keeping him there, as he did. Bragg was a bantam in success & a dunghill in disaster."

found some of the big logs from behind which the Federals fought, just bristling with ramrods: we account for this on the ground that we rebels were in such hot haste while advancing, shooting and loading, that we did not take time to return the ramrods to their place but let the Federals have ramrods and all. We saw many whose hands and arms were in the exact position of holding their guns taking aim. We saw many who had been stripped of all their clothing, and many whose pockets had been rifled and turned inside out. Men were wounded in every shape and place imaginable. Boone Daugherty, of Denton, and a member of Company G., of the 18th Texas regiment says he is going back there one of these days to see "if the thirteen teeth the Yankees pulled for him and planted there have sprouted and produced any of their kind."

A pair of holsters rest on the pommel of Lieutenant Colonel Isaac L. Clarke's McClellan saddle. Clarke, who fought with the 95th Illinois, was shot from this saddle "bravely cheering his men" in their defense of Snodgrass Hill in the final hours of the battle on September 20. He died of the wound two days later.

REVEREND JOHN M. CARLISLE
7TH SOUTH CAROLINA INFANTRY, KERSHAW'S BRIGADE

Following the savage slaughter on Snodgrass Hill where Kershaw's men suffered terribly, Carlisle, a minister and regimental chaplain from Pendleton, South Carolina, faced the painful task of writing to Congressman Richard F. Simpson, a family friend, of the death of his son.

Ringgold Geo R R
Sept 22nd 1863.
My dear Bro Simpson

It is my mournful duty to communicate to you and your dear family the fact that your son and my dear young friend, Tally, fell on the bloody field of Sunday last, 20th inst. He was shot through the heart by a minnie ball, his left arm was broken, and either a grape or canister shot passed through his head, supposed to be after he fell. He was doing his duty and met his fate as a brave soldier. He fell with his face to the foe.

I buried him yesterday, putting him away as carefully as the circumstances allowed. I placed him by the side of Capt Williams whom you know. The grave is marked. It is near the home of R. H. Dyer, Walker County, Geo, 4 miles from Crawfish Springs. Harry Miller's boy, Jim, was with me, and should you at any time desire to remove him, Jim can identify the spot.

My Bro, you have my prayers and sympathies under this sore bereavement, for though I know that as much as possible you were prepared for such an event, yet you can but mourn for your first born and noble son. I feel as though I too had lost a child. I have known him since he was a boy, and then he was the son of you whom I number among my dearest friends. May God's grace sustain you and the family and enable you to say "Thy will be done."

Tally was a good soldier & loved by every one for his gentle demeanor. Few have fallen more lamented. I had several close conver-

"We must drop a soldier's tear upon the graves of the noble men who have fallen by our sides."

sations with [him] on his religious condition, and I assure you you have good grounds to hope that he is now in the heavenly land. I believe he tried to live right, and he died in the discharge of duty. I hope to see you before long and will give you whatever additional particulars I may. . . .

Yours in sadness
John M. Carlisle

Taliaferro Simpson of the 3d South Carolina was only 24 when he was killed at the foot of Snodgrass Hill and buried in a grave shared with a comrade. They were disinterred later and moved to family plots in Pendleton, South Carolina.

GENERAL BRAXTON BRAGG
COMMANDER, ARMY OF TENNESSEE

In this message to his troops two days after Chickamauga, Bragg praises them for their hard-won victory while hinting at bloody work ahead. But he issued no orders for a major attack on the Federals in Chattanooga. The officers in his command fired off angry letters to President Davis demanding Bragg's removal, to no avail. The cantankerous general would command the Army of Tennessee until recalled to Richmond in early 1864 to serve as Davis' military adviser.

Headquarters Army of Tennessee
Field of Chickamauga, September 22, 1863.
It has pleased Almighty God to reward the valor and endurance of our troops by giving to our arms a complete victory over the enemy's superior numbers. Homage is due and is rendered unto Him who giveth not the battle to the strong.

Soldiers, after two days of severe battle, preceded by heavy and important outpost affairs, you have stormed the barricades and breastworks of the enemy, and driven before you in confusion and disorder an army largely superior in numbers, and whose constant theme was your demoralization and whose constant boast was your defeat. Your patient endurance under privations, your fortitude and your valor, displayed at all times and under all trials, have been meetly rewarded. Your commander acknowledges his obligations, and promises to you in advance the country's gratitude. But your task is not ended. We must drop a soldier's tear upon the graves of the noble men who have fallen by our sides and move forward. Much has been accomplished. More remains to be done before we can enjoy the blessings of peace and freedom.

Braxton Bragg.

PRIVATE BENJAMIN R. GLOVER
6TH FLORIDA INFANTRY, TRIGG'S BRIGADE

Thirty-one-year-old Glover was a planter and engineer from Greenwood, Florida, when he signed up to fight for the Confederacy. In the midst of murderous fire on the 19th, Glover saw many of his comrades fall in battle. Despite taking a hit on the head, Glover was none the worse for wear—a plight, the hapless soldier lamented, that would keep him in the fighting.

Ringold Sept the 22, 1863
    Dear Betty
    I expect you are getting uneasy about us by this time. We got in the fight last Saturday. We came out better than I expected. I was nocked down by a spent ball which did not hurt me very long. It gave me the head ache for a day or two, but I am as well as ever this morning. Dr Holden sent me with some of the wounded down the rail road. I do not now where they will be sent, but I supose to Atlanta or Columbus, one. I will write to you as soon as I get there. I am going to put on a long face and limp about when I get there and try and get a furlow, but I look so well I am afraid I will fail. . . . I will write in a few days. I am well.
    Yours B R Glover

PRIVATE BENJAMIN MABREY
82D INDIANA INFANTRY, CONNELL'S BRIGADE

Mabrey answered the call to arms in August 1862, leaving behind his wife, Louisa, and infant daughter, Alice. He was enraged by the loss of his knapsack and, along with it, his family's photographs during the battle. He was somewhat mollified later when he had occasion to take a Rebel's haversack during the Battle of Missionary Ridge.

September the 24 1863
    At Chattanga
    dear wife: it is with great plasure that i onst more lift my pen to let you now that i am still alive and in tarable gud helth although nearly worn out. i have lost so much sleap latley and bin run so hard. Well, deare wife, we have had an aful hard fight and lost a greadeal of our men. We was in the fight last saterday and last sunday. our redgement was badley cut up. . . . it was the hardest fight that ever was none in the same lengeth of time. we have now fell back on Chattanuga and are bisy fortifing. we are agoing to hold this place or die on the ground. they are now falling back but thay may come again. we are redy for them. we have not lost nere as meny men yet as thay have. thay have a larger force than we have but we will Whip them or die atriing. i was vary luckey my self. i only got one shot in my left sholder . . . but the skin on my neck and ben Wildman got one through his pance gist but

Benjamin Glover's hat bears the entry and exit holes made by a spent ball during the battle. The shot knocked Glover down and kept him out of commission for a couple of days. The felt hat is missing its bands and appears to have been stretched and folded for storage.

"Thare was but fore men in our Company when we Quit fighting asunday evening."

CORPORAL MILTON BARRETT
3D BATTALION GEORGIA SHARPSHOOTERS, WOFFORD'S BRIGADE

One of three brothers in the service, Barrett was 31 when his unit went to reinforce Bragg's troops in Tennessee. The 3d arrived too late to fight at Chickamauga, but in late September the men found themselves on duty near Chattanooga, where the Yankees were holed up. Writing to his relatives, Barrett minces no words expressing his opinion of his commanding general.

to the skin. me and Ben Wild Man shot one hundard and twenty roundes apeas at them. thare was but fore men in our Company when we Quit fighting asunday evening. thare was about fiftey houls shot through our flag. our flag Carier was abrave man. Well, Lou, i must tell you something about you and Alis. the rebes sons of bitches got you both and my nap sack and all of my Close onley what i have on. they got my paper and envelops and ink and everything i had but i will make it all right with them yet for that for i will take twist as much from them the first Chans i get. i got revenge from them for that. i shot one of them from behind our one brest wirks. well, deare Wife, i now will have to Close. so gud by. take gud care of your self and dont be oneasy about me. Ben Mabrey

to Lou Mabrey

Sept the 24th 1863
On the Battlefield near Chattanooga Ten

Dear Brother and sister   I seit my self behind a bluff to pertect me from the Yankee bums that have bin a whirling a round us in grand stile this morning.

i have bin on the front line two days a poping a way. on last tuesday even we had a hard crurmish had several kild and wounded. we did not get hear in time to take a part in the battle last Sat and Sunday. i past over the Battle field last monday. it was a terable slauter. the dead lay thick for a bout three miles. the Yankees have made a stand hear at this place. the right of ther line rest on the lookout mountain and the left rest on the river. tha are strongly fortified hear and have all ready open two battles on us. we have no hight for battle. we will have to flank them by crossing the rivor or fall back a few miles. i can not tel what our genreals aim to do but i am shore tha will take us thrue right. Jinkins Brigade took ther place on the line last night. i have not saw any of them yet.

the Yankees is advancen. i must lay down my pen and go to shooting.

September the 25th   we had a lively time last night. we had a heavy crurmishing for three hours. we drove ther crurmishinges in and kill sevrel. we had non kild a few wounde. every thing is quite this morn-

ing. our line of Battle have move back a bout one mile and ar a fortifying. we still hold the lines that we first establish. we will have to fall
back a few miles to drive the enemy out. Bragg is not the genral that
Lee is and the western army cant fight like the virgina army. if genral
Lee was hear he would have had the yankees drove out of Tennesee.

these lines leves me well. i will close hopeing to hear from you soon.
i am a ever your loving Brother

Milton Barrett

MAJOR CLINTON M. WINKLER

4TH TEXAS INFANTRY, ROBERTSON'S BRIGADE

*Soon after the Federals fell back
to Chattanooga, Winkler and his
comrades on Lookout Mountain
confronted increasingly fortified
Union lines as they looked down
from their position. Winkler's
appraisal of the situation and his
dour predictions in this letter were
to prove all too correct.*

Camp near Chattanooga
September 27, 1863. . . .
On Friday last a party, of which I was one, obtained permission
to visit Lookout Mountain, and about noon, the day being beautiful,
set out and, in the course of an hour, had ascended as far as our horses
could carry us, and dismounting, were climbing up its steep and rugged
sides, when I disengaged myself from the balance of the party and sat
down upon a shelving rock, to contemplate the grandest scene my eyes
ever beheld.

Looking away to the northward, the Tennessee River could be seen
winding its way through the mountain range southward, until it seemed
to empty itself into the foot of the mountain where I sat, it being so
high and steep, as seemingly, to overhang and exclude from view the
river sweeping its base. The town of Chattanooga, situated on the east
side some half mile from the river, is plainly seen, together with the
large depot and railroad creeping down the valley, while across a large
horse-shoe bend of the river, in which the town is located, may be
traced the line of fortifications some time since evacuated by General
Bragg, and within which Rosecrans has taken shelter since his defeat at
Chickamauga. The enemy's encampment, along and within the heavy
works, are plainly visible to the naked eye, and viewed through a glass
presented a scene of life and bustle, interesting to contemplate, especially when we consider them our mortal enemies.

Their batteries are planted and frowning down upon us, their long
lines of bayonets glistening in the sun, their rows of tents, the cloud of
dust that is constantly ascending as they move to and fro, as officers
dash along the lines, or their trains of wagons passing down to the pontoon bridge, and crossing the river, lose themselves among the mountains to the right, the whole surrounded and surmounted by mountains
grand and gloomy, and as I gazed in amazement at the scene I thought
of the exclamation of Bascomb at the falls of Niagara: "God of grandeur,
what a sight!"—almost bewildered by the beauty spread out before me.

I do not believe it is the intention of our general to make another di-
rect attack at present, but to cut off Rosecrans' supplies and compel him
to come out of his stronghold and give us a fair fight in an open field.

We have greatly strengthened our position by throwing up earthworks, behind which we are safe from any shelling the enemy may hon-
or us with. The opinion prevails that when our artillery opens upon the
place, Chattanooga will become too warm for the cold blood of the
North, but I have no confidence in shelling them out. I believe, unless
we interrupt their communication, so as to compel them to withdraw,
we will be compelled to storm their works to get at them. There is little
likelihood that General Rosecrans will attack now that we are fortified.
I fear we have been too tardy in our movements; we should have followed up the victory of the 20th, before the enemy had time to recover
from the shock of defeat.

MAJOR GENERAL JOHN M. PALMER
Division Commander, Army of the Cumberland

Late on September 21, Palmer and his division began to fortify against the Rebels gathered on Lookout Mountain and Missionary Ridge. The following morning the Illinois lawyer and legislator watched with trepidation as Confederate guns massed on the heights. Consternation turned into complacency when the artillery barrage aimed at the Federals made more noise than damage.

The Rebel army appeared on Mission Ridge to our front, and about the same time they took possession on Lookout Mountain, which at a distance of less than two miles overlooked the city. . . . there were probably a hundred guns of different caliber looking into our camps and threatening our annihilation. I will never forget the feeling of awe with which I contemplated this spectacle; and as all parts of our camps seemed equally exposed to danger, I determined to take a position where I could watch the "grand opening." I confess I expected that from the commanding position of the Rebel artillery, hundreds of feet above us, and within what seemed to be easy range of all points in the city, our loss in killed and wounded would be heavy. With this impression on my mind, I seated myself with a few officers on one side of the earthworks on my line where I could observe all points on the Rebel line, and waited for what I imagined would be the coming storm. I did not wait long until the Rebel guns at all points along their line opened as if by a single command, and then in a few moments the roar of the cannon on the hills was repeated by the bursting of the shells high up in the air, and near to and upon the earth around us. My first impression, produced by the roar and apparent confusion, was, that the artillery had inflicted immense injury, but, after looking in every direction, I could not see a sign of harm. After the first volley, the fire from the hills was kept up slowly, but regularly, so that it was comparatively easy to watch its effect. For a half hour, perhaps, our attention was active, but as we saw no evidence of injury done by it, our apprehensions relaxed, so that I noticed many men, who at first seemed excited and alarmed, sound asleep.

Viewed from Lookout Mountain, the Tennessee River arcs around Chattanooga and the entrenched Federals. From Lookout Mountain and Missionary Ridge, Bragg began to bombard the Union army and choke off its main supply lines.

CHIEF MUSICIAN WILLIAM J. WORSHAM

19TH TENNESSEE INFANTRY, STRAHL'S BRIGADE

Facing the Yankees on the outskirts of Chattanooga, Worsham, a regimental fife major who had been in the service for just over two years, saw little peril in being so close to the enemy. Sporadic exchanges of artillery fire did minimal damage, and soldiers on both sides considered their proximity to one another a source of entertainment.

Bragg and Rosecrans settled down to work with pick and spade, directly under each others' guns with all their might as if preparing a grave each one for the other. Bragg kept pushing the enemy's lines in on the city until he held the river from Lookout Point to about half way to the city and from Sherman Heights to the river above. For days the videttes of each army stood in two hundred yards of and gazed at each other like grim monsters. The valley out and around Chattanooga was literally blockaded with breast works and plowed up with rifle pits. The crest of Mission Ridge, its base and sides were furrowed with rifle pits and covered with cannon. Every now and then from the summit of Lookout Mountain were sent savage, hissing shells which would fall and burst in the camp of the enemy. For days the pickets of each army sat in their "Gopher Pits" cracking jokes with each other, while from the top of Mission Ridge and the rocky peak of Lookout went shrieking messengers of death over their heads unnoticed and uncared for by them, and the signal flags from the mountain tops talk with each other in their silent way over the enemy's camp.

A peculiar scene is here presented in the two encampments of supposed hostile foes; both armies were under the range of a single shot; the bands of each played for the entertainment of the other; while the sweet notes of "Dixie" were wafted towards the city over the encampment of the enemy, they were met by those of "Yankee Doodle" coming over to us. Another uncommon feature of these two encampments was while the enemy could plainly see the men and officers moving around Bragg's headquarters, we in turn from the top of Lookout and the ridge with glasses could see what the Yankees had for dinner.

PRIVATE JOHN W. COTTON

10TH CONFEDERATE CAVALRY, DAVIDSON'S BRIGADE

As the Confederates besieged Chattanooga, Cotton, a 31-year-old father of seven, took time to write to his wife, Mariah. He would remain with his regiment until its surrender at Bentonville, North Carolina, in 1865. Cotton then returned to Alabama to farm, only to die of measles a year later.

Tennessee Camps near Chattanooga September the 29. 1863 Dear and most beloved wife and family I once more take my pen in hand to try to rite you a few more lines to try to let you no where I am and what I am doing I am well and doing as well as any can in the place I am in our regiment is in site of the yankeys all the time and have been for fore days they are in there brest works here at chattanooga and we are standing picket around them in gun shot of them and we have some fireing backwards and forwards at them but they wont come out nor we wont go to them our men are planting there cannons as fast as they can to try to shell them out of there brest works but I dont no how they will come out we have got the advantage of a big hill to shell them from and the lookout mountain we can here there drums and fifes and horns and here them crossing the river on their pontoon bridge and we can go out on a big hill and see all over there fortifications and them too they say that there is a heap of our forces crossing the river to cut them off from there pervisions but I dont no how many I think ould brag is trying to get them out of chattanooga without a fite if he can it will bee the best for if we have to whip them out we will loose a many a man and mayby get whiped I think they are fortifying on the other side of the river it may bee some time before we get them away from here if we get them away at all. . . . I stood picket the other nite in shooting distance of the yankeys there was three of us on the same post and one stood while the others slept the yankeys say we have whiped

"In a few moments the surgeons did the work, and left me with a lasting recollection of Chickamauga's bloody field."

them the worst they ever have been I reckon I have said enough about the yankeys I had rather reed a letter from you than rite about them a weak I have not got nary letter from you yet and there ant no use in trying to tell how bad I want to here from you all. . . . I dont no what to rite unless I could here from you di-rect your next letter to tennessee Chickamogga station nothing more at present only I remain your true devoted husband til death dont bee uneasy about me

   John W Cotton

PRIVATE FRANK T. RYAN
1st Arkansas Mounted Rifles (Dismounted), McNair's Brigade

Wounded on the 19th, Ryan suffered for 18 hours before his leg was amputated. After the surgery Ryan would endure a two-week wait before he could be moved. As he lay in the hospital camp, his only real comfort was a blanket taken off a dead Federal at Murfreesboro nine months before. Ryan preserved it for his children.

On reaching the hospital camp I inquired for our regimental surgeon—Dr. Hussy—who had solemnly promised me that, in the event I was ever wounded, he would make a critical examination of the same, and ascertain for certain that amputation was actually necessary before such should be done. I had exacted this promise of him for the reason that I had seen so much unnecessary amputation that I wanted to know sure, should I be wounded, that it was absolutely necessary. Soon after reaching the hospital camp, Dr. Hussy made his appearance whereupon I reminded him of his promise, and asked him to examine my wound. During the whole time he was making the examination I was watching his countenance closely to see if I could detect any signs of his opinion, at the same time was questioning him. He made me no reply, but walked off and left me. Soon after the brigade surgeon came and made a thorough examination. He made no reply to my questions

but finishing, walked off as Dr. Hussy had done. The division surgeon came next, and examined my wound as the other two had done, but made me no reply, and walked away without giving me any satisfaction. Soon Dr. Hussy returned and said that a thorough and complete examination had been made, to which I agreed, and remarked that I had a feeling recollection of the same. The doctor further said that the leg would have to be amputated, as there was no hopes of saving it, to which I replied: "There is no use of being in a hurry about it, is there, doctor?" He quickly said: "Yes, it must be done at once; it has already been postponed too long and should have had earlier attention."

Very near where I was lying was the so-called amputating table. It was constructed in this wise: Four sharpened posts, forked at one end, was driven in the ground with pieces laid across at each end upon these; laid lengthwise were small saplings, a sufficient number of them to make it the proper width, over these were thrown a blanket. This was what the surgeons operated on. Already had they been at their bloody and ghastly work for one whole day and night, and beside this rudely arranged affair, lying in heaps, were arms, legs, fingers, and other members of the body, that presented a sickly looking sight and to one who was about to undergo the same, it had anything but an inspiring effect. The sight of the doctors, too, had a tendency to weaken one's nerves. There they stood with their coats off, their shirt sleeves rolled up to their elbows, their shirt fronts bespattered with blood, with their sharp and glistening instruments lying around.

Soon after Dr. Hussy had informed me that I must submit to an amputation, I was taken up by four comrades, and placed upon the amputating table, where, in a few moments the surgeons did the work, and left me with a lasting recollection of Chickamauga's bloody field. Soon thereafter I was removed from the amputating table, and laid upon a small pile of straw, where I lay and suffered such agonizing pain as no language can describe for fourteen days. My wound was of such dangerous nature, it being above the knee, and the doctors afraid of hemorrhage, that not until fourteen days after the fight was I removed.

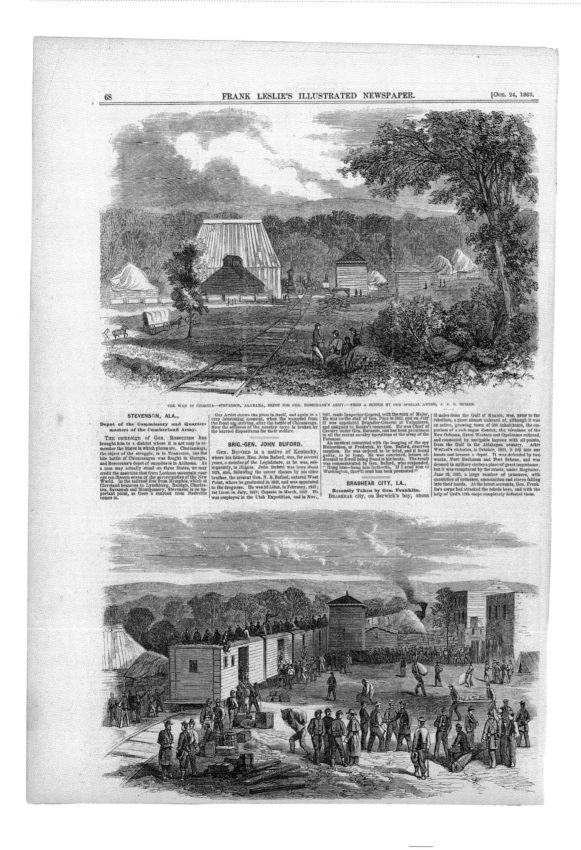

These two engravings from Frank Leslie's Illustrated Newspaper portray the Union-controlled railroad depot at Stevenson, Alabama, nearly 40 miles southwest of Chattanooga. In the bottom view, carloads of wounded Federal soldiers pull into town after the Battle of Chickamauga. The Nashville & Chattanooga Railroad ran through the town, so Stevenson also served as Rosecrans' main supply base before and after the Battle of Chickamauga. Because their rail and river routes to Chattanooga were cut by Confederate shelling from Lookout Mountain and Missionary Ridge, the Yankees had to move supplies by mule-drawn wagons overland along a 60-mile trail.

LIEUTENANT ISAAC H. C. ROYSE

115TH ILLINOIS INFANTRY, WHITAKER'S BRIGADE

Wounded in the left shoulder on the 20th, Royse sought medical attention in Chattanooga two days later. He was treated by a surgeon who "had neither eaten nor slept since the battle, but with many others had constantly worked day and night, being sustained by the excitement and an occasional sip of brandy."

he siege was on at once. Very soon the Confederates had taken position on Missionary Ridge, with their advance line extending across the valley to Lookout Mountain, threateningly near our works. The Union forces were working night and day putting the old rebel forts in order, building new ones, digging trenches and throwing up earthworks. The whole place was on "rush orders." As early as the 24th the Confederates were on Lookout Mountain and had taken possession of the road to Bridgeport. Thus our lines of communication to Nashville were cut off, except the very difficult one over Walden's Ridge and down Sequatchie Valley, a distance of seventy-five miles of little used mountain roads to Stevenson, Ala.

The difficulty of securing supplies for such a large army was at once apparent, and the danger that the Confederates who were daily receiving large reenforcements would attempt to take the place by storm, made it imperative that all the wounded who were able to travel should be sent to the rear. The danger of the situation becoming known to the wounded through the excited surgeons and nurses, what was very nearly a stampede to the North began on the 23rd. Every man at all capable for the journey, and very many so badly wounded that to attempt it was at the imminent risk of life, scrambled for a chance to get away. All the ambulances and wagons available were soon filled. Hundreds with arms and legs bandaged, and many more or less severely wounded but whose wounds had received no attention, took to the

road afoot. And thus the crowds streamed over the pontoon bridge and up the slopes of Walden's Ridge. The jolting of the ambulances and wagons was excruciating to the badly wounded, but regardless of the cries of pain the procession moved on. A dozen or more died that night and were buried in rude graves, without coffins or ceremony, on the summit of the ridge.

In early October, Confederate nurse Kate Cumming traveled to a hospital in Ringgold, Georgia. In her diary she wrote of treating the wounded, "some of whom were suffering for want of water. They all seemed perfectly resigned, the more so as we had been victorious. How they seemed to glory in it!"

"After it was all over I and my brothers picked up as many bullets as we could find and carried 'em home."

Found on Horseshoe Ridge some 20 years after the battle, this brass eagle finial topped the flagstaff of a Federal regiment engaged in the desperate fighting on September 20. Seven skulls found near the eagle attest to the gallant resistance of the color guard before they were overrun by the onrushing Confederates.

ANONYMOUS CONFEDERATE SOLDIER'S SON

After the battle, the family of the boy whose account appears here was put at risk by Confederate foragers who appropriated their livestock. "Things were so unsettled that several families here decided to refugee, and our family was one 'em," the boy recalled years later. They moved in with relatives some 90 miles farther south and did not return until after the Confederate surrender two years later.

After it was all over I and my brothers picked up as many bullets as we could find and carried 'em home. Among other things we come across a broken cannon cassion with a box on it that had a hundred little sacks of powder inside. Each sack held a pound or two—just a load. We had fun with those sacks for a month, I guess. We'd string the powder from one of 'em along on a plank and touch a match to it to see it burn. Sometimes we'd wet it, and then it would fiz and sparkle as it burned on the plank. We did n't know the danger of the thing. One of us found a gun. The barrel was bent as if some one had struck it against a tree. We picked up several boxes of cartridges in the woods, and we fired the cartridges off in that bent gun. Bumbshells were lyin' around everywhere, and I know Mother pried the tap out of one with a table knife. That was pretty risky, and so was our fooling with the gun.

LIEUTENANT GEORGE B. GUILD

4TH TENNESSEE CAVALRY, WHEELER'S CORPS

By moonlight one night in late September, 5,000 Confederate cavalry forded the Tennessee River about 30 miles northeast of Chattanooga, seeking to intercept a Federal supply train on its way to that besieged city. Guild recalls the action that ensued a few days later when the horsemen found their quarry.

The command then moved toward Middle Tennessee across the mountains into the Sequatchie Valley, where we went into camp for the night at a crossroads. Nothing of note occurred during the day. About daylight the following morning we were aroused by an order to saddle up and mount our horses, as the bugle sounded "boots and saddles." In a few moments more we were moving down the valley at a rapid rate, not knowing at the time what was up.

A few miles away we commenced overhauling Federal wagons, partially plundered; then the cry of a wagon train was raised. As the pace quickened, these captures thickened along the way, and after going ten or twelve miles down the valley to the vicinity of Jasper, there opened the richest scene that the eye of a cavalryman can behold. Along the side of the mountain hundreds of large Federal wagons were standing, with their big white covers on them like so many African elephants, solemn in their stately grandeur. They had been rushed up there by the teamsters and abandoned.

The sketch portrays an attack by Wheeler's Rebel cavalry on a Federal supply train in the Sequatchie Valley northwest of Chattanooga on October 2. After scattering the Yankee escort, the Rebels spent hours looting and burning the wagons until driven off by Union cavalry. "There was a delicious quota of sutlers' wagons filled with good things to eat and wear," wrote Colonel Avery of the 4th Georgia, "and the hungry and soiled Confederates went after the unwonted luxuries with a gusto born of long deprivation."

This was too rich a bonanza to be left without an escort; and in a few minutes the rifles sounded from the mountain sides, indicating that we would have to do some fighting for such booty. Men were dismounted in haste and hurried to the right and left. A vigorous fire was kept up for a while when the enemy, seeing that they were greatly outnumbered, surrendered after some casualties on both sides. The escort numbered 1,200, with many drivers of the wagons. Some of them had escaped by cutting loose the mules and mounting them.

We knew that there was a large infantry force not many miles away, and we set to work destroying everything at once. Orders were given that no plunder was to be carried off. This, however, was but partially enforced. The wagons were loaded with all manner of clothing and rations for the army of General Rosecrans. Among the wagons were a number belonging to sutlers, with rich stores of all kinds. The result of the capture was seven hundred and fifty wagons, twenty-six hundred fat mules and twelve hundred prisoners. The wagons, or the most of them, were loaded with rations for the army. The enemy was afraid to risk railroad transportation, and was endeavoring to provision their army at Chattanooga by means of wagons from McMinnville. It had rained the night before and left the roads so slippery that the wagons could not go over the steep mountain pass.

Such of the mules as we could not take off were destroyed. The wagons and the greater part of their contents were destroyed on the spot, the debris covering acres of ground. I was particularly struck with the fine harness that had been stripped from the mules, as it lay chin-deep over ten acres of ground. Such a calamity as this would have been most seriously felt by us, and would have retarded movements for months; but with "Uncle Sam," with all the world at his back, it made no perceptible difference. If it created a ripple of discomfort anywhere, we never had the satisfaction of knowing it.

"The private and the major-general rode on side by side down the Sequatchie Valley road 'after the enemy' and munching cheese and crackers."

PRIVATE JOHN A. WYETH
4TH ALABAMA CAVALRY, RUSSELL'S BRIGADE

Wyeth recalled the October 2 attack on the Federal wagon train. "Some of the wagons were overturned, blocking the road in places, some of the mules still standing, some fallen and tangled in the harness, and all in inextricable confusion." Amid the chaos, Wyeth grabbed a chance for a small repast, which he generously shared with his corps commander.

After a run of six or seven miles, I ventured to stop for a few minutes to help myself to a tempting piece of cheese and some crackers which I saw in one of the wagons. Filling my haversack, I was on the point of remounting when General Wheeler galloped up, sword in hand, and said to me, "Get in your saddle and go on after the enemy." As he and I were the only Confederates in sight just then, I said, "All right, General. Have some cheese," and the private and the major-general rode on side by side down the Sequatchie Valley road "after the enemy" and munching cheese and crackers.

By this time the smoke of the burning train was visible for many miles, and soon the explosions of fixed ammunition, with which a number of wagons were loaded, sounded along the valley road, not unlike the firing of artillery in action.

The capture and destruction of this immense train was one of the greatest achievements of General Wheeler's cavalry. Its loss was keenly felt by the Federals, for it added to the precarious situation of the army in Chattanooga, and reduced rations to a cracker a day per man for several days in succession.

PRIVATE PETER B. KELLENBERGER
10TH INDIANA INFANTRY, CROXTON'S BRIGADE

Although an occasional shelling by Confederates on Lookout Mountain might make things unpleasant within the Federal encampment in Chattanooga, Kellenberger writes of much greater concerns. By mid-October, Bragg's stranglehold on the Federal supply lines had taken its toll, and the loss of the wagons to the Rebel cavalry attack earlier in the month had become more keenly felt in the Union camps.

Our boys are very poorly off for clothing having piled their knapsacks in the fight, and lost all but what they had on their backs. So far we have been very short of rations. Part of our train was captured by the Rebs. The road is long and miserable bad, and what teams were left are worn down. Half rations has been the go for some weeks and no clothing—However they are bringing supplies to within 7 miles by boat now, and already we are beginning to do better.

Our position is considered impregnable, and in time all will go right —The Rebs have a battery on a point of Lookout Mountain with which they shell our train on the other side of the river, and occasionally throw a shell at some of our forts, but it all amounts to nothing— There has been not less than twenty shots fired since I commenced this letter. I can see the smoke of their guns from my tent door. This is an every day thing and we pay no attention to it anymore. They spoiled some dinner for us one day that was cooking in the quarters but have not shelled our camp lately.

At this place has been the hardest siege we have ever had in the way of short supplies, not a can of corn is to be had nearer than 40 miles and not a dimes worth of anything to eat can be bought at stores, or sutlers. If it was not for the beef driven here on foot, we would have a serious time indeed—Half rations hard bread, and pork, and quarter rations coffee and sugar has been the allowance until this morning when it is raised to 2/3 all round. Daily beef, and a little mixed vegetable for soup —Mind you I am not making long faces, only telling you what it is to be a soldier—Teamsters watch their horses as close as you would have your gold dust.

SERGEANT ROBERT D. JAMISON
45TH TENNESSEE INFANTRY, BROWN'S BRIGADE

In mid-October, between lethargic exchanges of artillery fire, Jamison wrote to his wife, Camilla (standing, left), recalling happier times. Being immobilized in Chattanooga wore on the rank and file, who, like Jamison, could not begin to guess where and when their next fight would be.

Near Chattanooga,
October 10th, 1863
Mrs. C. P. Jamison

My own dear, darling wife,

After another long rainy spell of weather I again embrace the opportunity of writing to you this beautiful sunshiny morning. . . . The weather now reminds me very much of the time we were up at Lookout several years ago when we were *sweethearts*. But now, instead of that place being one of amusement and enjoyment, it is covered with the guns of Lieut. Gen. Longstreet's corps opening fire every once in a while upon Chattanooga, near its center, dealing death and destruction to Rosa's Yanks. We are still here in sight of the army, as we have been for nearly a month, and as a general thing are as quiet as if there was not a Yankee in a thousand miles of us. When there is any excitement at all in the lines of warfare, the artillery does it all, and we gather round on the most prominent points of the ridge and witness the shooting. It is one of the most magnificent sights I ever saw to witness the movements of these two large armies. Just imagine two large armies of one hundred and fifty thousand men in the same valley in sight of each other, and everything quiet as to fighting. It is indeed a strange circumstance, but each one is afraid to attack the other in his present situation, and it seems each one is afraid to make a move in any direction. When we first came here nearly every one thought we would stay here but a few days at farthest, and then would flank Rosa. However, we are astonished to find ourselves here yet with just the same prospect of leaving as at first, with the exception that we have one or two pontoon bridges completed. For what purpose we know not. Therefore, we are in as much doubt about what we are going to do as we were when we first got here. There are many opinions but we know nothing for certain. . . . Never since I have been in the army have I seen the time that we knew as little of what we were going to do as we are just at the present time. . . .

    Your devoted husband,

    R. D. Jamison

ILLUSTRATIONS OF THE WAR IN AMERICA, BY OUR SPECIAL ARTIST.

VIEW OF CHATTANOOGA AND THE FEDERAL LINES FROM THE LOWER RIDGE OF LOOKOUT MOUNTAIN.

VIEW OF CHATTANOOGA AND THE FEDERAL POSITIONS FROM THE LEFT CENTRE OF THE CONFEDERATE LINES.—SEE PAGE 662.

THE ILLUSTRATED LONDON NEWS

664

Dec. 26, 1863

The engravings show views of besieged Chattanooga (background) from different Rebel vantage points on the slopes of Lookout Mountain. Union and Rebel positions around the city remained unchanged for weeks following the battle. Only after the reinvigoration of the Federal armies under Major General Ulysses S. Grant would the siege stalemate at Chattanooga be broken.

"But it seems to me that the *élan* of the Southern soldier was never seen after Chickamauga—that brilliant dash which had distinguished him was gone forever."

LIEUTENANT GENERAL DANIEL H. HILL
CORPS COMMANDER, ARMY OF TENNESSEE

Although the censure of General Bragg by his officers was nearly unanimous, Hill was one of the most vocal of the critics. Having quarreled violently with Bragg after Chickamauga, Hill was relieved of duties and returned to his native North Carolina. His harsh criticism of Bragg, demonstrated by his account here, cost him his promotion, and he never received another substantial command.

There was no more splendid fighting in '61, when the flower of the Southern youth was in the field, than was displayed in those bloody days of September, '63. But it seems to me that the *élan* of the Southern soldier was never seen after Chickamauga—that brilliant dash which had distinguished him was gone forever. He was too intelligent not to know that the cutting in two of Georgia meant death to all his hopes. He knew that Longstreet's absence was imperiling Lee's safety, and that what had to be done must be done quickly. The delay in striking was exasperating to him; the failure to strike after the success was crushing to all his longings for an independent South. He fought stoutly to the last, but, after Chickamauga, with the sullenness of despair and without the enthusiasm of hope. That "barren victory" sealed the fate of the Southern Confederacy.

U. S. Grant, shown in a sketch by Adolph Metzner, called for reinforcements on arriving in Chattanooga and established a new supply route nicknamed the Cracker Line. Reinforced, Grant attacked in late November and dislodged Bragg's forces from the mountains, sending the Rebels fleeing into Georgia.

GLOSSARY

adjutant—A staff officer assisting the commanding officer, usually with correspondence.

ambuscade—An ambush.

battery—The basic unit of artillery, consisting of four to six guns.

bee gum hat—A broad-brimmed slouch hat with a conical crown resembling a bee gum, or hive.

bivouac—A temporary encampment, or to camp out for the night.

breastwork—A temporary fortification, usually of earth and about chest high, over which a soldier could fire.

canister—A tin can containing lead or iron balls that scattered when fired from a cannon. Used primarily in defense of a position as an antipersonnel weapon.

cap—Technically a percussion cap. A small metal cover, infused with chemicals and placed on the hollow nipple of a rifle or revolver. When struck by the hammer the chemicals explode, igniting the powder charge in the breech.

carbine—A lightweight, short-barreled shoulder arm used especially by cavalry.

case shot—*Case shot* properly refers to shrapnel or spherical case. The term was often used mistakenly to refer to any artillery projectile in which numerous metal balls or pieces were bound or encased together. See also *shrapnel*.

claybank horse—A horse of a yellowish color.

Colt revolving rifle—A rifle constructed on the principles of Samuel Colt's six-shot pistol. The .56-caliber, five-cylinder 1855 model weighed nine pounds 15 ounces.

Enfield rifle—The Enfield rifle musket was adopted by the British in 1853, and the North and South imported nearly one million to augment their own production. Firing a .577-caliber projectile similar to the Minié ball, it was fairly accurate at 1,100 yards.

enfilade—Gunfire that rakes an enemy line lengthwise, or the position allowing such firing.

flank—The right or left end of a military formation. Therefore, to flank is to attack or go around the enemy's position on one end or the other.

forage—To search for and acquire provisions from nonmilitary sources. To soldiers of the Civil War it often meant, simply, stealing.

garrison—A military post, especially a permanent one. Also, the act of manning such a post and the soldiers who serve there.

grapeshot—Iron balls (usually nine) bound together and fired from a cannon. Resembling a cluster of grapes, the balls broke apart and scattered on impact. Although references to grape or grapeshot are numerous in the literature, some experts claim that it was not used on Civil War battlefields.

hardtack—A durable cracker, or biscuit, made of plain flour and water and normally about three inches square and a half-inch thick.

haversack—A shoulder bag, usually strapped over the right shoulder to rest on the left hip, for carrying personal items and rations.

howitzer—A short-barreled artillery piece that fired its projectile in a relatively high trajectory.

Minié ball—The standard bullet-shaped projectile fired from the rifled muskets of the time. Designed by French army officers Henri-Gustave Delvigne and Claude-Étienne Minié, the bullet's hollow base expanded, forcing its sides into the grooves, or rifling, of the musket's barrel. This caused the bullet to spiral in flight, giving it greater range and accuracy. Appears as minie, minnie, and minni.

musket—A smoothbore, muzzleloading shoulder arm.

muster—To assemble. To be mustered in is to be enlisted or enrolled in service. To be mustered out is to be discharged from service, usually on expiration of a set time.

Napoleon—A smoothbore, muzzleloading artillery piece developed under the direction of Napoleon III. It fired a 12-pound projectile (and therefore was sometimes called a 12-pounder). The basic light-artillery weapon of both sides, Napoleons were originally cast in bronze; when that material became scarce in the South, iron was used.

Parrott guns—Muzzleloading, rifled artillery pieces of various calibers made of cast iron, with a unique wrought-iron reinforcing band around the breech. Patented in 1861 by Union officer Robert Parker Parrott, these guns were more accurate at longer range than their smoothbore predecessors.

picket—One or more soldiers on guard to protect the larger unit from surprise attack.

prolonge—A stout rope on a gun carriage that allowed soldiers to maneuver an artillery piece over short distances without having to attach it to a limber.

ration—A specified allotment of food for one person (or animal) per day. The amounts and nature of rations varied by time and place throughout the war. *Rations* may also refer simply to any food provided by the army.

rifle pits—Holes or shallow trenches dug in the ground from which soldiers could fire weapons and avoid enemy fire. Foxholes.

right shoulder shift—A position for holding a musket in which the butt of the gun was held in the right hand at just below chest height, the breech area rested on the right shoulder, and the muzzle pointed skyward. The rough equivalent of the modern *shoulder arms*.

shrapnel—An artillery projectile in the form of a hollow sphere filled with metal balls packed around an explosive charge. Developed by British general Henry Shrapnel during the Napoleonic Wars, it was used as an antipersonnel weapon. A fuse ignited the charge at a set distance from the gun, raining the balls down on the enemy. Also called spherical case.

skirmisher—A soldier sent in advance of the main body of troops to scout out and probe the enemy's position. Also, one who participated in a skirmish, a small fight usually incidental to the main action.

Spencer rifle—A repeating carbine with a seven-shot magazine, designed for the Union just before the war by Christopher M. Spencer.

spherical case—See *shrapnel*.

tattoo—Drum or bugle call signaling the time to return to quarters in the evening. Taps, initiated in 1862, calls for lights out.

vedette—A sentry on horseback.

worm fence—Also known as a snake fence, in which split rails were stacked alternately and at an angle producing a zigzagging line.

ACKNOWLEDGMENTS

The editors wish to thank the following for their valuable assistance in the preparation of this volume: Eva-Maria Ahladas, Museum of the Confederacy, Richmond; E. Burns Apfeld, Oshkosh, Wis.; Jane Grafft Apfeld, Somerville, Ohio; Joe Blunt, Chickamauga, Ga.; Keith Bohannon, East Ridge, Tenn.; Judy Bolton, Louisiana State University, Baton Rouge; Mildred Bradley, Staten Island, N.Y.; John Culp, Nashville; Greg Dainwood, Columbia, Tenn.; Randy W. Hackenburg, U.S. Army Military History Institute, Carlisle Barracks, Pa.; Corinne P. Hudgins, Museum of the Confederacy, Richmond; Mary Ison and Staff, Library of Congress, Washington, D.C.; Diane Kessler, Pennsylvania Capitol Preservation Committee, Harrisburg; Scott McKay, Roswell, Ga.; Don MacPhee, Mogodore, Ohio; Sheila A. Menzies, Tile Heritage Foundation, Healdsburg, Calif.; Sue Miller, Civil War Times Illustrated, Harrisburg, Pa.; James Ogden, Ft. Oglethorpe, Ga.; Diane Rocklin, Hamilton Packer Tile Co., Columbus, Ohio; Dana B. Shoaf, Frederick, Md.; Edward Whitson Simpson Jr., Clemson, S.C.; Jennifer Songster, Ohio Historical Society, Columbus; Christie Stanley, Kansas State Historical Society, Topeka; Kristoffer Lee Tinney, Chattanooga; Geoff Walden, Stockbridge, Ga.; Michael J. Winey, USAMHI, Carlisle Barracks, Pa.

PICTURE CREDITS

The sources for the illustrations are listed below. Credits from left to right are separated by semicolons, from top to bottom by dashes.

Dust jacket: front, Library of Congress, Neg. No. LC-B8184-10260; rear, National Portrait Gallery, Art Resource.

All calligraphy by Mary Lou O'Brian/Inkwell, Inc.

6,7: Map by Paul Salmon. 8: Collection of C. Paul Loane, copied by Arthur Soll. 15: Map by R. R. Donnelley & Sons Co., Cartographic Services. 16: Courtesy Seward R. Osborne. 17: Library of Congress. 18: Courtesy E. Burns Apfeld Collection, Oshkosh, Wis., photographed by Bill Krueger. 19: L. M. Strayer Collection, Dayton. 20: Sketch by Adolph Metzner, courtesy E. Burns Apfeld Collection, Oshkosh, Wis., photographed by Bill Krueger. 21: Philip Daingerfield Stephenson Papers, Louisiana and Lower Mississippi Valley Collections, LSU Libraries, Louisiana State University. 22: From *Generals in Gray*, by Ezra J. Warner, Louisiana State University Press, Baton Rouge, 1959. 23: Illinois State Historical Library, Springfield—Civil War Library and Museum, Philadelphia, photographed by Larry Sherer (3). 24: Painting by Horace Rawdon, courtesy Frank F. Marvin. 26: Illinois State Historical Library, Springfield. 27: Blue Acorn Press. 28: William J. Warner, Ashton, Ill.; from *The Story of the Sherman Brigade*, by Wilbur F. Hinman, published by author, 1897, copied by Philip Brandt George. 29: Frank and Marie-Thérèse Wood Print Collections, Alexandria, Va. 31: L. M. Strayer Collection, Dayton. 32: From *History of the Sixth Regiment Indiana Volunteer Infantry*, by Charles C. Bryant, published by Wm. B. Burford, Indianapolis, 1891. 33: From *With Sabre and Scalpel: The Autobiography of a Soldier and Surgeon*, by John A. Wyeth, Harper and Brothers, New York, 1914. 34: Herb Peck Jr. 35: The Jesse Ball Dupont Library, The University of the South, Sewanee, Tenn. 36: From *The Photographic History of the Civil War*, Vol. 2, edited by Francis Trevelyan Miller, published by the Review of Reviews Co., N.Y., 1911. 37: Massachusetts Commandery, Military Order of the Loyal Legion and the U.S. Army Military History Institute (MASS-MOLLUS/USAMHI), copied by A. Pierce Bounds. 39: Map by R. R. Donnelley & Sons Co., Cartographic Services. 40: From *Soldier in the West: The Civil War Letters of Alfred Lacey Hough*, edited by Robert G. Athearn, University of Pennsylvania Press, Philadelphia, 1957, copied by Philip Brandt George. 41: Courtesy E. Burns Apfeld Collection, Oshkosh, Wis., photographed by Bill Krueger (2). 42: Painting by William Travis, Smithsonian Institution, Washington, D.C., Photo No. 49433-H. 43: American Documentaries, Walpole, N.H. 44: Brad L. Pruden Collection, Marietta, Ga. 45: Frank & Marie-Thérèse Wood Print Collections, Alexandria, Va. 46: Library of Congress, Neg. No. LC-USZ62-11967. 47: Painting by William Travis, Smithsonian Institution, Washington, D.C., Photo No. 49432-G. 48: MASS-MOLLUS/USAMHI. 49: Illinois State Historical Society, Springfield, copied by Richard Baumgartner. 50: Alabama Dept. of Archives &

History, Montgomery. 51: From *The Civil War Journal and Correspondence of Matthias Baldwin Colton*, edited by Jessie Sellers Colton, Macrae-Smith, Philadelphia, 1931, copied by Philip Brandt George; From *Column South: With the Fifteenth Pennsylvania Cavalry, from Antietam to the Capture of Jefferson Davis*, compiled by Suzanne Colton Wilson, edited by J. Ferrell Colton and Antoinette G. Smith, J. F. Colton, Flagstaff, Ariz., 1960, copied by Philip Brandt George. 52: William L. Clements Library, University of Michigan. 53: Courtesy Gil Barrett, copied by Richard Baumgartner. 54: L. M. Strayer Collection, Dayton. 55: MASS-MOLLUS/USAMHI, copied by A. Pierce Bounds. 56: From *A Carolinian Goes to War: The Civil Narrative of Arthur Middleton Manigault, Brigadier General, C.S.A.*, edited by R. Lockwood Tower, University of South Carolina Press, Columbia, 1983. 58: The Western Reserve Historical Society, Cleveland. 59: Courtesy Byron J. Ihle. 60: Library of Congress, Waud Collection. 62: Map by R. R. Donnelley & Sons Co., Cartographic Services, overlay by Time-Life Books. 63: Map by Walter W. Roberts. 64, 65: MASS-MOLLUS/USAMHI, copied by A. Pierce Bounds. 66: National Portrait Gallery, Art Resource. 67: Courtesy George Wray, photographed by Larry Sherer (2). 68: From *Battles and Leaders of the Civil War*, Vol.3, edited by Robert Underwood Johnson and Clarence Cough Buel, Century, New York, 1887, copied by Philip Brandt George. 69: Herb Peck Jr., copied by Philip Brandt George; Mark Weldon Collection, Ft. Wayne, copied by Richard Baumgartner. 70: From *The Truth about Chickamauga*, by Archibald Gracie Jr., Houghton Mifflin, Boston, 1911, copied by Richard Baumgartner; L. M. Strayer Collection, Dayton. 71: From *The Civil War Letters of Col. Hans Christian Heg*, edited by Theodore C. Blegen, Norwegian-American Historical Association, Northfield, Minn., 1936. 72: From *Battles and Leaders of the Civil War*, Vol. 3, edited by Robert Underwood Johnson and Clarence Cough Buel, Century, New York, 1887, copied by Philip Brandt George. 73: L. M. Strayer Collection, Dayton, Ohio. 74, 75: Blue Acorn Press. 76: MASS-MOLLUS/USAMHI, copied by A. Pierce Bounds. 77: Frances H. Evans, Tupelo, Miss., copied by Philip Brandt George. 78: From *The Old Guard in Gray*, Press of South Carolina Toof and Co., Memphis, 1897, copied by Philip Brandt George. 79: From *Battles and Leaders of the Civil War*, Vol. 3, edited by Robert Underwood Johnson and Clarence Cough Buel, Century, New York, 1887, copied by Philip Brandt George. 80: Courtesy of the North Carolina Division of Archives and History; *Confederate Veteran*, Vol. 22, August, 1914, copied by Richard Baumgartner. 81: From *The Mountain Campaigns in Georgia*, by Joseph M. Brown, Matthews, Northrup,

Buffalo, 1895. 82: From *The Truth about Chickamauga*, by Archibald Gracie Jr., Houghton Mifflin, Boston, 1911, copied by Richard Baumgartner. 83: Carter House Museum, Franklin, Tenn., copied by Richard Baumgartner. 85: Kansas State Historical Society, Topeka. 86: The Valentine Museum, Richmond, Va. 87: The Museum of the Confederacy, Richmond, Va., photographed by Larry Sherer. 88: The State Historical Society of Wisconsin, Madison. 89: Blue Acorn Press; L. M. Strayer Collection, Dayton. 90, 91: MASS-MOLLUS/USAMHI, copied by A. Pierce Bounds. 92, 93: Pastel drawing by Sadie Waters, Tennessee State Museum, photographed by Bill LaFevor—courtesy of the Atlanta History Center, Georgia (3). 94: From "On the Field at Chickamauga," by Robert H. Hannaford, edited by Robert F. Russell, *Military Images Magazine*, Vol. IV, No.3, November-December, 1982, copied by Philip Brandt George; courtesy Stamatelos Brothers Collection, Cambridge, photographed by Larry Sherer. 95: Library of Congress, Waud Collection. 96: From *Fourteen Hundred and 91 days in the Confederate Army*, by W. W. Heartsill, edited by Bell Irvin Wiley, Broadfoot, Wilmington, N.C., 1987, copied by Philip Brandt George; MASS-MOLLUS/USAMHI, copied by A. Pierce Bounds. 98: Robert Van Dorn. 99: Library of Congress, Neg. No. LC-USZ62-47483; Museum of the Confederacy, Richmond, photographed by Larry Sherer. 100-103: Maps by R. R. Donnelley & Sons Co., Cartographic Services, overlay by Time-Life Books. 104: From *Observations of an Illinois Boy in Battle, Camp and Prisons: 1861-1865*, by Henry H. Eby, published by author, 1910, copied by Philip Brandt George; from *Confederate Veteran*, Vol. XI, No. 10, October 1903, Nashville, Tenn., copied by Philip Brandt George. 105: Blue Acorn Press. 106: Painting by Katherine Helm, courtesy Mrs. Joseph Murphy, "Helm Place," Lexington, Ky., photographed by Joey Oller. 107: L. M. Strayer Collection, Dayton. 108: Courtesy E. Burns Apfeld Collection, Oshkosh, Wis., photographed by Bill Krueger. 109: Sketch by Walton B. Taber, Tennessee State Museum, photographed by Bill LaFevor. 111: Austin History Center, Austin Public Library, Texas. 112: Library of Congress. 113: Library of Congress, Neg. No. LC-B811-2430. 114: Collection of Timothy D. Bowman, Elizabethtown, Ky. 115: Courtesy Richard F. Carlile. 116: Museum of the Confederacy, Richmond—Sketch by Frank Vizetelly, by permission of The Houghton Library, Cambridge, Mass. 117: L. M. Strayer Collection, Dayton. 118, 119: Library of Congress. 120: Frank and Marie-Thérèse Wood Print Collections, Alexandria, Va. 121: Alabama Department of Archives and History, Montgomery, photographed by Robert Fouts. 122: Library of Congress. 123: Courtesy Daniel W. Strauss;

L. M. Strayer Collection, Dayton. 124: Courtesy Illinois State Historical Library, Springfield; L. M. Strayer Collection, Dayton. 125: MASS-MOLLUS/USAMHI, copied by A. Pierce Bounds. 126, 127: Civil War Library and Museum, Philadelphia, photographed by Larry Sherer. 128, 129: Civil War Library and Museum, Philadelphia, photographed by Larry Sherer (2)—Mike Miner Collection. 130: Confederate Museum, Charleston, S.C., photographed by Michael Latil; courtesy Collection of William A. Turner, copied by Philip Brandt George. 131: Ohio Historical Society, Columbus. 132: From *The Truth about Chickamauga*, by Archibald Gracie Jr., Houghton Mifflin, Boston, 1911, copied by Richard Baumgartner. 134: *Confederate Veteran*, Vol. 17, February 1909, copied by Richard Baumgartner. 135: MASS-MOLLUS/USAMHI, copied by Richard Baumgartner. 136, 137: Artist: Harry J. Kellogg, Minnesota Historical Society, St. Paul. 138: The Western Reserve Historical Society, Cleveland. 142: Vann R. Martin Collection, Madison, Miss., copied by Richard Baumgartner. 143: Don Troiani Collection, photographed by Larry Sherer; Ed and Maureen Simpson. 144: Ed and Maureen Simpson. 145: Alabama Department of Archives and History, Montgomery, photographed by Robert Fouts; from *Benjamin Benn Mabrey: Yankee Soldier*, by Verle Procter Sutton, Crown Printers, San Bernardino, Calif., 1978, copied by Philip Brandt George. 146: From *The Confederacy Is on Her Way up the Spout: Letters to South Carolina, 1861-1864*, edited by J. Roderick Heller III and Carolynn Ayres Heller, The University of Georgia Press, Athens, 1992, copied by Philip Brandt George. 147: From *Confederate Capitol & Hood's Texas Brigade*, by A. V. Winkler, published by Eugene Von Boeckmann, Austin, 1894, copied by Richard Baumgartner. 148, 149: MASS-MOLLUS/USAMHI, copied by A. Pierce Bounds. 150: From *Yours Till Death: Civil War Letters of John W. Cotton*, edited by Lucille Griffith, University of Alabama Press, University of Alabama, 1951. 152: Frank and Marie-Thérèse Wood Print Collections, Alexandria, Va. 153: From *History of the 115th Regiment Illinois Volunteer Infantry*, by I. H. C. Royse, Windsor and Kenfield, 1900; from *Gleanings from Southland*, by Kate Cumming, Roberts & Son, Birmingham, Ala., 1895. 154: Tennessee State Museum, photographed by Bill LaFevor. 155: From *Military Annals of Tennessee, Confederate*, by John B. Lindsley, published by J. M. Lindsley and Co., Nashville, 1886, copied by Richard Baumgartner—General Research Division, The New York Public Library, Astor, Lenox and Tilden Foundations. 157: Henry D. Jamison III. 158: Frank and Marie-Thérèse Wood Print Collections, Alexandria, Va. 159: Sketch by Adolph Metzner, courtesy E. Burns Apfeld, photographed by Bill Krueger.

BIBLIOGRAPHY

BOOKS

Allardice, Bruce S. *More Generals in Gray*. Baton Rouge: Louisiana State University Press, 1995.

Andrew, A. Piatt, III. *Some Civil War Letters of A. Piatt Andrew, III*. Gloucester, Mass.: private printing, 1925.

Atkins, Smith D. *Chickamauga: Useless, Disastrous Battle*. Freeport, Ill.: Journal Printing, 1907.

Baumgartner, Richard A., and Larry M. Strayer. *Echoes of Battle: The Struggle for Chattanooga*. Huntington, W.Va.: Blue Acorn Press, 1996.

Beatty, John. *The Citizen-Soldier; Or, Memoirs of a Volunteer*. Cincinnati: Wilstach, Baldwin, 1879.

Bierce, Ambrose. *Ambrose Bierce's Civil War*. Ed. by William McCann. New York: Wings Books, 1956.

Blackburn, Theodore W. *Letters from the Front: A Union "Preacher" Regiment (74th Ohio) in the Civil War*. Dayton: Press of Morningside Bookshop, 1981.

Carnahan, James R. "Personal Recollections of Chickamauga." In *Sketches of War History, 1861-1865: Papers Read before the Ohio Commandery of the Military Order of the Loyal Legion of the United States, 1883-1886* (Vol. 1). Wilmington, N.C. Broadfoot, 1991 (reprint of 1888 edition).

Carroll, John M. *List of Field Officers, Regiments & Battalions in the Confederate States Army: 1861-1865*. Mattituck, N.Y.: J. M. Carroll & Co., 1983.

Chesnut, Mary. *Mary Chesnut's Civil War*. Ed. by C. Vann Woodward. New Haven, Conn.: Yale University Press, 1981.

Collins, R. M. *Chapters from the Unwritten History of the War between the States*. Dayton: Morningside House, 1988.

Colton, Matthias Baldwin. *The Civil War Journal and Correspondence of Matthias Baldwin Colton*. Ed. by Jessie Sellers Colton. Philadelphia: Macrae-Smith, 1931.

The Confederacy Is on Her Way up the Spout: Letters to South Carolina, 1861-1864. Ed. by J. Roderick Heller III and Carolyn Ayres Heller. Athens: University of Georgia Press, 1992.

The Confederate General (6 vols.). Ed. by William C. Davis. Harrisburg, Pa.: National Historical Society, 1991.

Connolly, James A. *Three Years in the Army of the Cumberland: The Letters and Diary of Major James A. Connolly*. Ed. by Paul M. Angle. Bloomington: Indiana University Press, 1959.

Cotton, John W. *Yours Till Death: Civil War Letters of John W. Cotton*. Ed. by Lucille Griffith. University: University of Alabama Press, 1951.

Cumming, Kate. *Kate: The Journal of a Confederate Nurse*.

Ed. by Richard Barksdale Harwell. Baton Rouge: Louisiana State University Press, 1959.

Dana, Charles A. *Recollections of the Civil War: With the Leaders at Washington and in the Field in the Sixties*. New York: D. Appleton, 1902.

Dyer, Frederick H. *A Compendium of the War of the Rebellion* (Vols. 1 and 2). Dayton: Press of Morningside Bookshop, 1979 (reprint of 1908 editions).

Eby, Henry H. *Observations of an Illinois Boy in Battle, Camp and Prisons: 1861 to 1865*. Mendota, Ill.: Henry H. Eby, 1910.

Fitch, Michael H. *Echoes of the Civil War As I Hear Them*. New York: R. F. Fenno, 1905.

Fullerton, J. S. "Reenforcing Thomas at Chickamauga." In *Battles and Leaders of the Civil War: Retreat from Gettysburg*. New York: Castle Books, 1956.

Giles, Val C. *Rags and Hope: The Recollections of Val C. Giles, Four Years with Hood's Brigade, Fourth Texas Infantry, 1861-1865*. Comp. and ed. by Mary Lasswell. New York: Coward-McCann, 1961.

Green, Johnny. *Johnny Green of the Orphan Brigade: The Journal of a Confederate Soldier*. Ed. by A. D. Kirwan. Lexington: University of Kentucky Press, 1956.

Heartsill, W. W. *Fourteen Hundred and 91 Days in the Confederate Army*. Ed. by Bell Irvin Wiley. Wilmington, N.C.: Broadfoot, 1987.

Heg, Hans Christian. *The Civil War Letters of Colonel Hans Christian Heg*. Ed. by Theodore C. Blegen. Northfield, Minn.: Norwegian-American Historical Association, 1936.

Hicks, Borden M. "Personal Recollections of the War of the Rebellion." In *Glimpses of the Nation's Struggle*. Wilmington, N.C.: Broadfoot, 1992 (reprint of 1909 edition).

Hill, Daniel H. "Chickamauga: The Great Battle of the West." In *Battles and Leaders of the Civil War: Retreat from Gettysburg*. New York: Castle Books, 1956.

Hinman, Wilbur F. *The Story of the Sherman Brigade*. Alliance, Ohio: Wilbur F. Hinman, 1897.

Hood, J. B. *Advance and Retreat: Personal Experiences in the United States & Confederate States Armies*. Ed. by Richard N. Current. Bloomington: Indiana University Press, 1959.

Hough, Alfred Lacey. *Soldier in the West: The Civil War Letters of Alfred Lacey Hough*. Ed. by Robert G. Athearn. Philadelphia: University of Pennsylvania Press, 1957.

Hughes, Nathaniel Cheairs, Jr.. *The Battle of Belmont: Grant Strikes South*. Chapel Hill: University of North Carolina Press, 1991.

Johnson, Clifton, comp. *Battleground Adventures*. Boston: Houghton Mifflin, 1915.

Kiene, Ralph E., Jr. *A Civil War Diary: The Journal of Francis A. Kiene, 1861-1864*. Kansas City, Mo.: Yearbook House, 1974.

Krick, Robert K. *Lee's Colonels: A Biographical Register of the Field Officers of the Army of Northern Virginia*. Dayton: Press of Morningside Bookshop, 1979.

Longstreet, James. *From Manassas to Appomattox: Memoirs of the Civil War in America*. Ed. by James I. Robertson Jr. Bloomington: Indiana University Press, 1960.

Magee, B. F. *History of the 72d Indiana Volunteer Infantry of the Mounted Lightning Brigade*. Ed. by William R. Jewell. Huntington, W.Va.: Blue Acorn Press, 1992 (reprint of 1882 edition).

Manigault, Arthur Middleton. *A Carolinian Goes to War: The Civil War Narrative of Arthur Middleton Manigault, Brigadier General, C.S.A.* Ed. by R. Lockwood Tower. Columbia: University of South Carolina Press, 1983.

Miller, William Bluffton. *"I Soldiered for the Union": The Civil War Diary of William Bluffton Miller*. Ed. by Robert J. Willey. N.p., n.d.

Owen, William Miller. *In Camp and Battle with the Washington Artillery of New Orleans*. Boston: Ticknor, 1885.

Palmer, John M. *Personal Recollections of John M. Palmer: The Story of an Earnest Life*. Cincinnati: Press of the Robert Clarke Co., 1901.

Quintard, C. T. *Doctor Quintard: Chaplain C.S.A. and Second Bishop of Tennessee*. Ed. by Arthur Howard Noll. Sewanee, Tenn.: University Press, 1905.

Simpson, Richard Wright, and Taliaferro Simpson. *"Far, Far from Home": The Wartime Letters of Dick and Tally Simpson, Third South Carolina Volunteers*. Ed. by Guy R. Everson and Edward W. Simpson Jr. New York: Oxford University Press, 1994.

Stanley, David S. "The Tullahoma Campaign." In *Sketches of War History, 1861-1865*. Vol. 3. Wilmington, N.C.: Broadfoot, 1991 (reprint of 1890 edition).

Stephenson, Philip Daingerfield. *The Civil War Memoir of Philip Daingerfield Stephenson, D. D.* Ed. by Nathaniel Cheairs Hughes Jr. Conway, Ark.: UCA Press, 1995.

Sutton, Verle Procter. *Benjamin Benn Mabrey: Yankee Soldier*. San Bernardino, Calif.: Crown Printers, 1978.

Thruston, Gates P. "The Crisis at Chickamauga." In *Battles and Leaders of the Civil War: Retreat from Gettysburg*. New York: Castle Books, 1956.

Tourgée, Albion W. *The Story of a Thousand*. Buffalo: S. McGerald & Son, 1896.

United States War Department:

The War of the Rebellion: A Compilation of the Official Records of the Union and Confederate Armies. Series 1, Vol. 30, 4 parts. Part 1: Reports. Washington, D.C.: Government Printing Office, 1890.

Vieux Seconde. "The Second Tennessee Regiment at Chickamauga." In *The Annals of the Army of Tennessee and Early Western History: Including a Chronological Summary of Battles and Engagements in the Western Armies of the Confederacy* (Vol. 1). Ed. by Edwin L. Drake. Nashville: A. D. Haynes, 1878.

Warner, Ezra J.:
Generals in Blue: Lives of the Union Commanders. Baton Rouge: Louisiana State University Press, 1964.
Generals in Gray: Lives of the Confederate Commanders. Baton Rouge: Louisiana State University Press, 1959.

Watkins, Sam R. *"Co. Aytch": A Side Show of the Big Show.* New York: Collier Books, 1962.

West, Granville C. "Personal Recollections of the Chickamauga Campaign." In *War Papers Being Read before the Commandery of the District of Columbia Military Order of the Loyal Legion of the United States* (Vol. 4). Wilmington, N.C.: Broadfoot, 1993.

Wilder, John T. "Paper of John T. Wilder." In *Sketches of War History, 1861-1865.* Wilmington, N.C.: Broadfoot, 1993.

Wilson, George S. "Wilder's Brigade of Mounted Infantry in the Tullahoma-Chickamauga Campaigns." In *War Talks in Kansas: A Series of Papers Read before the Kansas Commandery of the Military Order of the Loyal Legion of the United States.* Wilmington, N.C.: Broadfoot, 1992 (reprint of 1906 edition).

Wilson, Suzanne Colton (comp.). *Column South: With the Fifteenth Pennsylvania Cavalry, from Antietam to the Capture of Jefferson Davis.* Ed. by J. Ferrell Colton and Antoinette G. Smith. Flagstaff, Ariz.: J. F. Colton., 1960.

PERIODICALS

Anderson, Kellar. "The Rebel Yell." *Confederate Veteran,* January 1893.

Chalaron, Joseph A. "Memories of Major Rice E. Graves, C.S.A." *The Daviess County Historical Quarterly,* January 1985.

Coxe, John. "Chickamauga." *Confederate Veteran,* August 1922.

Hannaford, Robert H. "On the Field at Chickamauga." *Military Images,* November-December 1982.

Jarman, Robert A. "The History of Company K, 27th Mississippi Infantry." *Aberdeen Examiner,* March 7, 1890.

McMurray, W. J. "The Gap of Death at Chickamauga." *Confederate Veteran,* November 1894.

Ridley, B. L.:
"Southern Side at Chickamauga." *Confederate Veteran,* September 1898.
"Southern Side at Chickamauga" (Parts 2 and 3). *Confederate Veteran,* November 1898.

Vance, Wilson. "On Thomas' Right at Chickamauga." *Blue and Gray,* February 1893.

Wyeth, J. A. "The Furlough That I Did Not Get." *Confederate Veteran,* November 1900.

OTHER SOURCES

Brindley, Thaddeus Marion. Letter, September 3, 1863. Collinsville, Ala.: V. M. Brindley.

Ely, John. Diary, n.d. Fort Oglethorpe, Ga.: Chickamauga and Chattanooga National Military Park.

Fenton, James. Memoirs, September 19, 1863. Springfield: Illinois State Historical Library.

Glover, Benjamin R. Letter, September 22, 1863. N.p.

Jamison, R. D. Letter, October 10, 1863. In "Letters and Recollections of a Confederate Soldier, 1860-1865," compiled by Henry Downs Jamison Jr. Unpublished manuscript, 1964. Nashville.

Kellenberger, Peter B. Letter, November 15, 1863. Indianapolis: Indiana Historical Society.

McCaffrey, James M. "Only a Private: The Civil War Memoirs of William J. Oliphant, Company G, 6th Texas Infantry Regiment." Thesis presented May 1987. N.p.

Magee, John Euclid. Diary, 1861-1863. Durham, N.C.: Duke University.

Miller, Gerald J. "Middletown Yank's 'Journey to War and Back.'" Unpublished manuscript, February 1985. Champaign, Ill.

Petzoldt, Theodore. "My War Story: As Told Fifty Years after the War." Unpublished manuscript, 1917. Portland, Oreg.

Records, William H. Unpublished manuscript, n.d. Manuscript Collection, Indiana Division. Indianapolis: Indiana State Library.

Reed, Axel H. Diary, July 1863. Fort Oglethorpe, Ga.: Chickamauga and Chattanooga National Military Park.

Ryan, Frank T. "Surrender of Vicksburg, and the Battle of Chickamauga." In *An Historical Sketch of the Georgia Military Institute, Marietta, Ga.* By Robert L. Rodgers. Atlanta: Kimsey's Book Shop, 1956.

Wagner, Levi. "Recollections of an Enlistee, 1861-1864." Unpublished manuscript. *Civil War Times Illustrated* collection. Carlisle Barracks, Pa.: U.S. Army Military History Institute.

INDEX

 Time-Life Books is a
division of Time Life Inc.

TIME LIFE INC.
PRESIDENT and CEO: George Artandi

TIME-LIFE BOOKS
PRESIDENT: John D. Hall
PUBLISHER/MANAGING EDITOR: Neil Kagan

VOICES OF THE CIVIL WAR

DIRECTOR, NEW PRODUCT DEVELOPMENT:
Curtis Kopf
MARKETING DIRECTOR: Pamela R. Farrell

CHICKAMAUGA

EDITOR: Henry Woodhead
Deputy Editors: Philip Brandt George (principal),
Harris J. Andrews, Kirk Denkler
Design Director: Barbara M. Sheppard
Art Director: Ellen L. Pattisall
Associate Editors/Research and Writing: Connie Contreras,
Gemma Slack
Senior Copyeditors: Donna D. Carey, Judith Klein
Picture Coordinator: Lisa Groseclose
Page Makeup Specialist: Monika D. Thayer
Editorial Assistant: Christine Higgins

Initial Series Design: Studio A

Special Contributors: John Newton, David S. Thomson (text);
Michael Bub, Charles F. Cooney, Robert Lee Hodge, Susan
V. Kelly, Henry Mintz, William Lee White (research); Roy
Nanovic (index).

Correspondents: Christina Lieberman (New York).

Vice President, Director of Finance: Christopher Hearing
Vice President, Book Production: Marjann Caldwell
Director of Publishing Technology: Betsi McGrath
Director of Photography and Research: John Conrad Weiser
Director of Editorial Administration: Barbara Levitt
Production Manager: Marlene Zack
Quality Assurance Manager: James King
Chief Librarian: Louise D. Forstall

Consultants
Richard A. Baumgartner, a former newspaper and magazine
editor, has written, edited, or published 16 books dealing with
Civil War and World War I history, including *Blue Lightning:
Wilder's Mounted Infantry Brigade in the Battle of Chickamauga.* A longtime student of the Civil War's western theater, he
served as editor of *Blood & Sacrifice: The Civil War Journal of a
Confederate Soldier,* and coedited *Yankee Tigers* and two volumes in the award-winning Echoes of Battle series: *The
Atlanta Campaign* and *The Struggle for Chattanooga.* Focusing
on the experiences of the common soldier, he has written
numerous articles for several military-history journals.

Larry M. Strayer, an editor with Blue Acorn Press, has written
or contributed to more than a dozen titles on the war's western
theater, including *Yankee Tigers* and the award-winning
Echoes of Battle volumes on the Atlanta and Chattanooga
campaigns. Well known in living-history circles, he currently
serves as adviser for Accuracy Historical Productions. His next
publication will photographically chronicle Ohio's involve-
ment in the Civil War, with its focus on the common soldier.

Library of Congress Cataloging-in-Publication Data
Chickamauga / by the editors of Time-Life Books.
    p. cm.—(Voices of the Civil War)
    Includes bibliographical references and index.
    ISBN 0-7835-4710-2
    1. Chickamauga (Ga.), Battle of, 1863.
    I. Time-Life Books. II. Series.
E475.81.C48 1997
973.7'359—dc21   96-48665
                                   CIP